THE CHICAGO COLLEGE PLAN

THE UNIVERSITY OF CHICAGO PRESS
CHICAGO, ILLINOIS

—

THE BAKER & TAYLOR COMPANY
NEW YORK

THE CAMBRIDGE UNIVERSITY PRESS
LONDON

THE MARUZEN-KABUSHIKI-KAISHA
TOKYO, OSAKA, KYOTO, FUKUOKA, SENDAI

THE COMMERCIAL PRESS, LIMITED
SHANGHAI

THE CHICAGO COLLEGE PLAN

CHAUNCEY SAMUEL BOUCHER, Ph.D.

Professor of American History, Dean of the College
The University of Chicago

38168

THE UNIVERSITY OF CHICAGO PRESS
CHICAGO · ILLINOIS

TO

THE MEMBERS OF THE COLLEGE FACULTY
WHOSE IMAGINATION, COURAGE, AND
LABORS HAVE MADE POSSIBLE THE DE-
SIGN AND ADMINISTRATION OF THIS
EDUCATIONAL ADVENTURE

this series of studies and thoughtfully designed experiments was an entirely revised program launched with an incoming Freshman class in September, 1931.

We believe that the basic principles of the plan we have developed have been demonstrated to be sound. Though our plan was developed in the light of our own situation, we believe that at many points this situation is so similar to that of most other institutions that, with appropriate adaptation of various details to a local situation, many features of the plan could be adopted by many other colleges, with profit to all concerned. We are glad to share our experiences with others for whatever these experiences may be thought to be worth.

Permit me to state at once my conviction that the administrative organization of any educational institution (including all administrative officers, regulations, policies, and practices) has valid reason for existence only to the extent that it encourages and facilitates the attainment of desired educational objectives; and whenever the administrative organization is found to impede the attainment of these objectives, it should be altered accordingly or perhaps even be abolished to make way for one that will serve the ends desired. I hold this view because I have known more than one administrator who seemed to comport himself as though the only rôle appropriate for a student or faculty member was that of a perfectly articulated cog in his administrative machine.

Change in the organization of administration or change of the curriculum merely for the sake of change is quack doctoring. Administrative reorganization is legitimately called for only as a needed accompaniment of a change, usually professedly directed at improvement, of educational objectives, which improvement, in turn, is usually attempted through a change in curriculum organization. Though administrative reorganization may be the first step actually taken in the launching of a new educational policy and program previously agreed upon, the determination of the extent and character of the administrative reorganization should come as the last step in the design of the new educational plan. The logical—and, it seems to me, the only defensible—sequence in the development of a new educational program in any institution is the following: (1) agreement should be reached on a restatement of educational objectives; (2) the curriculum best adapted to the attainment of these objectives should be designed; (3) full consideration should be given to a selection of the seemingly best combination of methods of instruction to be used in the attempt to attain the objectives; (4) full consideration should be given to a selection of the seemingly best combination of methods to be used in the attempt to measure the attainment of the objectives; (5) lastly, the administrative organization should be designed solely with a view to maximum service to the attainment of the desired educational objectives by the two parties most vitally concerned, students and faculty, since the major educational purpose of the faculty is to assist the students and the sole purpose of administration is to serve both students and faculty.

To educate one's self is an arduous process that may be painfully dreary or delightfully exhilarating, depending upon the attitude of the individual and the character of the process pursued, but never has been, and never can be, facilitated by any kind of pedagogical twilight sleep. Students and faculty alike have found our New Plan educational process delightfully exhilarating and quite the antithesis of anything resembling pedagogical twilight sleep.

Long as it is, this book is too short to present the entire story. Each one of the four introductory general courses is worthy of a chapter longer than the one chapter devoted to the four courses. In each one of a dozen of the departmental year-courses and year-sequences new departures of very significant educational value, that have not even been mentioned in these pages, have been developed and successfully put into practice. However, if this narrative report gives the reader a reasonably clear picture of the New Plan as a whole and in some of its more important details, the book will have served its purpose.

To acknowledge individually my indebtedness to those who have given me reports of various types that have been invaluable in the writing of these pages would require a listing of most of the members of the College Faculty. Hence I have dedicated the book to them as a group. Professor Edith Foster Flint, chairman of the English composition staff, Professor A. J. Brumbaugh, Dean of Students in the College, and Mr. John M. Stalnaker, the Humanities Examiner, gave special assistance by reading in manuscript chapters v, viii, and vi, respectively, for inaccuracies. Mr. Donald P. Bean, Manager of the University of Chicago Press, gave many helpful suggestions in the final stages of the preparation of the manuscript.

C. S. BOUCHER

COBB HALL
January 1, 1935

TABLE OF CONTENTS

xi

CHAPTER I
REORGANIZATION

DURING a considerable period, while the University of Chicago was winning eminence in graduate education and research, much of the undergraduate work was grossly neglected; even worse, the College came to be regarded by some members of the family as an unwanted, ill-begotten brat that should be disinherited. Nearly all finally agreed that we had reached a situation that necessitated a decision either to abandon the College or to develop it to a position of strength in its field comparable to that of our graduate schools in their fields.

Approximately ten years ago President Burton announced that our objective would be to develop the best possible College. A proposal was then put before the Faculty to segregate the junior college completely from the other schools of the University, placing it across the Midway with its own faculty, budget, dean, buildings, and equipment. The debate over this issue resulted in a stalemate that was generally interpreted as defeat of the proposal. Under President Mason it was decided that the College should be not merely *of*, but effectively *in*, the University.

In the meantime, a campaign was launched to study carefully every phase of life and work in the College with a view to the development of a constructive program. The most significant early step actually taken was the development of a greatly improved guidance program. This, in turn, brought clearly to light the need of fundamental cur-

1

riculum revisions and the need of improvement in the quality of instruction, which in turn showed the need of improvement in College faculty personnel and the devotion of serious attention to instructional methods. As this study progressed, many of us became convinced that there was also need for a radical change in the method of measuring the student's progress, away from the course-credit and course-marking system, that would change fundamentally the relationship between student and instructor, that would improve student motivation, and that would make provision for the great differences in capacity and in the effectiveness of applying their capacity among students.

In view of what had been learned from a study of student-guidance problems, from experimentation with new selections and new organizations of subject matter for presentation in courses, from improved methods and combinations of methods of instruction, and from improvement of old types and the development of new types of examination techniques for use in comprehensive examinations, it seemed that little more could be done to improve the educational process at the college level unless the most basic structural element in the system were changed by a substitution of the requirement of a demonstration of genuine achievement for the bookkeeping and adding-machine requirement in terms of semester-hours or course-credits. A few of the best educators in the country seemed to be agreed that the course-credit system was the most formidable impediment in the path of progress in college education. We happened to have a larger proportion of members in our Faculty who saw the situation in this light than was true of faculties of most other institutions, and who, seeing the light, had courage enough to follow where it directed. Though college faculties are proverbially so much the slaves of custom in regard to administrative practices and machinery once adopted that they instinctively react unfavorably to proposals that involve radical departures, the majority of our Faculty seemed ready to regard this proposal for a fundamental revision of the system merely as the next logical and necessary step in the path toward the best attainable educational results.

Under date of May 1, 1928, a special Senate[1] Committee on the Undergraduate Colleges—a committee of nine members, including the present writer as chairman—sent to members of the Senate, the Faculty of the Colleges of Arts, Literature, and Science, the Faculty of the College of Education, and the Faculty of the School of Commerce and Administration, copies of a report to be considered by these various bodies later in the month.

The covering letter included the following paragraph:

The modifications here proposed in the operations of the Junior and Senior Colleges of Arts, Literature, and Science are an attempt to remedy defects in the present system that, in the opinion of the Committee, are serious and deep-seated and demand courageous measures for their correction. The nature of these defects is considered at some length in the accompanying Supplementary Statement prepared by Dean Boucher. Briefly, the plan seeks, among other things, to encourage in the student an attitude of mind in accordance with which he views his college course more in terms of opportunity and less in terms of requirements; more in terms of developing competence in fields in which he is interested and less in terms of required total of courses and grade points. It proposes to offer to the exceptional student the opportunity to make more rapid progress than the mediocre student, and it proposes to place upon the shoulders of all students a larger measure of responsibility for their own educational progress.

Prior to our administrative reorganization in October, 1930, the "Dean of the Colleges" was Dean of the Junior

[1] The University Senate is composed of all professors of full rank in all colleges, schools, and divisions of the University.

College and the Senior College of Arts for the award of the
A.B. degree, the Junior College and the Senior College of
Literature for the award of the Ph.B. degree, and the
Junior College and the Senior College of Science for the
award of the S.B. degree. Our distinction between the
junior-college status and the senior-college status of the
student had come to have little more significance than that
prior to attaining eighteen "majors" (quarter courses) of
credit the student registered on yellow cards, and after
attaining eighteen "majors" of credit he registered on
white cards, until he attained the mystic number of course
credits (thirty-six) necessary for a degree.

Under the heading "Junior College and Admission to
Senior College," the Report stated the following "Guiding
Principles":

The essential educational requirements for admission to the senior
colleges from our own junior colleges or from other institutions are (1)
an appropriate degree of attainment in respect to general education,
and (2) a demonstration of the power of independent and informed
thinking. In our own junior colleges we should offer opportunities for
the pursuit of the early stages of special education in some field of particular interest to the student. Hence, the program of our junior colleges
should include not only studies aiming toward general education but
also studies in the early stages of special education in some field of particular interest to the student. In both general and special education
the University should aim to give its junior-college students ample opportunity to receive inspiration by work under, and by contact with,
men who, by their research work, are contributing to the advancement
of the boundaries of human knowledge.

The junior-college requirements were stated in terms of
five comprehensive examinations: (1) English Composition and English Literature, (2) Foreign Language, (3)
Natural Science and Mathematics, (4) Social Science, (5)
an elective that might represent the early stages of specialization in a chosen field of knowledge. The accompanying

proposed regulations provided that any student might take the examinations for the completion of junior-college requirements and admission to senior college any time they were offered, regardless of the length of time the student had been in residence.

Similarly, the requirements for the completion of senior college and for the Bachelor's degree were stated in terms of three comprehensive examinations, including a major and two minor fields, which the student might take whenever ready; but no degree was to be granted to any student who had been in residence less than one academic year.

Provision was made for the establishment of a College Board of Examiners, and departments were given encouragement to restudy their course offerings with a view to reducing the number of isolated and unrelated course units, and to conduct experiments in methods of instruction which might involve considerable deviation from the then existing stereotyped methods and routine.

The supplementary statement by the chairman of the Committee began by pointing out that the features of the plan presented were designed:

(1) to establish educational standards with measurements of achievement (for the mental and intellectual development of each student) which are more meaningful than those we are now using;

(2) to give more meaning to the Bachelor's degree than it now has, since it too frequently represents only so much time served in order to accumulate a required number of course credits;

(3) to give the student an opportunity, which he will gladly seize, to assume more responsibility for his own education, and thus give greater opportunity and encouragement for self-development and growth in power;

(4) to encourage the student to think of his education as a lifelong and continuous process, which, to be effective, must be a well-ordered process, at various stages of which he should have rather definite objectives and should demonstrate his capacity for successful achievement;

(5) to encourage the student to take a broader perspective and to work and to think in terms of fields rather than small, isolated, and sometimes meaningless, units;

(6) to save time for the better students, who are able to develop both faster and more thoroughly than the average student, by awarding the degree on the basis of demonstrated accomplishment, rather than on a required number of course credits, and thus break up the lock-step system;

(7) to award the Bachelor's degree to no student who cannot demonstrate a certain degree of attainment in mental and intellectual development, even though the student may have "passed" any number of courses;

(8) to set for high-school administrators, teachers, and students a fairly definite goal at the end of the period of secondary education, which, in our present scheme of institutional divisions, begins with the first year of high school and ends with the second year of junior college;

(9) to give assurance to high-school administrators, teachers, and students that, the more thoroughly and the more wisely a student applies himself in high school, the sooner, possibly, and certainly the more surely, will the student be prepared to demonstrate by examination his fitness for entrance into senior college.

The report was to have been presented to the Senate on Monday, May 7, 1928, not for action at this meeting, but merely for information and as a report of progress. The recommendations were to have been presented to the various faculties concerned later in May. If these faculties had seen fit to approve the recommendations, with or without amendments, another meeting of the Senate was to have been called for consideration of the actions of the respective faculties.

On Sunday, May 6, President Mason's resignation was announced in the newspapers. In order that we might not seem to be acting with inordinate haste while the matter of the presidency was unsettled, the chairman of the Senate Committee, at a meeting of the Faculty of the Colleges of Arts, Literature, and Science, May 15, 1928, offered the following motion, which was passed:

(1) that there be created an Administrative Board of the Junior Colleges of Arts, Literature, and Science, to consist of at least five members;

(2) that there be created a similar Board of the Senior Colleges;

(3) that to these Boards shall be referred the parts of the Report of the Senate Committee on the Undergraduate Colleges dated May 1, 1928, which concern the Junior Colleges and the Senior Colleges, respectively;

(4) that these Boards shall be requested to study, respectively, the educational and administrative problems of the Junior and Senior Colleges of Arts, Literature, and Science, and to report with recommendations to this Faculty;

(5) that in making such studies, the Boards shall have in mind, as ends to be attained so far as may be practicable,

(a) the substitution of fields of study for the present course units,

(b) the provision of opportunity for the exceptional student to make more rapid progress,

(c) the abolition of the present system of counting credits for a degree and the substitution therefor of either comprehensive examinations or of some other method of demonstrating accomplishment, and

(d) in general, greater emphasis upon the student's opportunity and responsibility for his own education.

Two Boards of nine members each were appointed, with the Dean of the Colleges serving as chairman of each Board. Each Board devoted time and effort periodically to further study of the report and particularly to the problem of comprehensive examinations, though it was realized by all that little real progress could be made until a President of the University had been appointed.

Shortly after his election as President, Robert Maynard Hutchins indicated to the Dean of the Colleges that he was thoroughly in sympathy with the objectives set forth in the report of the Senate Committee on the Undergraduate Colleges.

President Hutchins soon pointed out that this study of the college program had been carried to the point that the time was ripe for the proposal of appropriate administrative changes. Thanks to his vigorous and constructive leadership, our new divisional organization was framed in the manner best suited to the attainment of our objectives at the junior-college level and for the appropriate adaptation of some of the basic principles of the junior-college plan to the upper-divisional and professional-school programs at the senior-college and graduate levels.

Thus, having agreed that our major educational objective for the junior college should be general education, with reasonable provision for the pursuit of special interests, we decided that there was need for fundamental revision both of the curriculum and of the method of measuring the progress of the student as shown through his demonstration of attainments worthy of a junior-college certificate. The administrative reorganization then suggested by President Hutchins as the one best adapted to the achievement of our newly defined educational purposes was adopted enthusiastically by the University Senate in October, 1930.

The administrative plan adopted created five divisions in Arts, Literature, and Science: the College (a lower division for the junior-college program) and four upper divisions (the Biological Sciences, the Humanities, the Physical Sciences, and the Social Sciences) for the senior-college and graduate programs. Each of the five divisions has a faculty, a dean, and a budget. The objects of the reorganization were stated as follows:

. . . . to improve administration by placing greater responsibility on officers who are familiar with the work of their respective divisions, to reduce the number of independent budgets presented to and administered by the President's Office, to promote co-operation in research, to co-ordinate teaching, and to open the way to experiments in general higher education.

Under this organization each division is presided over by a dean, who receives the budgets of the departments in his division and co-ordinates them into a divisional budget, which then is transmitted to the President's Office. The budget of the College consists of that portion of the salaries of members of the faculty that represents the share of their time and service that is devoted to College work. A faculty member may appear in the College budget for all of his salary, or for as little as one-ninth of his total salary. Most of the members of the College Faculty are also members of one or another of the four upper divisional faculties. Appointment recommendations receive the approval of the appropriate divisional dean or deans before being transmitted to the President.

The function of the College is to do the work of the University in general higher education. A student passes from it on completing his institutionalized general higher education and is admitted to one of the other divisions on presenting evidence of his ability to do advanced work. Specialized study in Arts, Literature, and Science, whether professional or non-professional, is carried on in the upper divisions. Though the College is a separate administrative unit with all the freedom needed, it is so closely knit into the upper divisions that it has at its command all of the educational resources of the entire University. Many departmental chairmen and professors who are scholars of international renown are interested participants in College instruction. This is one of the notable advantages of a college in a great university—a strong teaching organization set against a research background. "Teaching" is the passing-on of truth and the tested methods of search for truth; "research" is finding new truth and new methods of finding truth which will later be passed on and may be applied in life. The two go naturally together; and they should be done best, though they are not always actually done best, where they are done together—in a university which supports both teaching and research, at both the undergraduate and graduate levels.

In December, 1930, upon recommendation of the President, the Senate authorized the appointment of a new administrative officer, co-ordinate in rank with the divisional deans, to be known as "Dean of Students and University Examiner," to co-ordinate all of the University's relations with students, including admissions, recording and reporting, health service, the administration of entrance, placement, and comprehensive examinations, the educational and social supervision of residence halls and clubhouses, the direction of social affairs, vocational guidance and placement, student aid, the administration of fellowships and scholarships, and student advisory service in Arts, Literature, and Science. Upon request these functions may be extended to the professional schools.

The report of a special committee on the constitution of a Board of Examinations was adopted by the Senate in March, 1931, as follows:

1. The creation of a Board of Examinations to consist of three members appointed by the President; a representative from each of the divisions, to be chosen as hereinafter provided; a representative from each professional school using comprehensive examinations; and the University Examiner, chairman ex officio.
2. The appointment by the dean of each division and by the Dean of the College of divisional committees on examinations. The chairmen of these committees should serve ex officio on the Board of Examinations provided for in paragraph 1.
3. The three members of the Board of Examinations to be appointed by the President should be selected primarily because of their competence in examination methods.

4. The Board of Examinations would be responsible for: (*a*) determination of policies to be used in the formulation and administration of comprehensive examinations (Comprehensive examinations should not be interpreted as being restricted to any particular type of examination. In the opinion of this Committee they should include any kind of test, investigation, problem, assignment or creative work by which the abilities, achievements, or performance of students may be measured. The examination techniques designed to achieve these ends with the greatest degree of reliability should be the subject of study by the Faculty and the Board of Examinations); (*b*) the recommendation for appointment of a Chief Examiner to be in charge of preparing and conducting such comprehensive examinations as are desired by the several faculties. The Chief Examiner would be responsible for recommending the appointment of his technical staff and office force.

5. The Board of Examinations, after consultation with the deans of the divisions and the heads of the departments concerned, should recommend the appointment of members of the instructional staff who have shown interest and competence in the development of examinations to work with the Chief Examiner in the preparation of examinations. Persons chosen for this work should be freed from such portion of their regular responsibilities as may be necessary.[2]

6. The divisional committees on examinations should be called into council when examinations which concern their respective divisions are being planned, they should report to the Board of Examinations regarding the adequacy of the examinations as a test of the objectives and the methods of instruction of their divisions, and such additional information as may be of assistance to the Board in the development of an adequate program of examinations.

Upon suggestion of the President and with the recommendation of the Senate Committee on University Policy, the Senate adopted the following in November, 1932:

That the requirement that all members of the College Faculty be members of departments and divisional faculties be abrogated, and that the Dean of the College be empowered, in consultation with the chair-

[2] During the depression it has proved necessary for members of the Faculty to assume an immense burden in connection with the preparation of examinations without release from any of their regular responsibilities.

men of the departments and deans of the divisions concerned, to recommend to the President members of the College Faculty who may or may not have departmental or divisional affiliations. It is understood that members of the faculties of other divisions will continue to teach in the College by arrangement between the Dean of the College and the dean of the division concerned. For the guidance of the Dean it is considered desirable that a large proportion of the College Faculty be members of departments and divisional faculties.

The attention of the Senate was called to the action of the Senate, in the preceding March, providing that appointments to departments are made only on approval of the department concerned. Only one faculty member has as yet been appointed who does not have departmental affiliation, but such appointments can and will be made whenever the need arises.

The Dean of the College prepares the agenda for, and presides at, College Faculty meetings; serves as chairman of the College Curriculum Committee and of the College Executive Committee; represents the College on the Board of Examinations; is responsible for the preparation and printing of the syllabi for College courses; is responsible for the character, amount, and quality of College instruction; recommends persons to the President for appointment to the College Faculty; recommends faculty members for promotion in rank and increases in salary; is responsible for the preparation of copy for the College *Announcements* and the quarterly *Time Schedule;* and prepares and administers the College budget.

CHAPTER II

THE CURRICULUM—PHILOSOPHY, CONTENT, AND ADMINISTRATION

FOR generations, in the early history of American colleges, there was very little provision for the individualization of student programs, because the curriculum was almost entirely prescribed. There was no choice of meat offerings or of dessert offerings; each student was fed the same intellectual menu as every other student who entered at the same time. Came a time, however, when research broadened the limits of old fields of knowledge and opened up entirely new fields. New courses could be introduced only if electives were introduced. In order that the curriculum might reflect the widened boundaries of knowledge, electives were introduced, at first sparingly, and then wholesale. As is typical of us in so many phases of life, we went from one extreme to another—from the rigidly fixed curriculum to the almost completely elective curriculum.

Twenty years ago, in many colleges, entering students faced a formidably large catalogue with literally hundreds of course offerings, not clearly described and not properly related, with the elective system in vogue and with no faculty member and no administrative officer available to help them solve the puzzle of course elections. Throughout his four years a student with no definite professional aim, finding no one on the college staff to guide him, would likely drift from one subject to another, depending upon chance, caprice, or student gossip for his guidance (or, if he had a professional objective, he would concentrate almost

13

solely in a single departmental field), and would come out at the end of four years with an academic record sheet that should now be considered worthy of a place in a museum of educational monstrosities. And yet, a student with a constitution strong enough to withstand such a stuffing of utterly indigestible educational hash, would come out triumphantly with a diploma and a degree—though frequently without anything worthy of being called an education—provided only that he had accumulated a certain number of course credits. It is no wonder that in this period our college students developed for themselves, as never before, outlets for their best thought and efforts, "student activities"—athletics, publications, dramatics, and a vast number of purely social activities. In this period Woodrow Wilson, as President of Princeton University, complained that the "side shows" were overshadowing the "main tent;" and a Chinese student, after observing the hysteria of a football season and the hectic days of a fraternity rushing season, wrote that "an American college or university is a great athletic association and social club in which provision is made, merely incidentally, for intellectual activity on the part of the physically and socially unfit."

After seeing from experience the folly of both extremes—the rigidly fixed curriculum and the wide-open elective system—the better colleges endeavored to strike a happy medium. In recent years it has been common practice to prescribe a number of group requirements—English, foreign language, mathematics, natural science, and social science—designed to furnish a proper balance in an introduction to general education to be completed by the end of the second year, and a sequence or concentration requirement for the last two years.

The introduction of group requirements was a step taken

in good faith to introduce at least a modicum of order and
balance into a student's total college program without
interfering seriously with the individualization of student
programs. After careful study of the situation over a
period of several years we concluded, at the University of
Chicago, that group requirements, stated merely in terms
of a course or two in each of a few large groups of departments, achieved too little as a guaranty, for the individual
student, of an appropriate breadth of educational contact
and experience, with departmental introductory courses
what they were.

In what may be termed the "chaotic" period, when the
wide-open elective system ran riotously into utter confusion—a period which lasted in most institutions until ten
or less than ten years ago, and still persists in some institutions—most departmental introductory courses were designed for the sole purpose of preparing students for advanced courses in the respective departments. Most departments seemed to think only in terms of specialization,
as though the intellectual sun rose and set within their
boundaries, and seemed to be interested not at all in students who wanted and needed an introduction to several
departmental fields of thought as essential parts of a general education.

In the last decade, a basic theory of college education has
been put before us more and more frequently and with increasing forcefulness: Though a student who enters college
with a specific educational and perhaps vocational aim
should be given the opportunity to pursue that aim to a
reasonable extent even in his Freshman year, the major
emphasis in the junior-college years should be devoted to
breadth of general education; and, though general education should continue in senior college, the major em-

phasis of the last two years should be upon concentration in, and depth of penetration of, a single, though fairly large and individually selected, field of thought. This basic principle has come to be so generally accepted that in recent years one department after another, in our better colleges, has studied its course offerings as not before, in a generation, and has had the courage to scrap many of its old courses and introduce a new set, fewer in number and arranged in a well-ordered, progressive sequence, with elementary courses designed not only to furnish the foundation material necessarily prerequisite for the departmental advanced courses but also to serve the needs of students who are interested in a particular department only in so far as it contributes to general education.

In a few instances a department concluded that a single course could not meet both objectives satisfactorily, and that two introductory courses were needed: one for students planning to do advanced work in the department, and another for students interested in an introduction to the departmental field merely as part of general education. Our Department of Geology designed, and offered simultaneously and very successfully, introductory courses of both types in our period of experimentation prior to the framing of the New Plan; and their experience with the one-quarter introductory course in geology for students who wanted an introduction to the field of geology merely as part of general education was of great value when we designed the present Introductory General Course in the Physical Sciences as one of a group of four such courses.

One of the most significant products of the study recently devoted to educational objectives and the curriculum has been a new type of course called an "orientation" or "survey" course, designed to orient the student in a large field of thought which runs through and across many of the artificial boundary lines established by the growth of the numerous departmental compartments which universities have developed and formalized.

Our most successful course of this type developed at the University of Chicago was one covering the whole field of the physical and biological sciences in two quarters. This course was given for eight years, a period long enough for a careful study of results. Again and again, Seniors, who had taken the course in their Freshman year, testified that, in looking back over their educational careers, they were clearly convinced that the most stimulating and most profitable intellectual experience ever afforded them was this survey course in the sciences, entitled "The Nature of the World and of Man." For a student who wanted no more than an introduction to the field of science, this course seemed to be more profitable than any one of the old-style departmental introductory courses; and for the student who expected to specialize in one of the sciences, this course gave an excellent background for later concentration—it showed him the true position of his specialty in a larger field of thought, together with the contributing values of each specialized department for the others in the larger field of thought.

Our success with this science survey course was probably the most significant one of the considerations that led us to frame and adopt the imposing program of four introductory general courses in as many large fields of thought that we now offer. It is not likely that we could have brought ourselves to face the heroic efforts necessary to design and administer this program, with any assurance of success, had it not been for what we had learned from our previous experience in the field of the sciences regarding the possibilities and values of such courses.

Shortly after the divisional organization, described in the

preceding chapter, was adopted, a new College Curriculum Committee was appointed, with the Dean of the College as chairman. At a meeting of the College Faculty on January 14, 1931, a preliminary report was made, not for action but for discussion. Members of the Faculty were requested to submit in writing criticisms and constructive suggestions for use by the Committee in preparing a later and more definitive report. The impressive number of valuable suggestions submitted gave clear evidence that many members of the Faculty were genuinely and constructively interested in the problems to which the Committee was devoting its efforts.

Under date of February 7, 1931, the Curriculum Committee sent a mimeographed report of eleven pages to members of the College Faculty, with a covering letter that read in part as follows:

We are submitting herewith a program which we believe combines proposals for new departures and experiments together with the retention of the best fruits of past experience in a manner which is in harmony with nearly all of the suggestions received, and promises, if adopted, to place us nearer the attainment of our goal, namely, the best educational program that we can offer at the College level.

We realize that no program can be successful without the enthusiastic co-operation of the Faculty. The inclosed draft, therefore, is to be regarded as tentative. We plan to have numerous departmental and divisional group meetings, with one or more members of the Committee present at each meeting to answer questions and to receive criticisms and suggestions. The Committee will welcome criticisms and suggestions in writing from any individual or group, provided they may be in the hands of the chairman by February 23. The Committee will then meet as often as may be necessary to give full consideration to all suggestions offered. We hope to have a revised draft, if revision proves necessary or desirable, in your hands several days before a meeting of the Faculty, which we hope may be called during the first week of March, for action on the report.

The program of group meetings was carried out (with the Dean present at most of them), but revision of the report proved unnecessary; and the report was adopted by the College Faculty March 5, 1931, at an exceptionally well-attended meeting, by a vote of approximately three to one, and was approved by the Senate a few days later.

For the benefit of those who may wish to read the report on the curriculum as officially adopted, it is printed in Appendix A, followed by some additional New Plan legislation and some explanations and amendments of the original legislation. For the uninitiated reader who did not participate in the discussions that accompanied the framing and adoption of the original and succeeding legislative enactments, the plan as now administered can perhaps be presented in a manner more readily understandable than from the official documents.

The requirements for the College (junior-college) Certificate and the title of Associate in Arts are stated solely in terms of educational attainments, and not at all in terms of course credits or residence requirements; these attainments are measured by examinations which may be taken by the student whenever he is prepared to take them, at any scheduled examination period. Each student must pass seven examinations, of which five are specifically required and two are elective.

One of the five required examinations, the English qualifying examination, requires a demonstration that the student has developed acceptable and reliable habits of writing. The other four required examinations demand the attainment of the minimum essentials of factual information and an introduction to the methods of thought and work in each of four fields—the biological sciences, the humanities, the physical sciences, and the social sciences—

such as may be expected of a student who has pursued through an academic year a general course at the junior-college level in each of the four fields. These five examinations represent a common core of educational experience and background for all students who complete the requirements of our College: they constitute the major part of our definition of the minimum essentials of a general education.

A course in English composition, English 102A, B, and C, running through the Autumn, Winter, and Spring quarters, is offered for those who are shown by a placement test in Freshman Week to need instruction to develop satisfactorily the required attainments that are measured by the English qualifying examination. Approximately 15 per cent of the entering Freshmen are advised, on the basis of a placement test, that they do not need the course in English composition. They are advised to take the English composition qualifying examination when offered in November. Most of them pass the examination. The few who fail are advised to attend the course the remainder of the year and take the examination again the following May, or to take the course the following year.

As aids to students in attaining the level of mastery required in each of the four general fields, the following four courses, running through the academic year, are offered: Introductory General Course in the Biological Sciences; Introductory General Course in the Humanities; Introductory General Course in the Physical Sciences; Introductory General Course in the Social Sciences.[1] It should be noted that we do not require course credits in these fields, but do require the demonstration of attainments by means of a comprehensive examination in each of the fields. Course credits are not given, and hence cannot be counted. A

[1] These introductory general courses are described at length in chapter iv.

student may take any one of the examinations any time it is offered, whether he has attended only part or none of the sessions of the corresponding course. Even if a student does all of the work suggested in one of the courses, and is reported by the instructor as having done it satisfactorily, in his judgment, still the student has no "credit" on the College Certificate until and unless he passes the official Board examination in that field. This is true of all College courses and all of the seven required Board examinations.

In order that each student may have at least a modicum of experience in *depth* of penetration in addition to what we believe to be an appropriate *breadth* of educational contact, and also in order that each student may have an opportunity to pursue a special interest to a reasonable extent even in his junior-college years and acquire the necessary prerequisite training for specialization in an upper division or professional school, we give him free choice in the selection of two of the seven required examination fields, and leave room in the program of an average student for an additional free elective beyond College requirements. The two elective examinations are designed to require the attainment of such mastery of the subject matter, techniques, skills, habits of thought, and methods of work in any two divisional or departmental fields as may be expected of a student who has pursued through an academic year in each of two divisional or departmental fields a second-year general course or a sequence of three quarter-courses in a departmental subject or an approved combination of subjects in a divisional field.

As aids to students in acquiring the attainments required in the two elective examinations, year-courses or three-quarter sequences are offered in Art, Biology II, Chemistry, English Literature, French, Geography, Geology,

Geology and Astronomy, German, Greek, Italian, Latin, Mathematics, Military Science, Music, Philosophy, Physics, Social Sciences II, and Spanish.[2] A student may offer his two elective year-course or year-sequence examinations in the same divisional field. In the case of the Department of Romance Languages and Literatures a student may offer a sequence in each of two languages, but not two sequences in the same language.

In fulfilment of the College requirement of two elective sequence examinations, a student may offer any College sequence examination regardless of whether the sequence examination includes units of work for which the student has offered entrance credit, except that a student may not offer as a College sequence examination one in a foreign language that includes units of work offered to meet the specific College foreign-language requirement.

In addition to the seven requirements listed above, there are specific minimum requirements in a foreign language and in mathematics; but these requirements are met by almost all our students at entrance. If a student enters the College with two acceptable units of a foreign language, he is not required to take any further foreign-language examination for the College Certificate unless he elects a language sequence. If a student enters the College without two units of acceptable credit in a foreign language, he must satisfy the language requirement by a Board examination in addition to the seven regularly required examinations. Any one of the beginning foreign language sequences (numbered 101, 102, 103) provides adequate preparation for the average student for this requirement.

Similarly, if a student enters the College with two ac-

---

[2] A list of the year-courses and year-sequences offered in the College is given in Appendix B. Sample student programs are given in Appendix C.

ceptable units of mathematics, he is not required to take any further mathematics examination for the College Certificate unless he elects a mathematics sequence. If a student enters the College without two units of acceptable credit in mathematics, he must satisfy the mathematics requirement by a Board examination in addition to the seven regularly required examinations. Courses in elementary algebra and elementary geometry are offered by the Home-Study Department, but not in the College program, as aids to the attainment of the mathematics requirement.

A student who offers two entrance units in each of two foreign languages may use the two units in one of the languages to meet the College foreign-language requirement, and may offer the examination on the first-year College course in the other language as an elective sequence examination for the College Certificate without taking the sequence in residence in the College, even though he used the two units in this language for entrance requirements. A student who offers four entrance units in a single foreign language may use two of the units to meet the College foreign-language requirement, and may offer the examination on the second-year College course in the same language as an elective sequence for the College Certificate without taking the sequence in the College, even though he used all four units in this language for entrance requirements.

The normal program for a student in the College is three or four courses in each of the three quarters. The program of each student in his first year includes a combination of general courses and sequence courses that seems advisable in the light of his ability and interests. The normal program for the first and second years comprises two general courses and one or two sequence courses each year. We do not recommend that a student take more than two of the general courses at a time, except in rare instances and for special reasons. The student takes four courses each quarter if he has average or better-than-average ability, unless handicapped by poor health or by having to work part time for self-support. Most courses meet four times a week, and thus a student carrying a full program spends sixteen hours a week in classes.

Since all College courses are year-courses or year-sequences, college students are registered in the Autumn for the entire year. This means that the quarter system is of little significance to College students. A superior student may enter the College at any time during the academic year after the opening of the Autumn quarter, register for less than a full program, or in some instances for a full program, make up the work he has missed in the courses he elects, and take the corresponding examinations in June. Several students do this successfully each year. Under the old plan, with course credits based at least in part upon time-serving, this was impossible.

Since four courses at a time constitute a full program, and since only seven examinations are required, a superior student can in the two College years anticipate two or more year-courses on upper-divisional requirements while completing the College requirements; an average student can anticipate one; while a below-average student may carry three courses the first year and four courses the second year, or, if he elects four courses the first year and fails one examination, he will have an opportunity to repeat that course the second year without loss of time.[3] Measured in terms of effective application of capacities to the work in

[3] See sample student programs in Appendix C.

hand, and in terms of genuine attainments, the seven required examinations represent much more than the old junior-college requirements in terms of course credits.

A student who enters the College with advanced-standing credit for a full year or more of college work may, at the discretion of his Adviser, arrange for a modified program under the New Plan. In such cases, some of the courses credited by advanced standing may be substituted for some of the comprehensive examinations. A modified New Plan program does not entitle the student to the College Certificate of the Associate in Arts title; but by passing certain prescribed examinations (usually from three to five) that fill in the lacunae in his general education as shown by his certificate of advanced-standing credits, he may fulfil the requirements for admission to an upper division or professional school.

All our students, who either end their institutional education upon the completion of the junior-college requirements or who continue in one of our four upper divisions, or in a professional school, have in common this much educational experience and mastery: an introduction to each of four large fields of thought, an essential minimum of proficiency in English usage, and a respectable minimum training in a foreign language and in mathematics.

Since all our students offer the same two units of mathematics and take the same examinations in the four large fields of thought and in English usage, and since individualization is provided only in the foreign-language requirement and in the two elective examinations, it would seem that we have taken a rather vigorous step in the direction of return to the idea of the old fixed curriculum. In a sense this is true, but there is a vast difference between the fixed elements in our curriculum and the old fixed curriculum,

and there are great differences between the reasons for
their respective adoptions. Even though the prescribed
items in our curriculum may seem, at first glance, to bulk
large, the average student has the opportunity in his
junior-college program to pursue half of his work (four out
of eight courses), and the superior student even more than
half, in his chosen divisional field, if he cares to do so.[4]

The old fixed curriculum that in a previous generation
was regarded as *more probato*, in the light of present standards and in view of a long process of "enrichment of the
curriculum"—to use a favorite phrase of education specialists—is now judged to have been meager, narrow, limited,
stilted, and not sufficiently integrated with life. Occasionally today one encounters a devotee of the old classical
school who bewails the passing of the old-style fixed curriculum and proclaims with vehemence that most of the
courses introduced with the elective curriculum are bilge
water or worse. The successful advocates of the elective
system insisted, however, that they were "enriching" the
curriculum.

This "enrichment" of the curriculum, accompanied by
the development of the elective system to an absurd extreme, resulted not infrequently in a pronounced case of
intellectual anemia or jaundice for the student. It happened too frequently that graduates of the same institution and of the same student generation discovered that
they had nothing in common in intellectual experience,
background, or outlook; and yet they had been members
of the same university community, where now members of
the same civic and social community, and were confronted
with many common problems in the same physical and
social world. Each discovered in the other fatal lacunae in

[4] See sample student programs in Appendix C.

his training as a supposedly educated person. Each at first would make mental note of the ignorance and lack of educational balance of the other. Second thought, however, was likely to place the blame and responsibility on Alma Mater.

A few years ago some of us, who gave thought and study to the total intellectual menu offered to our students with the privilege of selecting their own diet, came to the conclusion that most students did not get a properly balanced intellectual diet, and, even worse, that it was impossible for them to do so, even with the best of guidance, in spite of the fact that our offerings were legion. This impossibility arose from the overenrichment of the curriculum with the multiplicity of highly specialized departmental offerings. We concluded that our students, as citizens in the modern world, could be offered a properly balanced program to be pursued within a reasonable length of time only if co-operative attempts at selection and synthesis were made. The accumulation of knowledge in so many fields of thought had become so vast, and the refinement of skills, techniques, and methods of thoughtful work in each of these numerous fields had become so great, that it seemed impossible for a student to attain anything approaching a satisfactory general education; the only educational goal with adequate provision for attainment was that of a specialist.

The problem of the training of specialists has been adequately and admirably solved. The great problem of provision for even passably adequate general education has not been solved; and yet, in the present stage of development of man in his so-called "modern civilization," it would seem that our greatest need is provision for adequate general education for citizens in the modern world.

It seemed to us, at the University of Chicago, that this provision could be made only with the earnest and effective co-operation of our best specialists, working in logically related groups, in an effort to select judiciously and to synthesize meaningfully the most significant knowledge and methods of work in the various specialized fields of thought. Our new College curriculum represents our effort to cope successfully with the problem of general education.

Though to a certain extent we have returned to the old plan of a fixed curriculum, though of a distinctly new type, and to this extent have abandoned the individualization of student programs, we have made complete provision for individualization in regard to the attainments and the capacity of each student. Since we require the demonstration of achievement in both prescribed and elective fields rather than course credits, each student is saved from what for him may be boring repetition or routine, perfunctory, lock-step procedure. Each student can capitalize to the fullest his past achievements and his present capacity for achievement—he may save time in the fulfilment of the junior-college requirements in exact conformity with his degree of superiority over the average student in regard to past achievements and present capacity for achievement. A student may present himself for any examination at any regular examination period, whether he has participated in all or any part or none of the class work of any course. We have found that some students either are prepared or can prepare themselves without instructional assistance for one or more examinations; others need only part of the regular work of a given course; while the majority need all of the class work offered as an aid to the attainment of the knowledge and intellectual power necessary to pass each prescribed and each elective examination. Though the requirements are set to demand of the average student two years for the junior-college certificate, each student is advised according to his needs in order that he may always be engaged in work that challenges his interest and his capacity. We believe that this type of individualization of student programs is the one most needed to bring home to each student the true meaning and significance of the educational process for him individually.

It was early decided that grades on official Board examinations were to be reported in terms of "A," "B," "C," "D," and "F," with "D" passing. It was also decided that each instructor should report his estimate of each student's progress in his course each quarter in terms of: "S," indicating that the instructor had sufficient positive evidence to indicate that the quantity and quality of the student's work in the course were satisfactory; "U," indicating that the instructor had sufficient positive evidence to indicate that the quantity and quality of the student's work in the course were unsatisfactory; "R," indicating that, though the student was registered for the course, the instructor had insufficient evidence regarding the quantity and quality of the student's work to justify either an S or a U report.

Beginning in July, 1934, the marking system for the quarterly reports of instructors, in terms of "S," "U," and "R," was changed; since that date, in the College and in the upper divisions, the following marks have been used in the reports filed by instructors each quarter to indicate the quality of the student's work in courses: "A," excellent; "B," good; "C," fair; "D," low pass;[5] and "F," unsatisfac-

[5] The word "pass" in this connection has no significance except for transfer of "credit" to another institution. With us the "D" mark given by an instructor signifies merely the instructor's judgment, for guidance purposes, that the stu-

tory; the mark "R" is used to indicate that there is insufficient evidence to justify an estimate regarding the quantity and quality of the student's work in a course; "Inc." (incomplete) indicates that the quality of the student's work is judged to be satisfactory but that the student has failed to submit all the evidence required by the instructor for a passing mark. No stigma is attached to the mark "R" (or, for that matter, to the mark "F"), as far as attainment of the College Certificate is concerned. Each year we have some instances in which students who have repeatedly been reported "R" by instructors have written Board examinations that were scored well above the passing mark. These students are effective independent workers.

This change in the marking system was adopted primarily to protect the interests of the student who might wish to transfer to another institution; these marks are called "transfer marks" and are reported to the Registrar. Though these quarterly marks filed by instructors have no effect upon the status of a student as a candidate for the College Certificate, they are of value to the Advisers in counseling with students. Besides these marks, the Advisers receive from instructors for each of their advisees the much more valuable quarterly personnel reports, described and illustrated in some detail in chapter viii.

Under the old plan we had rather mechanical regulations concerning probation and dismissal on a grade-point basis. Probationary status had significance as a warning to the student and rendered the student ineligible for "student activities." Under the New Plan it was decided to abolish

---

dent's work is barely passably satisfactory. The "D" mark attained on an official Board examination, however, means definitely that the student has "passed" for College Certificate purposes.

probation as an official status. Each Adviser is responsible for warning students and their parents in writing that a student's work is unsatisfactory when such is the case to the extent that a warning is deemed by the Adviser to be advisable for the student or for the University. Each student in the College is eligible for participation in any and all student activities with the exception that in intercollegiate athletics we follow the regulations of the Intercollegiate Conference, of which we are a member. The Advisers are charged with the responsibility of advising their students regarding participation in student activities.

The development of policies regarding dismissal for unsatisfactory work was intrusted to the College Executive Committee with instructions to make recommendations to the Faculty for appropriate legislation in the light of experience. Though former regulations provided for dismissal as early as at the end of one quarter of residence, it was decided under the New Plan to dismiss no student for poor work prior to the end of a full academic year, on the ground that each student should be given at least a year to demonstrate that he could or could not adjust himself satisfactorily to life and work in the College. Our present policy is as follows: At the end of each year a student is expected to pass at least one-half of the comprehensive examinations for which he is presumed to be prepared by the courses which he has pursued; a student who fails to meet these minimum requirements is denied the privilege of further registration until these requirements are met, but special circumstances affecting any particular case are considered by the student's Adviser and the Dean of Students in the College. A student who has been denied the privilege of further registration may re-register when he has passed the number of comprehensive examinations that were required for continuance in the College. Although an erstwhile resident student is not registered for residence work, he is eligible to take the comprehensive examinations at any time they are given. A student may also be granted the privilege of re-registering if he submits an acceptable record of work done in another institution of creditable standing.

Honorable mention for excellence in the work of the College is awarded to not more than the highest 15 per cent, selected on the basis of their performance in the examinations for fulfilment of the College requirements.

Each of the four upper divisions has adopted the basic principles of the New Plan and has developed appropriate programs for the Bachelor's, Master's, and Doctor's degrees. Though there are some differences among the four upper divisions regarding Bachelor's degree requirements, the general plan is that the student shall devote one third of his senior-college program to work in his chosen department and one third to work in related departments within the division, the remaining third to be elected by the student either in his division of registration or in any other division. This plan provides much individualization of student programs in the light of student interests and objectives at a time in his educational career when emphasis may appropriately be given to concentration or specialized training.

Each of the four upper divisions provides for each of the three degrees, as has the College for its certificate, individualization of student programs in the light of past achievements and present capacity, subject to the one limitation that a person, to be eligible for the College Certificate or for any divisional degree, must have been in residence in the University not less than one full academic year. This does not mean that a student who enters as a Freshman, must spend at least a year in the College; if he can pass the College examinations at entrance or after one quarter of residence work, he may at once enter an upper division and pass the examinations for the Bachelor's, Master's, or Doctor's degree as soon as he is able to do so. He cannot receive a certificate or a degree prior to the end of a full academic year (three quarters) of residence in the University; but he might then, as far as the residence requirement is concerned, receive the Doctor's degree.

CHAPTER III

THE PREPARATION OF THE SYLLABI

THE legislation enacted by the College Faculty requires a printed syllabus for each course offered in the College to assist students in preparation for the required examinations. This serves excellently several purposes.

In the first place, since the examinations are based on the syllabi, the student, who is qualified and desires to do so, may work independently in one or more fields and thus save both time and money. Secondly, courses are more likely than not to be better designed, organized, and presented, when the faculty members in charge are required to follow programs of work that they have had to make available in print for inspection by their colleagues and their students. Thirdly, the requirement of a printed syllabus for each course means that the proponents of a course must be able to show not only that it will vindicate its existence in general terms but that it will serve a specific purpose in the entire program of studies if the course is to pass muster before the Curriculum Committee. This means that the days when the curriculum just grew, like Topsy, under the wide-open elective system, when instructors and departments introduced or withdrew courses (frequently the former, but seldom the latter) almost solely in the light of their own whims or desires, are gone forever in our College. Fourthly, it means an end of the type of course (of which there were some in our institution, and still are far too many in not a few other institutions) that begins any place, drifts along at any pace determined by the caprice of the instructor, and ends any place attained by the end of the course.

As soon as the report of the Curriculum Committee was adopted by the Faculty, work was begun upon the preparation of the syllabi for the various courses. For each of the four introductory general courses—in the biological sciences, the humanities, the physical sciences, and the social sciences—and the course in English composition, a chairman was appointed by the Dean of the College, with the exception that in the case of the physical science general course the appointment of two co-chairmen proved advisable. In each instance the person selected was a full professor or an associate professor whose standing as a scholar was beyond question, and whose interest in, and capacity for, successful college teaching was widely known.

The number and variety of departmental courses offered as electives differs widely in the four general fields, as indicated in the previous chapter. In the biological sciences it was decided to offer, besides the introductory general course, only one year-course—a sequence in botany, zoölogy, and physiology, giving primarily and almost solely an intensive training and discipline in laboratory methods and techniques. In the humanities and in the physical sciences a considerable number and variety of year-courses or sequences are offered. In the social sciences it was decided to offer a second-year general course, built upon the introductory general course or its equivalent as prerequisite background, representing primarily economics, political science, and sociology; year-courses were also offered in geography and in American history—the former being listed also in the group of physical science electives and the latter in the humanities electives.[1]

---

[1] The course in American history was withdrawn at the end of the second year of the New Plan because of staff readjustments in the Department of History.

Since, in most instances, the preparation of these syllabi required an immense amount of careful and intensive study, it was necessary to relieve several persons of part or all of their regular teaching obligations for which they were scheduled during the Spring or Summer quarters of 1931, or during both quarters; in other instances persons who were scheduled to be out of residence during one or both of these quarters had to be employed for extra service. A generous grant from the General Education Board made the arrangement of such a program financially possible.

The chairman of each of the four introductory general courses, in consultation with the Dean of the College, carefully selected a group of colleagues vitally interested in the College program to co-operate in the design of the course, in the preparation of the syllabus, and in the laying of plans for the administration of the course. In most instances these course committee members were also to participate, to greater or lesser extent, in the offering of the course.

Each general course committee agreed at once to solicit suggestions from most or all of their colleagues in their divisional field. Many faculty members submitted, in writing, helpful suggestions that reflected an impressive amount of thoughtful consideration of the problem in hand.

As soon as a proposed preliminary outline of a course was agreed upon by a committee, copies were sent to most or all of the faculty members of that divisional field, with a request for criticisms and constructive suggestions. Extra typing and stenographic service was provided by the Dean to facilitate this program. All helpful criticisms and suggestions—and there were many of them—submitted by faculty members were carefully weighed by the committee in preparation of a longer and more detailed outline that began to approach syllabus proportions. Again copies were sent to faculty members—this time only to those who had shown an active interest—and further suggestions and criticisms were solicited. Again the committee spent many days evaluating the returns, and progressed one stage farther toward its goal.

In all four committees this process was followed at least three times, and in some instances five or six times. In the last stage of the preparation of a single syllabus, the final copy of a particular section was sometimes a tenth copy, to the preparation of which one or more specialists in the particular subject had made contributions. No single specialist, however, was permitted to dictate the content or form of a single section, which might have thrown the section out of proportion or perspective in the entire syllabus, because the committee, and in the final analysis the chairman, was responsible for adherence to the objectives and for the maintenance of proper proportions of the entire syllabus.

At each point in the work of each committee, educational objectives were seriously considered in the following order: the objectives of the four courses as a group; the objectives of each course as one of the four; the objectives of each large unit as part of a course; the objectives of each smaller unit as part of a larger unit. Then a similar careful consideration was given to each of several types of instructional methods to be used for the attainment of the objectives agreed upon, and to the extent to which each method should be employed in each unit of the course. Lastly, equally careful consideration was given to the methods of measuring the attainment of the objectives.

The immense amounts of time, careful study, pointed discussion, and downright hard work that were devoted to the weighing of objectives, the selection and organization of appropriate subject matter, the selection of reading and demonstration materials, and the selection of methods of instruction, for each smaller part of each larger part of each main section, in order to have the entire syllabus, and the course as given, a properly proportioned and thoroughly integrated structural unity, can be realized only by one who participated throughout the preparation of a single syllabus or who kept closely in touch with each chairman and shared with him some of his major difficulties, as did the Dean.

While the four introductory general courses are designed as a group and individually to serve the purpose of general education, the departmental or sequence courses are designed to serve still further the purpose of general education and at the same time provide the prerequisite training necessary for advanced divisional work.

For the preparation of the syllabi for the departmental year-courses or divisional field sequences, a single person was usually selected by the Dean after conference with the chairman or chairmen of the department or departments concerned, though in some instances a committee of two or three produced the syllabus of a three-quarter (academic year) course. In most instances where a single person's name appears on a syllabus as its author, however, the author solicited and received helpful suggestions from other members of the department at various stages of the preparation of the syllabus copy.

The extent to which faculty members, with the best of grace, inconvenienced themselves and their families, by postponing the pursuit of research projects and by changing plans of residence for the summer, and with genuine enthusiasm put their shoulders to the various wheels of the College cart, was most gratifying and inspiring to those of us who had been most concerned with the design of the program from the very beginning.

As soon as the program was adopted by the Faculty, evidences of the best of sportsmanship came from several of the minority who had voted against its adoption. In one instance, a chairman of a department called the Dean by telephone the next morning and said: "Though I voted against your Committee report yesterday, because I thought we should devote another year to study of the proposed program, now that the majority of the Faculty are shown to be clearly for it, I want you to know that I shall work whole-heartedly for the success of the experiment. I have given considerable thought to the proposed humanities course and have a suggestion to offer. . . . ." He was told that his suggestion would be most welcome. It was an excellent suggestion and was embodied in the plans for the course.

In another instance, when the Dean approached another of the few departmental chairmen who had voted against the adoption of the plan, regarding the preparation of the syllabus for the College sequence in his department, honest co-operation was accorded in the selection of the most appropriate member of the department. This member of the department also had voted against the adoption of the plan, but at once agreed to change his plans for the summer in order to work on the syllabus; and he produced an excellent syllabus that reflected clearly the immense amount of careful, thoughtful effort he had devoted to the cause.

In the whole period from the official adoption of the plan to the time when it was put into operation with the Freshman class entering in October, 1931, when dozens of faculty members were working most strenuously under great pressure, when basic questions were being considered in a fashion that meant trampling upon deep-seated prejudices and old vested interests in not a few quarters, there was only one instance of poor sportsmanship, and that one was in a department that did not offer work at the junior-college level but had a few members who were more dogmatic in their pronouncements on the junior-college program than any member of any other department.

At the very beginning of the preparation of the numerous syllabi it was decided that no specific style, form, or size should be prescribed for all. Each syllabus was to be written in the style—outline or running discourse, or a combination of both—that would serve best the needs of students interested in educating themselves in the specific field, both in the course and independently. If an extended syllabus were needed in any course, well and good; if a short outline with appropriate bibliographical citations were all that was needed, so be it.

All agreed, however, that the first edition of each syllabus, for experimental use the first year, should be studied critically throughout the year in the light of student and faculty experience in pursuit of the course, and be thoroughly revised for the following year. No course should be allowed to "jell" or crystallize in the form of the first edition of its syllabus. Hence the legend appeared on each syllabus: "First Preliminary Edition." In succeeding years the faculty members rightly insisted on the maintenance of freedom of revision, and the result is that in September, 1934, we published the "Fourth Preliminary Edition" of many of our syllabi.

When the first editions of the syllabi were being prepared, the manager of the University of Chicago Press indicated a desire to be permitted to publish them and advertise them widely for public sale. Faculty members objected on two grounds: they feared that if the syllabi were set up in type, freedom of revision might be dependent upon publication costs and sales returns; and they did not want the syllabi to be widely distributed until tried out experimentally and revised in the light of experience. Hence it was decided to issue the syllabi for the four introductory general courses and a few other courses with large enrolments in planographed form, and most of the syllabi for the departmental and divisional field sequences in mimeographed form. When the Dean was asked by the printer in January of the first year of the New Plan whether the plates for the syllabi of the introductory general courses should be saved any longer, the Dean replied that they might be destroyed. In April, when the Dean set a date during the following summer for the delivery of copy for the new editions, he informed the course chairmen that he had taken them at their word in regard to opportunity for revision, he had given permission for destruction of the plates, and the syllabi could be completely rewritten.

To date it has been our policy to have each year's edition pay for itself so that each fiscal year and each academic year, as far as the publication of the syllabi is concerned, can be begun with a clean slate. The price at which each syllabus is sold to the students includes only the costs of printing, manufacturing, and distribution; no editorial costs are included. The syllabi are copyrighted by the Dean in the name of the University; but each author is told that if, at a later time, he should wish to incorporate any part or all of his syllabus in a book, he will have permission to do so. In one instance this has already happened, and bids fair to happen frequently in the near future.

Though copies of all syllabi are available through the University of Chicago Bookstore to any persons who may be interested, they have not been publicly advertised for public distribution. During the first two years over six hundred separate orders for one or more of the syllabi from outside the University were filled by the Bookstore. In a few instances requests have been received from other institutions for permission to use in their courses one or more of our syllabi, and in each instance the request has been granted. In most instances we can now honestly say that our syllabi have been restudied and re-written in the light of experience to the point that they are for us and our students successful instruments of instruction, and we shall be glad to have any other institutions use any one or more of our syllabi that seem to be adapted to their situation and meet their needs.

The syllabi for the various College courses offered the first year totaled 3,629 pages. The syllabi used in the fourth year, for virtually the same number of courses, totaled 4,328 pages.

In many courses, not only in the four introductory general courses, but also in several of the newly designed sequence courses, suitable texts and supplementary reading volumes have been difficult or impossible to find. To meet these needs three books that are directly the product of the New Plan have already been published for as many different courses, and many others are now being written. In each of two fields a series of texts and supplementary reading volumes has been planned for publication at the rate of a volume a year until the series is complete.

CHAPTER IV

THE FOUR INTRODUCTORY GENERAL COURSES

IN THE early period of planning the four courses in as many large divisional fields of thought, each including several departmental fields, we decided that they should be called "introductory general" courses rather than "survey" courses. In our period of preliminary experimentation we had designed and offered several "survey" courses, the most successful one being in the field of the natural sciences. Our new courses were to be a further development of the basic idea of the survey course, but were to be distinctly something more: they were to be broader in scope and deeper in penetration—they were to be less superficial than the survey courses of the then prevailing type.

The descriptions of the four introductory general courses, as printed in the current (1934–35) *Announcements*, are as follows:

INTRODUCTORY GENERAL COURSE IN THE BIOLOGICAL SCIENCES

The dominating objectives of this course are: (1) to cultivate the scientific attitude of mind through repeated illustrations of the scientific method of attack upon nature's problems; (2) to implant such practical information about biology as is desirable for a citizen in the modern world; (3) to awaken interest in the impressive machinery of the organic world and in the major concepts of biology.

The content of the course is arranged in four main sections: (I) Variety and relationship among living organisms; a brief survey of plant and animal kingdoms, with emphasis upon man's probable ancestry. (II) The dynamics of living organisms; an analysis of how the living machine works, with particular emphasis upon the physiology and psychology of man in health and in disease. (III) Organic evolution, heredity, and eugenics. (IV) Ecology; the relation of living organisms to their environment and to each other: the problems of social organization in lower organisms.

The normal week's program comprises three lectures, one conference period, and five or six hours of outside study. In addition, the students are encouraged to visit the laboratory once each week. Here they are provided first-hand experience with biological facts and materials by a new set of exhibits and demonstrations each week. The lectures are given by fifteen members of the regular staff of the division. Many of the lectures make large use of lantern slides and demonstrations. Students meet in small groups once a week for conference, each group having the same conference leader throughout the year. Conference periods are devoted to discussion, written work, and coaching in the technique of study.

Each student is expected to have a copy of the syllabus of the course, outlining the subject matter with appropriate reading references. Professor Coulter, with the assistance of other faculty members, is responsible for the organization and administration of the course.

Lecturers: COULTER (chairman), ALLEE, CANNON, CARLSON, COLE, DRAGSTEDT, EMERSON, GERARD, JOHNSON, MOORE, NEWMAN, STRANSKOV, SWENSON, TALIAFERRO, AND THURSTONE.

INTRODUCTORY GENERAL COURSE IN THE HUMANITIES

This course uses the materials of history as a foundation and framework for the presentation of the literature, philosophy, religion, and art of the civilizations which have contributed most conspicuously to the shaping of the contemporary outlook on life. The course begins with the civilizations of the Nile and the Tigris-Euphrates valleys, passes thence to Greek and Roman civilization, and concludes with our ruling Western civilization. As this, our own Western civilization, is the main object of attention, it is traced with increasing detail from its medieval beginnings around 500 A.D. through its successive phases down to our own day.

Each student is expected to have a copy of the syllabus of the course to guide his work throughout the year. To illustrate and supplement the syllabus three lectures a week are given, and each student has the opportunity to attend one session a week in a small discussion group with a particular instructor to whom he is assigned for consultation and guidance. The collateral reading in large part is directed to the actual masterpieces of the thought and literature of the past. In connection with the study of the arts the resources of the Art Museum, photographs, prints, and the stereopticon are used. By this method of direct contact with the creations of the philosophers, poets, and artists the effort is made to stimulate the senses, the emotions, and the imagination of the student while developing his critical judgment. In accordance with the very nature of the humanities, the ideal of the course is the well-rounded man.

Lecturers: SCOTT (chairman), ANDERSON, CATE, LOVETT, MACLEAN, MORRIS, OSBORNE, SCHEVILL, and guest lecturers.

INTRODUCTORY GENERAL COURSE IN THE PHYSICAL SCIENCES

The subject matter includes the following: (I) The earth as an astronomical body; the moon; the sun and its family of planets; the stars, star clusters, and galaxies with special reference to astrophysical methods for determining the masses, the composition, the temperature, and the velocity of heavenly bodies; questions of their origins and evolution. (II) The fundamental laws of energy; heat and temperature as manifestations of atomic and molecular motions; relations between matter and electricity and proofs of the atomic character of electricity and the electrical structure of atoms, the atomic character of energy; sound, light, infra-red, ultra-violet, and X-rays as examples of wave phenomena. (III) The many varieties of forms which matter assumes in our environment: chemical elements, compounds, mixtures, solutions, and their distribution in nature; atomic weights, atomic numbers, chemical transformations; periodic system; equilibrium and velocity of chemical reactions, catalysts, combustion; the atmosphere and its products; ionization, acids, bases, salts; carbon compounds and some of their relations to life, the relation of electrical and chemical phenomena, and of atomic structure to chemical properties. (IV) The analytical character and method of physical science: the place, character, and effectiveness of the contribution of mathematics to the development of the physical sciences. This presentation is descriptive, involving a minimum of mathematical technicalities. (V) The earth and its materials: rocks, minerals, earth features and the work of winds, waves, streams, and glaciers in forming them; the character of the geologic record and determination of a time scale; shift of land and sea areas; periods of mountain making and degradation; climatic changes, fossils in their aspect of a geological record of life. (VI) Meteorological processes and phenomena; the character and distribution of major types of climates; the problem of surveying and mapping the earth's surface; the earth as the home of man.

Lectures, given by men of experience as scientists, lecturers, and teachers, are illustrated with experimental demonstrations, stereopticon, and motion pictures. Collateral reading, group discussions, written work, and contacts in appropriate museums with phenomena wherever possible, are important parts of the course. A copy of the syllabus, outlining the work of the course, is available for each student. Professors Lemon and Schlesinger, with the assistance of several other faculty members, are responsible for the organization and administration of the course.

Lecturers: LEMON, SCHLESINGER (chairmen), BARTKY, BLISS, BRETZ, CHAMBERLIN, COMPTON, CRONEIS, HOGNESS, LOGSDON, MONK, TAYLOR, AND OTHERS.

INTRODUCTORY GENERAL COURSE IN THE STUDY OF CONTEMPORARY SOCIETY (SOCIAL SCIENCES I)

The course is concerned primarily with the impact of the complex of forces generally described as the industrial revolution on economic, social, and political institutions. It begins with an examination of the problems and methods of investigation peculiar to the social sciences. The economic, social, and political order that preceded the industrial revolution is then contrasted with contemporary society. The processes of transformation by which these changes were brought about is traced with a view to providing a suitable background for the understanding of the major social problems of the present day. This study of the economic, social, and political order gives occasion for the introduction of descriptive and analytical methods of approach. Opportunity for individual work on selected problems is offered in connection with the major divisions of the content of the course.

A syllabus of the entire course is available at the first meeting. It gives a detailed survey of the subject matter, the program of lectures and readings. Three lectures are offered weekly, and each student has the opportunity to participate in a small discussion group, meeting at least once a week, with an instructor who is also available for individual consultation.

The syllabus of the course has been prepared by Associate Professors Gideonse, Kerwin, and Wirth, with the assistance and advice of other members of the Faculty of the Division of the Social Sciences. These members of the faculty give the lectures and supervise and participate in the work in the small discussion groups.

Lecturers: GIDEONSE (chairman), KERWIN, WIRTH, AND OTHERS.

We realize fully that the classification and organization of knowledge into the four fields which we have set up for the design and administration of as many introductory general courses may advisedly be challenged as an arbitrary classification and organization. One may well ask: Why not two, or three, or five, or six fields; or, even if four, why not a different grouping? A case may well be made for any one of the following organizations: two fields—the humanistic and social phases of man's life and activities, and the nature of the physical and biological world; three fields—the humanities, the social sciences, and the natural sciences; four fields—the history of civilization, philosophy and religion, the social sciences, and the natural sciences; four fields—man in society, the history of ideas, the fine arts, and the natural sciences; five fields—the history of civilization, the fine arts, the social sciences, the biological sciences, and the physical sciences; six fields—the history of civilization, philosophy and religion, the fine arts, the social sciences, the biological sciences, and the physical sciences. Many more groupings into any number of fields from two to ten might be suggested and defended.

All that we claim for our particular organization into four fields is that, after protracted study of the problem in the light of our educational objectives to be pursued with our student and faculty personnel, we selected the plan of organization that seemed most advisable for the launching of our experiment. In the light of accumulating evidence, and in a never ceasing effort to attain the best possible educational results, we are continuously raising and discussing proposals for a fundamental regrouping and reorganization of fields. Any one who knows our Faculty knows that this means, not merely a readiness formally to tolerate proposals for change, but a readiness to consider proposals with an open mind and a readiness to act in the light of evidence and reason, with slight regard and much contempt for opposition to change based on considerations that smack of vested interests or on a blind appeal to past practice. This means merely that, though we have not, to date, seen sufficient reason to change our fundamental plan of organization, we may do so at any time in the future.

We realize also that the plan of organization of our introductory general course in any one of the four fields, as we have set them up, is only one of several possible and defensible plans. Perhaps primarily because of the nature of the subject matter, there is less serious disagreement among our faculty members over the organization and content of the introductory general courses in the biological sciences and in the physical sciences than over the general courses in the humanities and in the social sciences.

For example, some insist that the humanities general course as now offered is too historical; others claim that it is not historical enough; some others say that the present content is worthy of two year-courses—one in the history of civilization and the other in the fine arts; while still others maintain that we should introduce a new year-course devoted to ethics, logic, and philosophical concepts, or to the history of ideas. Having decided, for the present at least, that we shall have only one all-embracing general course in the humanities, the reactions of students seem to indicate that the present course—using the materials of history as a foundation and framework for the presentation of the literature, philosophy, religion, and art of the civilizations which have contributed most conspicuously to the shaping of the contemporary outlook on life—is a happy compromise (neither too much history nor too much philosophy and fine arts) that challenges and stimulates the students more effectively than might any one of the numerous alternative proposals. However, it should clearly be kept in mind that this is merely a tentative conclusion that may be altered by further study of results.

In the case of the social sciences general course, more than a dozen proposals for as many different plans of selection and organization of content were considered. Some were early discarded as least practicable and least promising. The final decision rested between three radically different proposals. The advantages and disadvantages of each of these three were seriously considered. It was finally decided that a course concerned primarily with the impact of the complex of forces generally described as the industrial revolution on economic, social, and political institutions was the one that would be most profitable to our students and could be offered best by our Faculty. We realized at the time the decision was made that this course would not satisfy all faculty members of the Division of the Social Sciences; indeed, it was evident from the great diversity of proposals made by the upper divisional faculty members that no course could possibly be designed that would meet with the approval of all. We simply had to use our best judgment in balancing gains and losses in determining whether this or that, or still another, proposed content and organization should be followed. In this instance, as in the case of the humanities course, results to date seem to show that a wise decision was made, though in the case of the social sciences the general course represents less of a compromise between different proposals than is perhaps true of the humanities general course.

In planning the offering of our new program it was seen that, since the four general field comprehensive examinations were required of all candidates for the College Certificate, and, though some students could and would prepare for one or more of these examinations independently, most students would wish to attend the four introductory general courses offered to assist students in preparation for these examinations, and that hence the enrolment in each course would be large. This in turn meant that the part of each of these courses that could advisedly be offered through the lecture method to large groups should be so offered.

Since we wished to give our Freshmen and Sophomores the opportunity to receive inspiration and instruction from many of our greatest scholars in each of the four divisional fields, the only way this privilege could be extended equally to all students was through large group lectures. Furthermore, it would seem to be a wasteful use of the best talent to have Dr. Anton J. Carlson (to give but a single example), a physiologist of international renown, talk to 25 students in a small section when he can give such remarkably impressive demonstration lectures very successfully to a group of 350 students.

Normally, in the second year of operation of the Plan and thereafter, there would be approximately 700 enrolled in each course. Since our largest class lecture room seated only 350, and in order to facilitate the framing of student programs without conflicts, it was decided to offer two lecture sections of each introductory general course. In the case of the physical science course, it proved necessary to offer three lecture sections, since our only lecture room properly equipped for demonstration lectures in this field seats only 235.

It was agreed unanimously that these courses should not be conducted merely as "talkies." The syllabus and the lectures given in each course should provide merely the points of departure for genuine work on the part of the student, with additional assistance from staff members in small group discussion sections, honor sections for superior students, "trailer" and special training sections for less capable and less adequately prepared students, special laboratory demonstration exhibits, field trips, and individual office conferences.

In the case of the biological sciences and the physical sciences, the question at once arose whether individual manipulatory laboratory work on the part of the student should be required. One of our most distinguished scientists represented the view of his scientific colleagues when he insisted that a science course without laboratory work would be "pale soup." When, however, it was pointed out that all of the introductory general courses were being offered primarily for general education rather than to train future scientists; that the scientific method in each particular field could be fairly adequately presented and illustrated, for purposes of general education, through laboratory demonstration lectures and through special laboratory demonstration museums; and that the requirement of individual manipulatory laboratory work by each student in all or even representative natural science fields would be unreasonably expensive in money and in student time, it was then decided to offer the introductory biological and physical science courses with frequent laboratory demonstration lectures, specially prepared illustrative laboratory demonstration exhibits, and without required student participation in laboratory manipulation.

For students who wished to do more intensive work in any of the natural sciences, the elective sequences in the various science fields would put special emphasis on training in laboratory methods, techniques, and skills for each student individually. For example, the student who plans to do advanced work in the Division of the Biological Sciences, or whose appetite has been whetted by the introductory general course to the point that he would like at least an introduction to intensive work in that field, follows the general course with a year sequence in botany, zoölogy, and physiology that is solely an intensive discipline in laboratory training. Similarly, the student who wants or needs special training in physics and chemistry has the opportunity to elect such courses conducted by the laboratory method in either his first or second year, or both.

To supplement the demonstration lectures and discussion sections of the introductory course in the physical sciences, a special physics museum was set up. There are about 125 experiments and exhibits, the majority of which are either self-operating or student-operated by means of push buttons or similar easily manipulated devices. This museum (described at greater length in chapter ix) is open throughout the year on an announced schedule of hours with a teaching assistant always in charge to answer questions. Special attention is called from time to time in the syllabus, in the lectures, and in the discussion sections, to particular experiments or exhibits housed in this museum. For this course also, the Museum of Science and Industry (founded by Julius Rosenwald), located only a few blocks from the University, has many exhibits that are of value and are used for instruction. Special demonstration lectures are also arranged for this course by the director of the Adler Planetarium and Astronomical Museum.

For the introductory general course in the biological sciences it proved impracticable to set up a permanent exhibit in a single place because of the nature of the materials needed and the expense. During most of the weeks of the year special demonstration exhibits are arranged for the first two days of the week in one of the research laboratories of the particular department whose field furnishes the subject matter for the week's work in the general course. This means that the junior-college students are introduced successively through the course of the year, in the order of the syllabus organization, to numerous laboratories in the biological field. Much ingenuity has been displayed in the design and arrangement of these special exhibits (described more fully in chapter ix). Frequently materials are used that must be specially prepared each day, and in many instances special operating and instructional assistants are employed. Many strikingly effective instructional demonstrations are presented in the course of the year. Also, special guide sheets for many exhibits in the Field Museum of Natural History are distributed to members of the course.

For the introductory course in the social sciences the city, with its many public institutions, its many industrial and financial institutions, and its neighborhoods of various types, furnishes a laboratory. During each quarter several trips to various institutions, industrial plants, and neighborhoods are conducted by staff members to illustrate economic, political, and social conditions, phenomena, and principles. Reports on some of these field trips by members of the course staff are presented in chapter ix.

The introductory course in the humanities uses to good

advantage the resources of the Art Institute of Chicago, the Field Museum of Natural History, and our own Oriental Institute, for trips of observation and study for special student papers and discussion in the sections.

The chairmen and staffs of the four introductory general courses do not follow a uniform policy regarding the number of lecturers used during the year. In the social science course most of the lectures are given by three men; guest lecturers are only occasionally invited. In each of the other three introductory general courses, from fifteen to twenty lecturers appear in a single course during the year. In each such instance the man who is the greatest authority (and who also can lecture effectively to junior-college students) in the field to which a certain section of the course is devoted is asked to give from one to as many as twenty lectures, depending on the amount of time allotted.

It is a matter of interest and gratification that many a one of our most distinguished scholars considers it a mark of honor to be asked to serve as a guest lecturer in the introductory general course in which his interest as a scholar lies. Many such men, who are identified primarily with our graduate work, have confessed that they devote more time, thought, and effort to a single lecture in one of the introductory general courses than to a half-dozen lectures to a graduate class. And many of them do it with most effective results. Merely because a professor, who is a distinguished scholar, sits high among the mandarins of his department or division, however, is no guaranty that he will be asked to lecture in an introductory general course. Some of them, though most effective with graduate students, simply cannot lecture successfully to junior-college students; and they and the students should not be asked to suffer together.

Guest lecturers who give only a few lectures receive no extra compensation for this extra service, but donate their services for the good of the cause. It has been arranged with the President's Office that when a guest lecturer has given a series of lectures that is long enough to be a significant drain upon his time and energies (say ten or more lecturers), for three or four years as extra service, he should be given partial release for a quarter from a full instructional load to pursue his research interest.

In three of the four introductory general courses the younger staff members are being given steadily increasing opportunities to do some of the lecturing. Many of these younger staff members of the rank of instructor are given opportunities to lecture first on the parts of the course that fall in their respective fields of special interest as scholars. In not a few instances they have proved to be among our best lecturers, and hence are asked to give a larger number of lectures, from year to year.

The normal minimum program for each student in each of the four introductory general courses is three lectures a week and one small-group discussion section. It was early decided that in each of the four introductory general courses, small-group discussion sections should be provided, of two types—"regular" sections and "special" sections. Each student in each course has the "privilege" of attending—has a place reserved for him, though he is not obligated to attend—one "regular" small-group discussion a week. By "small group" is meant a section of 25 or less. There is unanimous agreement that no "regular" section should become an old-fashioned quiz section (the instructor[1] quizzing the students for marking purposes) or another

---

[1] Here and in many following instances the word "instructor" is used generically to indicate a staff member of any rank, including full professors.

lecture. The primary purpose of these sections is to introduce each student personally, and more intimately than
can be done through the lectures, to methods of thought
and study in the field in hand.

Experimentation by discussion-section leaders in methods of conducting these sessions with greatest profit to the
students has been encouraged. At the weekly staff meetings of each course a large part of the time is often spent in
exchanging experiences in the use of different methods and
in agreeing upon the major instructional objectives for
the discussion sections of the next week. These weekly
"clinics" conducted by the several groups of staff members,
in order to enable them to be of steadily increasing service
to their students, have been quite productive of improved
performance.

Early in their experience staff members decided that it
was folly to attempt to cover in a discussion section all
points presented in the section of the syllabus and the
lectures of the previous week. Time was too short for anything but the dissipation of the energies of students and the
instructor alike in such a procedure. Perhaps the most
common practice is to agree in a staff meeting upon a few
of the points, covered in the current week's program,
which experience has shown present the most difficulty to
students, and regarding which a clear understanding is
most fundamental to satisfactory progress in the field of
thought in hand; discussion in the staff meeting is then
directed to the discovery of the best methods of approach
to achieve the agreed upon objectives in the student sections. Sometimes agreement is easily reached, and all sections are conducted in a similar manner; at other times
there is disagreement as to methods, and it is agreed that
two or more methods shall be used by different section

leaders, with reports on results a week later. Not infrequently the effectiveness of different methods can be, and is, tested by the use of a common objective test in all sections. There is general agreement that part of each "regular" section period must be devoted to answering questions that any students may care to raise concerning the work of the week.

There is no uniform practice in all of the four general courses regarding the character of organization and the method of conducting the "special" sections, which do not appear in the quarterly time-schedule but are voluntary and extra enterprises on the part of the students. All of these courses have special "honors" sections or "special interest" sections and "review" or "trailer" sections of one type or another.

"Honor" sections are always open only to superior students by invitation. In some instances they are small (from 5 to 20 students) and are conducted throughout the year by a single faculty member or by a pair of faculty members, both being present at each weekly session; while in other instances the honor section has as many as 60 students and is conducted each week by the faculty member who is the greatest specialist in the field under consideration that week. A student earns his invitation to attend an honor section by demonstration of superior attainment in the regular work of the course, and he may lose his right to attend the honor section by failure to maintain a high level of achievement in his work. There is abundant evidence to show that students regard these privileges as "honors" of genuine and not empty value. Some of the "special interest" sections are described in chapter vii and in Appendix E.

The "review" or "trailer" sections are usually small (20

or less); but occasionally for special purposes, when satisfactory results can be obtained through elementary exposition of a few basic points to a large group, with opportunity for questions from the floor, these sections may include as many as 100 students. In some courses the review sections are maintained continuously throughout the year, to provide a second or supplementary discussion section for students for whom one section meeting a week is not sufficient. The same instructor usually conducts a given section throughout the year. The student personnel of these sections may change from time to time: some students may need extra assistance in a course throughout the year, while others may need it on only one or a few parts of the course. In other courses review sections are organized from time to time, to continue but a few weeks, when it is evident that a significant number of students find a particular phase of a subject especially difficult, and hence need special assistance. As soon as these sections have achieved their purpose, they are disbanded; new ones are organized as the need arises.

In all courses the review sections of all types (save in rare instances) are announced to the class as a whole at the time they are organized, and any student who desires to do so may attend. In some instances instructors privately and personally call these special sections to the attention of students who seem to be in particular need of the type of instruction offered. In a few instances instructors have organized small review sections of four or five students on the private-invitation basis. One of our best instructors organized four such sections, giving several hours a week to these students, virtually on the tutorial basis. When he issued the invitation to the twenty lowest-ranking students (on the basis of a test taken by the entire class at the end of the Autumn Quarter) to attend these four sections of five each, he told the Dean he wished to discover whether the Admissions Office had made a mistake by admitting students of inadequate capacity, whether the students were not interested and hence not making sufficient effort to apply themselves effectively, or whether they merely needed coaching in how to work effectively. He found one or two of the first type and a few of the second type; but the majority were of the last type. Thanks to his effective efforts and their hearty co-operation, by the time of the comprehensive Board examination the majority had raised themselves from the bottom of the bottom quartile to a point safely above the passing mark, and in a few instances above the median.

During the current year more than a hundred students in the humanities course are each week attending an extra "regular" section besides the one for which they are registered, and a considerable number are attending two additional sections, in order to get the viewpoints of several discussion section leaders and to attain better mastery of the field.

Another important part of the opportunities for instructional assistance offered to students is found in the faithful keeping of an extended list of office hours by staff members. Students are encouraged to use these office hours for what amounts to tutorial service; and many voluntarily take advantage of the blanket invitation, while others are led to do so by special, private invitations. There is no doubt that students have more opportunities for, and more actual, personal contact with instructors under the New Plan than under the old one. Much of the most effective instruction is given through individual conferences or to groups of two or three students by faculty members in their offices. Though we do not have the tutorial system as developed at Oxford or at Harvard, we do provide an immense amount of tutorial service. Indeed, it may honestly be said that there is provided for each student as much instructional assistance as he may need or desire. This is shown clearly by the excerpts from some reports by faculty members presented in Appendix E.

Early in the conduct of these courses a need was discovered for mimeographing service. The Dean immediately informed the course chairmen that he wanted them to have all the mimeographing service needed to conduct the work successfully. Copy is brought to the Dean's office and 750 mimeographed copies are ready within two days, and occasionally, in case of necessity, on the following day. The materials prepared for distribution to classes are supplementary instructional materials of many kinds, study problems or assignments, and tests or examinations given for instructional purposes. In some courses a short test is given in the discussion sections each week. The amount of mimeographed materials prepared for the four courses during an academic year bulks impressively large.

The staff members of the four introductory general courses who are responsible for planning and carrying on the program of discussion sections include fifteen instructors, five assistant professors, four associate professors, and seven professors of full rank—an average of seven staff members per course. Only a minority of the instructors and assistant professors devote their entire time to conducting discussion sections and holding office conferences. Each of these full-time staff members conducts five "regular" sections and one "special" section. The majority of the staff members, including all of the full professors and associate professors, and slightly more than half of the assistant professors and instructors, devote part time (less than half time, half time, or more than half time) to an introductory general course, and give one or more other courses in the College or in an upper division.

An effort is made to have in the staff of each of the four general courses at least one member from each department whose subject matter contributes significantly to the program of the particular general course. In some instances two or three or even more members of the staff of a particular general course may be members of a single department. After each important departmental field is represented in the staff of a particular general course to the extent of at least one member (the best member available for the purpose), additional staff members are selected with a view to obtaining the most effective instructors, rather than with a view to the maintenance of definitely weighted departmental bloc representation. The establishment of anything approaching a vested interest in terms of departmental personnel representation is carefully avoided.

Each staff member in charge of a discussion section carries the section through the entire course and is responsible for correcting all of the papers and tests written by his students for instructional purposes. With an average of 25 students per section, if a staff member devotes full time to this work and has six sections (regular and special), he corrects the papers and tests and keeps office hours for conferences for a total of 150 students.

The full-time load for all faculty members of the University is three courses (when the faculty member is in full charge of each course), or the equivalent in teaching and research or in teaching and administrative work. Two discussion sections of an introductory general course are rated as one course, because each staff member shares in the work of preparing copy for syllabus revision, preparing copy for mimeographed instructional materials distributed frequently to supplement the syllabus, preparing examination questions for instructional tests and for Board examinations, conducting field trips or laboratory demonstrations, and attends weekly (and not infrequently bi-weekly) staff meetings, holds each week at least as many (and frequently more) office conference hours as he has discussion sections, and corrects all papers and tests written by his students. In addition, many of these staff members give some of the lectures.

All staff members, including those of the rank of instructor, are encouraged to keep alive their interests as scholars through pursuit of research interests. During the first year or two, when each staff member had to devote almost all his time to educating himself in the large divisional field of the course beyond his particular departmental field, opportunity for research was not infrequently out of the realm of possibility. During the third and fourth years of the operation of the plan, however, since most of the staff members have grounded themselves in the broader field sufficiently to feel that they are a comfortable distance "ahead of the hounds," many have found time and have been encouraged to pursue research projects.

The administration of four-sevenths of the College requirements through the four introductory general courses, even though they are conducted in part by the lecture method, has not reduced the size or cost of the instructional staff. Though the size of the staff has not been increased under the New Plan, the cost would have increased materially had the depression not descended upon us. The New Plan demands better instruction than the old plan, and many of the high-grade teachers and scholars we now have on the College Faculty at salaries below their worth would have received calls to other institutions at higher salaries if times had been normal. The comprehensive examination system is entirely an added expense over the cost of administering our old plan.

A tabular view of lecture sections and discussion sections for the four introductory general courses in the academic year 1934–35 is given in Appendix D.

CHAPTER V

FRESHMAN ENGLISH COMPOSITION

DURING the first year of the New Plan the part of our College program that was least successful was the work in English composition. This is no more a commentary on our staff than it is a commentary on the teaching of English composition to junior-college students in most of the colleges and universities of the country, for our course in English composition for Freshmen was apparently little better or little worse than the typical course in other institutions.

During the period of preparation prior to the inauguration of the New Plan, when syllabi were being prepared for several new courses and many old courses were being rehabilitated, the English composition staff planned no less than three experiments with as many different methods of instruction, together with control groups taught in the manner of all sections under the old plan. One experiment during the first year was conducted by having one instructor teach no regular class in English composition, but devote the time that would have been required to teach full time, three sections, to an equivalent number of students (approximately ninety) by a schedule of individual conferences, attempting to instruct them in English composition to the extent that need was evidenced by their papers written for other courses. The plan was unsuccessful and was abandoned in mid-year, because it was found that most of these run-of-mine students needed more instruction than could be given by this method to so many students by a single instructor. Furthermore, it was evident that most of them needed an amount and type of instruction that could be given more economically, and frequently more effectively, in a regular class program. The plan might have been successful had the instructor been assigned a group one-third as large, composed of students who were shown by the placement test to be only slightly deficient in English composition and to need special assistance on only a few particular points.

Another group of students were met, only three times in two weeks, in groups of three, for a half-hour at a time, to discuss papers which, so far as possible, were related to the work of other courses.

The experimental group of the largest number were divided into sections of thirty each and taught more or less in the traditional manner, with one notable difference: all subject matter for themes and exercises, and a very large proportion of the illustrative material used by the instructor, were taken from the four introductory general courses. All of the students of one section were registered in the biological sciences course; all in another section were registered in the humanities course; there was another section composed of students registered in the physical sciences course; and still another of students registered in the social sciences course. This plan, based upon the correlation of the writing for instructional purposes in English composition with the subject-matter materials of other courses, proved the most productive of fruitful results.

Of the four methods used, two proved failures, one was merely a continuation of the old course in the old way, while one proved partially fruitful. The lack of uniformity in the teaching of the various sections or groups of students robbed them of authority in the eyes of the students, who apparently thought that, since composition was taught in so many different ways, there was no body of essential information and skill to be got from the courses. The conclusion was justified, not because different methods were used, but because the various staff members had reached no common agreement on a precise definition of objectives. Not only were different methods being used, but different objectives were being pursued. By the end of the year it was clear that the staff had undertaken too many, and not too advisedly selected, experiments with different methods and sizes of groups, without having given sufficient attention to what was to be taught by the various systems.

It was the failure of the examination program in this field during the first year that precipitated a crisis and pointed clearly to the necessity of a new program in English composition. The instructional staff and the examiners were almost constantly at odds. The instructional staff complained that the "new-type," short-answer tests, of which the examiners were so fond, were not adequate and not valid for more than a small part of the objectives of the course. The examiners complained that the essay-type test, in which the instructional staff placed so much confidence, was not reliable; and the examiners demonstrated their point by having three instructors grade the same essay test paper independently, with resulting grades of A, C, and F.

The instructional staff, during the first year, seemingly could not bring themselves to a whole-hearted co-operation with the examiners. The examiners, without regard for the niceties of diplomacy, bluntly charged that the members of the instructional staff were not agreed on a clear-cut statement of objectives, were not agreed on the best

selection of materials or the most effective methods of instruction to use in an attempt to attain their objectives,
and could not measure the attainment of their objectives
in a valid and reliable manner.

Unfortunately, the Dean of the College was caught between the two millstones, since representatives of each
side of the controversy told their tales of woe to him and
asked assistance to bring the other side into line. By the
end of the year the Dean became convinced that the
examiners had the major weight of demonstrable facts on
their side. The Dean accordingly indicated to the instructional staff that, unless they could develop a defensible
program, the issue would have to be presented to the College Faculty; and in such event, there seemed to be no
alternative to a recommendation that we should drop all
pretense of requiring anything more than the rudiments of
the mechanics of grammar and rhetoric that could be
measured satisfactorily solely through objective tests, and
that the course offered to Freshmen should not attempt
or pretend to do anything more for students than to prepare, for such a qualifying test, those that a placement test
showed to be deficient.

The instructional staff then began in earnest to think
and work constructively. A new statement for a reorgan-
ized course and an experimental measuring program was
prepared and approved by the College Faculty. During
the second year the students suffered less and profited more
than in the first year; and, through effective co-operation
on the part of the instructional staff, the examinations
were materially improved.

In the spring of the second year the chairman of the
course and three members of the instructional staff, who
had worked faithfully and fruitfully on the development of

a new course program, came to the Dean and said that they now knew what they wanted to do and how to do it. The Dean expressed delight and extended congratulations. He was then informed that the further development of this program would require the labors of the three staff members through most of the summer. This meant an added burden on an already strained budget. Though times were hard and money was scarce, the Dean found the necessary amount, and the staff members went to work.

And how they worked! Computed in terms of cents per hour, the monetary compensation they received for what they did was disgracefully low. Their greatest compensation, however, came in the satisfaction derived from making a genuine contribution to the solution of one of the oldest and one of the most difficult of college instructional problems.

Approximately one hundred pages of student materials were prepared, a new English composition handbook was written, and an instructor's manual of over two hundred pages was prepared. But quantity is never as significant as quality in educational materials. In this instance the quality was even more significant than the extraordinary quantity.

The instructor's manual showed clearly that objectives and the methods of attaining the objectives had been given most careful consideration. The objectives of the course as a whole, of each of the three quarters, of each major subdivision of each quarter, and of each minor subdivision, including each day's program, were clearly stated. Many different methods of exposition and instruction were presented for the guidance and assistance of the instructors through the approximately ninety class-hours of the year-course (meeting three days a week), with each suggestion for each day designed in the light of the objective of the day.

In the student assignments for the numerous pieces of writing throughout the year's program there were none of the old-type bugaboos, such as a theme on "A Pleasant Vacation," or "A Trip to the Zoo," or "Building a Sailboat." Each piece of writing suggested for a particular purpose was integrated with the work of one of the four introductory general courses. For each piece of writing suggested, a topic with appropriate bibliographical citations, was offered for each of the four general courses. Since each student was normally registered for two of these courses while taking the work in English composition, he could write his papers in the field of the one that appealed most to him. Thus the reading that he did in preparation for each piece of writing, and the paper he wrote, were both in point in the pursuit of one of his other courses. His writing was therefore appropriately motivated. In the current (1934–35) year, writing assignments are given in each of the four general course fields and new possibilities are being discovered, particularly in the fields of the biological sciences and the physical sciences.

Each piece of student writing is carefully corrected by the student's English instructor, and frequently is returned to the student in private conference. Each instructor devotes at least as many hours a week to individual conferences with the members of a class as he does to class periods. Each piece of writing is used solely as an instructional device, and not at all as a marking device for recording purposes, for, as in all other courses, the instructor gives neither a credit nor a mark that counts for anything in the attainment of the College Certificate. Each student, to qualify for the certificate, must pass the English composition comprehensive qualifying examination of two three-hour sessions on the same day. The student and the instructor, therefore, are striving together to develop in the student the power to express himself with clarity and accuracy in written English—the ability to show that he has developed acceptable and reliable habits of writing.

During the third year, when the new materials of the new program were used for the first time, the instructional staff held long weekly meetings for a complete discussion of the week's work in the light of experience. Each staff member submitted to the chairman in writing (in advance of the meeting) his criticisms, favorable and unfavorable, and his suggestions for improvement of the week's program the next year. Frequently, of course, a day's or a week's program could be considered intelligently only in the light of its position in the program of the month or of the quarter or of the year. Hence the entire course, in its separate parts and as a whole, was continuously under consideration. Frequently in a staff meeting it would readily be agreed that a certain section and its materials were excellent; that another section should be shortened or lengthened; that the objective of another section was sound but that the materials and methods should be changed; or that a new section should be introduced at an appropriate place. Sometimes agreement on a single point regarding an objective, an instructional method, or illustrative material, was reached only after long debate.

During each of these meetings the two members of a specially designated syllabus revision committee took careful and complete notes, with a view to a thorough revision of all course materials for a new edition for the following year. During the following summer, 1934, these two staff members prepared the copy for the new edition. The same process, through weekly staff meetings, is being continued in the current year and now seems to have become a permanently established practice.

An interesting change of position has occurred among examiners and instructional staff members since their opening controversy. There has been a mutual conversion, a rapprochement. As the instructional staff have become educated in the possibilities of new-type (short-answer) tests that can be scored objectively, and have become expert in designing an ever increasing variety of types of increasing value, they have become less insistent upon the use of essay questions. As the instructional staff and the humanities examiner, by co-operative efforts, have succeeded in designing better essay questions and in training readers to attain very high reliability in scoring them, the examiner has become less insistent upon objective questions. In constructing the English qualifying examination for last November, we had the amusing experience of having the examiner suggest a piece of free writing in the form of a theme on a subject that was of the type of which the instructors three years ago were most fond, only to have the instructors balk so vigorously (on the grounds that we had progressed beyond that sort of monstrosity) that the proposal was not adopted.

During the third year and the current (fourth) year, student complaints against the English composition course have been almost conspicuous for their absence, while enthusiastic praise of the course has been frequently heard. At the present writing the prospects for an eminently satisfactory English composition program are excellent.

A brief outline of the program of the English composition course for the current year is as follows:

ENGLISH 102

1934–35

The general aim of the course is to train entering students in the efficient handling of problems involving written expression. The attempt to achieve this aim falls into three rough divisions, corresponding to the three quarters.

Autumn Quarter

The Autumn Quarter is devoted to: (1) laying a sound foundation for the work of writing by training students in the dissection and mastery of materials of the sort encountered in their introductory general courses; (2) training students in the handling of writing problems not involving original organization.

Section I. To train students in making outline analyses.—8 days.

Section II. To train students to write summaries of single pieces, with particular attention to sentence correctness and emphasis.— 12 days.

Section III. To instruct students in the unified summary of several pieces.—6 days.

Section IV. (1) To train students in writing examinations; (2) to prepare students for the work of the Winter Quarter by training them in the formulation of statements of purpose and program paragraphs.—8 days.

Winter Quarter

The Winter Quarter is devoted to training students in the writing of original papers. Students are trained in (1) the organization and development of ideas for presentation; and (2) the effective presentation of the materials gathered and organized.

Section I. To train students in the selection of subjects and in the location and collection of materials.—5 days.

Section II. To instruct students in organization.—10 days.

Section III. To train students in the development of paragraphs.— 6 days.

Section IV. To train students in diction.—8 days.

Spring Quarter

The Spring Quarter is devoted to giving students some elementary training in the specific writing problems that they will face both in examinations and in handling assignments made in other courses.

Section I. To train students in writing definitions.—2 days.

Section II. To train students in handling questions and assignments calling for analysis.—10 days.

Section III. To train students in writing accounts.—2 days.

Section IV. To train students in writing comparisons and contrasts. —5 days.

Section V. To train students in writing criticisms.—5 days.

Section VI. To explain to students what is expected of them in handling assignments phrased: "Discuss. . . . ."—1 day.

Section VII. To review the work of the quarter, and to give students drill in handling the kinds of papers discussed this quarter.— 6 days.

The present course in English composition, though given through the full academic year (three days a week through three quarters), is rated only as two-thirds of a year-course. Under the old plan, two quarters of English composition were required—one in the Freshman year and one in the Sophomore year. Under the New Plan it was decided that no more time was needed; but, since all other courses in the student's program were year-courses or year-sequences, student program-making would be facilitated by speading the work of two quarters over three quarters. Furthermore, the spread of the work over the slightly longer period would give additional time for the fixation of acceptable writing habits.

CHAPTER VI

THE COMPREHENSIVE EXAMINATIONS
AND THEIR RÔLES

THOUGH the primary purpose of the comprehensive examinations is the measurement of student attainments, the examinations have also furnished a significant measure of the effectiveness of the various parts of the educational program designed and administered by the College Faculty.

Though we have a relatively (not completely) independent Board of Examinations, the principle is well established and recognized by all, including the Board of Examinations, that the determination of educational objectives rests solely with the College Faculty. These objectives are defined first in general terms—in terms of the College curriculum as a whole. Then, in each large field the objectives are defined in terms of the general objectives of the College; in each year-course or year-sequence the objectives for each large unit, for each small unit, and for each smaller unit (until you get to a single-line item in a syllabus that may involve only five minutes in the classroom) are determined in the light of the objectives of the larger unit of which it is a part. Thus, the perspective of the position of each tree in the forest is constantly kept in view.

Since it was agreed at the outset that the plan and its administration were to be dynamic and not static (since any educational program to be able to vindicate its existence must react both to and upon the society it is presumed to serve), our educational objectives must at all times be subjected to critical evaluation, and hence subject to change at any time; and as educational objectives are changed, instructional materials and their organization, instructional methods, and the means of measuring results must all be changed accordingly.

At the outset it was decided that no single instructional method or combination of methods should be prescribed for any course or for any group of courses of similar type. The adoption of the New Plan meant that in each course a continuous restudy of instructional methods and their effectiveness was absolutely necessary. The proper uses and the unpardonable abuses of the lecture method (described by some wag as "that method by which the contents of the instructor's notes get into the notebook of the student, without passing through the brains of either"), the discussion method in large groups and in small groups, the quiz method, the tutorial method, the laboratory method, the project or problem method, the weekly and the term-paper method, the examination method for instructional purposes as contrasted with the examination for marking purposes, all must be continuously and critically studied in the ongoing program of each course, with a view to the ultimate selection of the best possible combination of methods in the best possible proportions for the attainment of desired educational objectives.

With educational objectives for a given course determined for a given year, course content and instructional methods on one hand, and the instrument for the measurement of results (the comprehensive examination) on the other hand, must both be framed in the light of the objectives. Neither the selection of instructional materials and methods nor the result-measuring instrument (the comprehensive examination) must be allowed to determine objectives, except in so far as either one or both may show that the attainment of a given objective is impossible, or that the attainment of an objective hitherto overlooked is desirable and possible.

Thus, the adoption of the comprehensive-examination method of measuring results, together with the establishment of a relatively independent Board of Examinations, established, in the first instance, the necessity of a clear-cut definition of objectives in each field of thought; secondly, it established the necessity of a most critical selection of subject matter and instructional methods for the attainment of the objectives. As the examination in a given field, through continuous critical analysis, has become increasingly valid and reliable, the results attained, as shown through this constantly improved measuring instrument, have shown clearly the advisability or necessity of changes in subject-matter content, in organization, in proportions and time allotments, and in methods of instruction. And the readiness of faculty members to become convinced of the necessity of such changes in the light of evidence, and their willingness to act upon such convictions, has been demonstrated again and again.

For generations we have centered our attention on the mechanical arrangements designed to facilitate the pursuit of education without having developed anything approaching an adequate method of measuring validly and reliably the educational product. We have proceeded with blind faith or with a pious hope that if the educational machinery were designed as well as possible, the educational results would be the best attainable. Recent attempts to measure results more scientifically have been conducted with sufficient success to show that at many points our faith and hope have been misplaced—that results from a given educational set-up are not what we had hoped or had taken for granted. Improved methods of testing educational outcomes, that have recently been developed, have forced in many quarters a more precise definition of attainable educational objectives and a more critical examination of instructional methods that have persisted for generations merely on a presumption.

It is my belief that the results of such enterprises as those now being conducted by the Pennsylvania Study, the Cooperative Test Service, the Educational Records Bureau, the Progressive Education Association, a few state-organized groups, and the University of Chicago and a few other colleges and universities, in the field of educational testing and measurements, will be judged by educators a few generations hence to have a significance comparable with that of the invention of the printing press and the steam engine. Just as we now regard the first printing press and the first steam engine as crude and feeble affairs in contrast with modern presses and engines, so will future generations regard our instruments of today for educational testing and measurement as crude and feeble affairs in contrast with what will then have been developed. But the pioneers in this new field in our generation will then rightly be regarded as the Gutenbergs and the Watts of educational testing and measurement. The important consideration is that a beginning, no matter how crude, has been made in a new and most significant field. This beginning will bring revolutionary advances in rapid succession. It means that at last we are centering our attention in education upon substance rather than upon forms.

Permit me to make it clear that I write not as a professional expert in this field—not as a member of the rapidly developing craft of "testers"—who has an ax to grind, in that he is anxious to establish a firm place for himself and his ilk in the educational system. I write as a faculty member and a faculty administrator who is interested primarily in effective instruction, and would cry "down with the testers" as vigorously as any member of my guild if I did not honestly believe that the testers are our best assistants at the present time in the determination of what are appropriate and attainable instructional goals for various types of individuals, as well as in the determination of the extent to which our instructional goals are actually attained.

Permit me to make it clear, also, that we recognize that we are at present making significant headway in the measurement of the attainment of only a few of the significant hoped-for outcomes of college education, and that there are many that we have not, as yet, attempted to measure scientifically. Our major efforts at present are confined to the measurement of some of the results in mental and intellectual attainments from the pursuit of our academic courses of study. Though we do all that we can to provide a setting conducive to the wholesome development of the social, moral, and physical well-being of our students, we have not as yet set up accurate measurements of attainments along these lines for the award of a degree. However, some significant experimentation is under way in an attempt to find accurate measures for these other types of significant products of the educational process.

Even in the realm of mental and intellectual attainments derived from the pursuit of our academic program, we realize that our examinations, though called "comprehensive," do not measure, and at the present stage of their development are incapable of measuring, all of the direct results and by-products. There are many intangibles and imponderables in the development of the mental processes

and the mental outlook of the individual that are important to him and to the society in which he lives, yet are too
subtle or too illusive to be caught and measured fully and
accurately in the written examinations that we now know
how to frame. This is particularly true, perhaps, of the
social sciences and the humanities fields. Most students
attain some phase or degree of many types of these intangi-
ble and imponderable factors from their educational experience in the lecture-room and in the discussion sections.
Some of these factors might possibly be partially caught
and subjectively evaluated to some extent in an hour of
oral examination conducted by three examiners—a little
Ph.D. examination—but such examinations seem out of
the question at the junior-college level because too costly
in time and man power.

However, in this whole educational business all things
are relative, and our present examinations are so much
better than examinations under our old plan—measure so
much more, and measure it so much more completely and
so much more nearly accurately—and contribute so much
to the diagnosis and remedy of defects in the design and administration of the educational program, that we have
reason to feel that we have made a big step forward, and
have reason to believe that this step will lead to still greater
strides toward the goal of the best attainable educational
results.

In colleges where the development of the curriculum was
left to chance, dependent only upon the caprices and pet
hobbies of individual faculty members who introduced
or withdrew courses of almost any type whenever they
chose, under the wide-open elective system, chaos resulted.
Whenever each faculty member is free to award course
marks in accordance with his own individual standard or

system (or lack of both) of evaluation, chaos results. Just as the curriculum must be a matter of co-operative faculty consideration and control, so must the measurement of results. In many institutions the development of a realization of the former necessity has preceded the development of a realization of the latter necessity, which progressive institutions are now endeavoring to meet through the improvement of measurement techniques and practices. The results of the measurement of the attainments of students from the pursuit of a program of one, two, or four years, by a faculty acting co-operatively through a group-controlled comprehensive-examination system, are more often than not quite different from a mere arithmetical average of individual faculty-member judgments for each student as registered *seriatim* through term marks on small unit courses; and the results of the former type of measurement are much more significant, because more nearly valid and reliable, than the latter.

Our faculty legislation says that "comprehensive examinations" shall not be interpreted as being restricted to any particular type of examination; they should include any kind of test, investigation, problem, assignment, or creative work by which the abilities, achievements, or performance of students may be measured, and the examination techniques designed to achieve these ends with the greatest degree of reliability should be the subject of continuous study by the Faculty and the Board of Examinations.

We are developing and using, not only comprehensive examinations for the measurement of student attainments for marking purposes, but also aptitude and placement tests for guidance purposes.

It is sometimes said that at the University of Chicago

we have divorced the examination function from the instructional function. This is only partially true. Though it is true that no instructor knows the mark of any one of his students in his field until the report of the examiners has been officially recorded, the examiners are not an independent group outside faculty control. The Board of Examinations is a faculty board, and the examiners, though they give full time to the preparation and the supervision of the scoring of examinations, are members of the Faculty and are responsible to the faculty Board of Examinations. The Chief Examiner is a faculty member. The statisticians, the examination technicians, and the specially employed readers are all responsible, through the Chief Examiner and the Board of Examinations, to the Faculty.

The Board of Examinations is a policy-framing body and not an active administering body. The board determines such matters of policy as the following: how often and when in each academic year each examination shall be offered; the marking scale (but not the distribution of marks); date limits for student registrations for examinations; fees to be charged students for taking a given examination a second or third or nth time; the amount of time to be allowed students for writing each examination; and any and all other matters of general policy.

The Board of Examinations employs a Chief Examiner, who is responsible for administering Board policies. Routine procedures entailed in the administration of Board examinations are conducted by the Registrar, who is not a member of the Board of Examinations: the registering of students for examinations, the scheduling of rooms and assignment of students to examination rooms (since frequently a given examination must be administered at the same time in several rooms to as many student groups), the recording of official examination marks, and the notification of students of examination results.

Though all members of the Board of Examinations are University faculty members, the Board is, for each division or school, mainly an outside agency in that the single representative of the division or school is a very small minority of the Board. Accidentally and indirectly, a division or school may have its representation slightly increased by having a member of its faculty, who is also and primarily a member of another faculty, appointed to the Board as a representative of the other faculty. The College, which is one of the five divisions, is thus represented on the Board not only by the Dean, as the official representative of the College, but by one of the other divisional representatives and by one of the three members appointed by the President because of interest and competence in examination methods, both of whom are members of the College Faculty; in each instance, however, the faculty member is not primarily identified with the College, since he devotes less than half-time to College instruction. Though the great majority of the examinations sponsored by the Board of Examinations to date have been College examinations, the direct and indirect representation of the College on the Board constitutes a small minority. Thus, for the College as for all other divisions and schools, the Board, though a University Board, is in one sense an "outside" agency, but in another sense is an agency of the University family.

The Chief Examiner is responsible for the selection of his staff of technicians and clerks. For each of the four divisional fields of thought—the biological sciences, the humanities, the physical sciences, and the social sciences—a special technician is employed. Each field technician is given appropriate faculty rank (most of them to date have been given the rank of instructor) and membership in the faculty that he serves. Each technician is usually a person who has pursued graduate work in the divisional field to which he is assigned, and in addition has acquired special training in examination methods, techniques, and statistical analysis. Each examination technician works closely with the instructional staff of each course offered in the field for which he shares the responsibility for framing and administering examinations.

For example, early in the first year of the New Plan, the humanities examiner was introduced to the chairman and staff members of the Introductory General Course in the Humanities. He expressed a desire to attend the weekly staff meetings and was invited to do so. He attended all lectures in the course and some of the discussion sections each week. After about a month he suggested to the staff that they begin consideration of some of the problems involved in framing and administering the comprehensive examination to be given the following June, some eight months hence. This was a new experience for most faculty members who, under the old plan, had customarily devoted no more than an hour (and frequently less than an hour) to framing a final examination.

Throughout the major part of the academic year the humanities staff, with the examination technician now regarded as a regular member of the staff, devoted many long sessions to the critical study of examination questions and materials. The instructional staff members trained the technician in the subject matter of the field, and the technician trained the instructional staff members in examination methods and techniques—he introduced them to the importance of such points as "validity" and "reliability," and the various possibilities of "new-type" short-answer tests.

Quite naturally the members of the humanities instructional staff thought of examinations almost solely in terms of "old-type" essay questions, the only type with which they were familiar and in which they had confidence; as for "new-type" tests, they knew almost nothing save the "true-false" type, for which they had little respect and much contempt. Gradually the technician introduced them to some of the enormously useful possibilities of several other more valuable forms of new-type tests and suggested that they all try their hands at framing samples. To make a long story short, within three months the technician told the Dean of the College that these staff members had co-operated so effectively that they had already taught him several "tricks of the trade" of which he had not dreamed, so skilful had they become in framing excellent new varieties of short-answer tests. One of the faculty members who had written a significant part of the syllabus and who had had prejudices against, rather than enthusiasm for, new-type tests at the beginning of the year, came to the College Dean's office after the test at the end of the Autumn Quarter had been given, to express enthusiasm over a group of short-answer questions on Oedipus Rex that could be answered in a few minutes; he registered the belief that with these questions and the few minutes devoted to them the staff could get a more accurate estimate of a student's knowledge and mastery of Oedipus Rex than from an essay to which the student might have been allowed to devote an hour.

As questions submitted by staff members and the technicians are discussed in staff meetings, each question is examined critically and is approved, or modified to make it satisfactory, or is rejected entirely. In the early days the technician criticized most of the questions submitted by instructional staff members on grounds of faulty technique, while the instructors criticized the technician's questions on the grounds of his lack of knowledge of the subject matter. By mutual education and self-help, nearly all so developed their capacity for framing satisfactory questions that criticisms and rejections of those submitted by individuals to the group became steadily less.

Of course, some staff members find that they have no capacity or facility for the development of interest and skill in examination-framing, while others soon develop a keen interest and remarkable skill. An equitable division of staff labors, among the many types of work necessary to run a course with several sections, that will use each man in the lines of activity in which he can give best service with genuine enjoyment is usually readily agreed upon. Thus, in nearly every field we have succeeded in developing, during the three years of operation of the New Plan, several expert test-makers among our faculty members.

Not only have faculty members developed skill in the framing of satisfactory new-type tests of great variety and usefulness, but they have also devoted an immense amount of time and effort to the improvement of the old-type essay questions, with a resulting significant increase in validity and reliability. The really remarkable reliability that we are now attaining in the scoring of essay questions is in large part due to the increased care and skill with which they are framed, and to the great care with which the specially employed readers are trained and brought to agreement in regard to what to read for and how to evaluate it.

Though in working on the comprehensive examinations for each of the fields of the four introductory general courses the appropriate examination technician works with

the entire instructional staff concerned or with a committee, in preparing examinations in the fields of the departmental sequences the technician is likely to work with a
single faculty member, or at most with two faculty members.

In the preparation of the entire battery of College examinations, the major part of the work falls upon members
of the instructional staff. This does not mean that any
faculty member works harder on, or contributes more to,
the production of examinations than any technician; but
the faculty as a group devote more man-hours and contribute more examination materials than do the technicians as a group. In the preparation of a single examination, in some instances a single faculty member devotes
more time and contributes more materials than does the
technician in whose field that examination falls; but the
technician, as a full-time examiner, is working on several
other examinations in his field.

The examination technicians do not know enough of the
subject matter of any field to produce adequate examination materials without assistance. The particular and important rôle of the technician is to give the criticism, guidance, and training to instructional staff members in examination methods and techniques necessary for improvement in the quality of the examinations. Thus, the examination part of the plan is distinctly a co-operative enterprise in the successful development of which two types
of training are necessary; neither the instructional staff nor
the Examiner's technical staff alone could produce satisfactory examinations; but, working together, each can contribute indispensable elements. At the end of three years of
training and experience, however, some faculty members
and some examiners have become masters of both subject-
matter and examination techniques sufficiently to be able

to frame creditable examinations in some fields without assistance. Nevertheless, the framing of all examinations continues on the co-operative basis, because this is a matter in which many minds are better than one.

At the time the organization was designed for the operation of our New Plan, a proposal was made for the establishment of an absolutely independent Board of Examinations responsible only to the President. Fortunately this proposal was not adopted, for it would have led to intolerable developments that would have wrecked our New Plan long ere this. Such an arrangement would have given control of the curriculum to the Board of Examinations. Our present plan forces the examiners to design their examinations in conformity with the curriculum, and leaves curriculum control entirely with the Faculty. The opponents of some examination programs now in operation or in process of development are right in all that they urge against "outside" examination agencies. The examination system used by any single institution or by any group of institutions (state, regional, or national) must be under control of the faculty or faculties concerned, through their duly accredited representatives, if it is to succeed. This is in accord with the viewpoint of the best test-making experts of the country, phrased by one of them as follows: "Test-making in the subject fields should follow, rather than precede or condition, the curriculum."

Our experience at the University of Chicago has shown that not only the determination of what is tested for, but also the form of the test, must be in the control of the Faculty. Specifically this means the determination of whether a given test or examination shall be "new-type" (short-answer), or "old-type" (essay), or a combination of both, and in what ratio.

As a result of critical and co-operative study by instructors and examiners we have had some interesting changes in attitude on the merits of the widespread controversy between advocates of the two types of examination questions. Some new-type advocates are overzealous and make unwarranted claims; some old-type advocates are stubborn and uneducated in the many excellent possibilities of new-type tests. Fortunately, most of our instructors and examiners have proved themselves openminded on the question, ready to be convinced by the evidence at each point in each field. In some instances it took time and patience to convince an instructor or an examiner that his prejudices or preconceived notions were wrong.

At the beginning of our first year the typical examiner's position was one of overconfidence, while the typical instructor's position was one of lack of confidence, in new-type tests. The instructor said, "Your new-type tests are not valid, because they do not measure what they are presumed to measure or what we want measured." The examiner said, "Your old-type test is unreliable, as witnessed by scores of A, C, and F on the same paper by three different instructors." Each was right in large part at the time. But in the course of three years, by long hours, days, and weeks of critical study and earnest effort by both instructors and examiners, we have learned to produce many new varieties of new-type tests that are valid; and we have learned to produce improved old-type questions that, with careful agreement in advance among readers as to what to read for and how to evaluate it, can be scored with a reliability in the nineties, which is very high reliability.

In the construction of each examination from the first year to the present, the ratio of new-type and old-type parts has been, and is, set by agreement between instructors and examiners, and not by the examiners alone. In some fields the proportion of new-type questions has steadily increased as the instructional staff members have become expert in framing questions and in recognizing the validity of new-type questions submitted by examiners for approval. As increasing reliability has been attained in the scoring of improved old-type (essay) questions, examiners have become their advocates. In one field at the present time we have the instructors urging a greater proportion of new-type questions, and the examiner urging a greater proportion of old-type questions, though three years ago their respective positions on this question of policy were the reverse. In not a few instances instructors, who at first were vociferously hostile to new-type examinations, have recently come to me to confess their conversion and to express their satisfaction with some of our most recent examinations that contain larger proportions of new-type parts than they believed three years ago they would ever approve.

Because of the ease and reliability of scoring new-type questions, our present tendency is to use this type in each specific examination to the extent that it can be validly used in that field. In some fields the proportions are now 50 per cent new-type and 50 per cent old-type parts, while in other fields the new-type parts constitute as much as 80 per cent of an examination. The ratio for each examination in each field is determined anew each time an examination is constructed, in the light of the study of previous experience. We have no set goal for a definite ratio in any field at any time in the future. We shall continue to be guided by reason in the light of evidence as it accumulates from experience.

Anyone who claims, as some have done recently in print, that new-type (short-answer) tests call merely for the development and exercise of the power to memorize—merely for the cramming of facts—simply demonstrates that he is not informed regarding the character of the most recently developed varieties of new-type tests. Though this charge was true of the particular variety of short-answer test that was at first widely used (the "true-false" question), this particular type is now used but little because so many more significant varieties have been developed and successfully used. Literally dozens of varieties of new-type tests have been developed in many fields in the last two years that measure validly powers and types of mastery that it was formerly thought even by test-makers, and is still thought by the uninformed in this area, could not possibly be measured by short-answer questions. And what is more, these questions can be scored with almost perfect reliability—something that could not be demonstrated for most of the old-type examinations.

The first half (three hours) of the examination in the field of the humanities given in June, 1934, was an "open-book" examination: students were permitted to bring and use textbooks and notebooks. Though the "open-book" examination led the faculty members and the examiner to devote the utmost care and effort to the preparation of the best possible examination questions, and led the students to prepare more elaborate and analytical notes, a comparison of results with those of the previous June examination shows that the effect of the open-book examination was not great.

Though any one of our instructors can honestly say to his students all during a year-course that he does not know what the comprehensive examination in that field will contain, he can give assurance that the examination will be fair (valid) and will be scored fairly (reliably). Though in many instances the instructional staff members in a given field work fairly continuously throughout the academic year with the examiner for that field on the preparation of examination questions and materials, these merely go into the hopper for future use and cover the entire field more completely than could possibly be done in any single examination. Thus examination materials are being accumulated almost continuously. Superior types or forms are constantly displacing old ones.

In some instances, when the time arrives for approving a particular examination for an announced date in the immediate future, the examiner for that field brings to the instructional staff a proposed selection of questions. The staff studies the proposed examination, suggests deletions, insertions, changes in proportions for various parts of the field, etc. In other instances, the examiner and the instructional staff together assemble a proposed examination and then study it carefully, item by item, until agreement is reached on the examination as a whole, including all component parts.

In the "Report of New Plan Examinations for the Period 1931–1933" prepared by the examiners and published in planographed form, December, 1933, the Chief Examiner, Dr. L. L. Thurstone, includes the following in his introductory statement:

The examiners have made numerous experimental studies of examination methods. These studies are published in various journals, and they have been listed in the bibliography at the end of this report. The bibliography includes all of the publications during a two-year period so that it is not limited to achievement examinations. The two principal problems in examining for achievement in college are (1) to ascertain to what extent each examination measures the objectives which the instructors may have had in mind, and (2) to ascertain the consistency with which the examinations record the achievement of individual students. These are the problems of validity and reliability. Problems of validity are always more difficult than those of reliability, because, in order to ascertain the validity of an examination, it is necessary to obtain some index of student achievement which is independent of the examination whose validity is to be ascertained. These indices are usually in the nature of estimates by the instructors of the achievement of students. These estimates usually vary among several instructors who may know the same student. Aside from statistical statements of this problem, it is evident that, in general, we cannot expect an examination to agree better with the judgment of instructors than the instructors agree among themselves. This problem is fundamentally the same whether we deal with the short-answer form or the essay form of examination.

The examiners favor the principle that examinations should place emphasis on the student's ability to reason with the principles of his subject, rather than the ability merely to repeat factual material by rote memory. One cannot demonstrate mastery of any subject without some factual material. The student should be asked, not only to supply whatever factual material he is expected to have mastered, but also to deal with it in such a manner as to involve, wherever possible, some degree of reasoning.

Occasionally we meet the notion that the short-answer form of examination lends itself only to the factual type of question, and that reasoning must be tested by an essay or by some form of free writing. This is a misunderstanding which we hope may be dispelled by the short-answer examinations that have been written during the last two years. It is possible to ascertain the student's power of reasoning with his material as well with the short-answer form as with the essay form; but there is, of course, no legislation or compulsion to use either form exclusively in any subject. The advantages of the short-answer form are usually that one can cover a much wider range of subject matter in a given time by the short-answer form, that it is much more consistent as to the grades that are assigned by several equally competent readers, and that it is less expensive for large classes than the essay form. It is clear, however, that it requires more ingenuity and labor by the instructors and the examiners to prepare an examination which shall test objectively the student's power to reason with the material of his subject than merely to ask him to discuss something. In grading student discussions, one is likely to find that equally competent instructors vary considerably in the grades that they assign to the same essay. The examiners are trying various methods of improving the essay form of examination both as regards its validity and its reliability.

In response to suggestions of the faculty, the examiners have collected a set of objective examination questions to illustrate the various ways in which the objective methods can be adapted to different types of subject matter. These examples, together with some explanatory material, have been assembled into a *Manual of Examination Methods* which is available in the University Bookstore.

Anyone familiar with modern examination techniques knows that a complete item analysis of a six-hour examination requires an immense amount of careful work; yet item analyses are frequently made. High degrees of validity and reliability can be attained and maintained only by continuous co-operative study by both instructional staff members and examiners.[1]

Occasionally during the first year the Dean of the College had to serve as an arbitrator of differences between examiners and faculty members. As instructors have come to appreciate more fully the character of examination problems, and as examiners have learned more of the subject matter and the educational objectives of instructors in their respective fields, serious disagreements have developed less frequently, and harmonious relationships are now the order of the day. In the most serious disagreement to date that arose in a most difficult field, the Dean, against his natural inclination, sided with the examiner, because the examiner demonstrated to the satisfaction of the Dean that the instructional staff members in question had not defined their educational objectives precisely, were not agreed upon the most effective instructional methods or materials to use in the attempt to attain their objectives, and were utterly unable to measure reliably the attain-

[1] See chapter x and Appendix H.

ment of the objectives—that instructors' course grades in this field in the past had been of little value. After this crisis was squarely faced, the instructional staff began to study their problems constructively and eventually succeeded in dissolving each of the three indictments of the examiner; and relationships between the examiner and the staff are now entirely harmonious. Needless to say, the students profited greatly from the development of an entirely new course in this field, with objectives clearly set forth, with instructional materials and methods better designed and administered, and with results measured validly and reliably.

Clearly, with the student's educational progress being measured for official recording solely by comprehensive examinations and not at all by course credits and course grades, and with instructors insisting and examiners admitting that in most fields sole reliance could not be placed upon new-type tests, if the examination were to test adequately the many types of power and mastery included in stated educational objectives, a greater degree of reliability in the reading and scoring of essay questions, than had characterized the reading and scoring of essay questions in the past, must be attained. In the three years (to date) of our study of this problem we have made remarkable progress. In the early days of our critical attack on the problem a reliability of .50 was high, while a reliability of .30 or even .20 was all too common. At the present time reliabilities of .90 and better are being commonly attained in the reading and scoring of essay questions. This achievement was attained only by co-operative effort on the part of both examiners and instructors.

At the present time reliability in the reading and scoring of essay questions is attained and maintained by the following typical procedure. When a set of papers is in hand to be read and scored, the readers are assembled to receive instructions from the examiner and one or more members of the instructional staff who may or may not be serving as specially employed readers for the examination in hand. The instructional staff members are qualified and authorized to represent the entire staff of the course as far as educational objectives and the evaluation of their attainment are concerned. The instructors explain to the readers the purpose of the first essay question to be read and scored—pointing out sins of commission and omission, and indicating what constitutes an entirely satisfactory answer worthy of the mark "A." A dozen or twenty papers are then selected at random and are read and tentatively scored by each reader independently. If the tentative scores of the several readers of a given essay in the dozen or more student papers approach uniformity to what is considered a satisfactory extent, the official scoring may proceed; if not, as frequently happens, another period of exposition and discussion follows, in preparation for another "trial heat" of scoring. When it is demonstrated that all have clearly in mind what to read for, and how to evaluate it, the official scoring proceeds. During the course of the official scoring, results are checked periodically for reliability if a hundred or five hundred or even more papers are to be scored.

Of course the objective or new-type parts of any examination can be scored by intelligent clerks. Readers for old-type (essay) questions are selected by the examiners only with the approval of the instructors concerned. All examination papers are scored anonymously—names are removed and numbers substituted. Thus, no special favors can be extended to athletes, children of trustees, or "teacher's pets." Occasionally an instructional staff member is employed (for extra compensation) as a reader in his field as well as to train the other readers in what to watch for in reading and how to identify and evaluate it. Since all examination papers at the time they are read and scored are anonymous, and since papers are allotted to readers purely by chance, even if an occasional instructor who is serving as a reader should happen to draw a few papers written by students whom he had instructed, he would not be aware of the fact and the number would be negligibly small.

The preliminary conferences in preparation for the scoring of a single examination are frequently several hours in length. Though expensive in time and money, the result (the attainment and maintenance of reliability in scoring) is worth the investment, because so crucially essential to the success of the examination system. With either validity or reliability open at all to serious question, the confidence and enthusiasm of faculty and students cannot be maintained.

The weighting of the various parts of a single comprehensive examination for scoring is a vitally important matter that is also determined by agreement between the examiners and the instructional staff concerned.

When the papers of a given examination are all scored, they are arranged in score order with percentile ranks computed. A conference is then held between the examiner for that field and one or more representatives of the instructional staff to agree upon the division points for the award of A, B, C, D, and F marks, with D passing. This is not done merely by looking for convenient "breaks" in the distribution of scores, but involves the reading by instructors of papers just above and just below a proposed division point. If the papers of the tentatively selected top group are not judged to be "A" papers and those of the group just below "B" papers, another division point in the distribution curve is sought and papers similarly examined. This process is continued until a satisfactory division point is found which may be at the 93d percentile or at the 85th percentile, or at any other percentile. Fairness to students in the light of their performance on the examinations is the primary consideration in selecting each division point between mark groups down to and including the division point between D and F marks, with D passing. While the A and B marks are of significance in the award of honors and scholarships, the F marks are the ones of most significance in determining whether a student should or should not continue in college.

Still the papers are anonymous. When the final-mark groups are agreed upon, they are reported to the Dean of the College for approval, merely that he may have an opportunity to investigate unusual or apparently unreasonable instances of percentage distributions among marks. We have no established "grade curve" for mark distributions; and though the Dean has investigated unusual distributions, he has in no instance to date ordered a review or re-reading, because a reasonable explanation was given in each instance. At one examination period the F marks on one examination were 8 per cent and on another examination 27 per cent, while the average for all examinations was 14 per cent. When the report in duplicate is signed by the Dean, he retains one copy and returns the other to the Examiner's Office for file. After the Dean has approved the distribution of marks, only then are the marks assigned from paper numbers to the names of the respective writers and reported to the Registrar for official recording.

We hope to attain, as soon as may be possible, something approaching an absolute standard in as many examination fields as possible. This seems more readily possible in some fields than in others. Our attention is forced to this problem because we early discovered that, while the group of students taking a given examination in June is typical, the group taking the examination in the same field in September is usually heavily weighted with two extremes—superior and inferior students. If it were easier for a student to pass at one examination period than at another in the same year, and if this discrepancy continued, the fact would soon be discovered by students and the effect upon student confidence in the examinations would be disastrous.

Thus, the effort is constantly made to keep examinations comparable from one period to another in regard to both difficulty and scoring standards, Though standards employed in the framing and scoring of the examination in a given field may wisely be raised or lowered slowly over a period of years, such changes should be consciously made, and should be kept carefully under control by examiners and faculty. Whether students are, or are not, directly and immediately informed of such changes by examiners and faculty, they will surely discover them fairly early.

Since all Board examinations become public property as soon as they have been given, and are available to students in the Bookstore or in the Libraries, one may ask whether a student might not prepare for a forthcoming examination in any field by use of past examinations in that field. To a certain extent this is true; indeed, we consider a careful study of past examinations in a field one of the useful and perfectly legitimate methods of attaining mastery of that field.

To date we have constructed a new form for each examination and have repeated no significant amounts of any previous examination. After we have constructed and used ten different forms of an examination in any field (and that point has been reached in a few fields and is about to be reached in all fields), we may begin to use several of the most valuable parts from various previous examinations. Even if we should construct the eleventh form of a particular examination by putting together parts selected from each of the previous ten (which we are not likely to do), it would be virtually impossible for a student to assemble correct answers for all questions in all of the previous ten forms, memorize them, and thus pass the eleventh form. Most of the questions are such that the exercise of the power to memorize is not sufficient to answer them satisfactorily; the examinations place emphasis upon the student's ability to reason with the principles of his subject, and therefore require an appropriate level of genuine mastery of the field. For a student to attempt to assemble satisfactory answers of all questions of ten previous forms of a certain examination, so that he might memorize them as a substitute for working out his own mastery of the field, would require the assistance for several weeks of someone who had mastered the field, and then would require a memorizing feat so stupendous that it would require more work and be less interesting and less profitable (even merely as a preparation for the next examination) than doing the regular work in the expected and customary manner.

Past examinations are of real value to the student as an indication of the type of examination to expect and as a legitimate auxiliary study-tool while endeavoring to master a field; one or two forms of previous examinations, kept available for study while the student is working his way through the various parts of a large field, may call to his attention points that he might otherwise overlook, and may assist him in clearing up doubtful points. Beyond this they will be of little service to him in preparation for a future examination.

Tests, quizzes, and examinations are frequently given in many courses for instructional purposes rather than for mark-recording purposes. The results of such examinations are never made a matter of record in the Registrar's Office. When test papers are carefully read and corrected, and returned to the student by the instructor in personal conference, as is frequently done, the test serves as an excellent instructional device. Students realize this and frequently ask for more tests in a course than the instructor has planned to give. The students realize that these tests or examinations are solely for their benefit, to assist them in their own education; a test does not furnish an occasion for the student to attempt to cheat or fool the instructor, because, since the instructor awards neither course credit nor a mark that counts for anything, it is impossible for the student to cheat the instructor out of a credit or an undeserved mark. Thus relationships between student and instructor are greatly improved.

These instructional tests given in courses furnish an excellent opportunity not only to instruct the students but also to instruct the instructors and the examiners regarding the value and soundness of examination questions concerning which they are in doubt. Many times questions are tried out experimentally in a course test, and their value proved or disproved. This reduces materially the number of questions in official Board examinations that have to be eliminated in calculating scores because results prove them to be faulty for one reason or another. Whenever a question is given in a course test that proves, on the basis of results, to be faulty, a complete explanation is given to the students in order to train them in the critical study of examination questions.

Toward the end of the Winter Quarter last year, one of the discussion section leaders in Social Sciences I (Introductory General Course in the Study of Contemporary Society) asked her students to submit questions on the work of the quarter that they would consider "fair" for a comprehensive examination on the year's work. Seventy questions were submitted that included many valuable suggestions for use in constructing future comprehensive examinations; they showed critical analytical thinking on the part of most of the students, and demonstrated that the project had been an excellent instructional device.

Each of the seven examinations required for the College Certificate is six hours in length, three hours in the morning and three in the afternoon of a given day. Thus, each student, to qualify for the College Certificate, must pass forty-two hours of examinations, either all at one examination period of two weeks, or spread over several examination periods, regardless of how many courses or parts of courses he has pursued in residence or the length of time he has been in residence. A student who has completed a course is not required to take the comprehensive examination in that field immediately upon the completion of that course; however, all seven required Board examinations must be passed within a period of two calendar years after the first comprehensive examination is passed. Nearly all Board examinations for the College Certificate are given at least twice a year. It is the desire of the Board that the examinations be given as often as once every quarter whenever there is sufficient demand to warrant the preparation of the examinations. Students are identified at Board examinations by signature and by photograph. The Board examinations are thoroughly proctored, with a proctor for each twenty-five students when a large room is used. To date only one student has been dismissed from the College for dishonesty in a Board examination, while three proctors have been discharged from service because of failure to follow strictly the carefully prepared and printed instructions for conducting examinations. There have been four instances in which a student was warned by a proctor, because of suspicious conduct, and reported to the Registrar; but in each case investigation showed that disciplinary action was not apropos.

No fee is charged the first time a student takes any Board examination. If the examination is repeated, a fee of $5.00 is charged for the first repetition and $10.00 for each subsequent one. There is no limit to the number of times a student may repeat any one of the examinations to attain a passing grade. The higher of the two grades is entered on the student's record: that is, if the second examination gives a higher grade than the first, the second grade stands; if the second grade is lower than the first, the first grade stands. A few students, as a matter of personal pride or to better their chances for honors or for a scholarship, pay the fee and repeat an examination in an attempt to raise a grade of B to A.

If a student questions the correctness of his grade, he may have his examination reviewed by presenting a petition to the Dean of College Students and making a deposit of $5.00. The deposit is refunded in case the letter grade is raised. The Board examinations are devices for measuring achievement, are not intended to be instruments of instruction, and hence are not returned to the students.

We have made significant improvement in the quality of design of examinations in our three years of experience and continuous critical study of results. We made good examinations in some fields the first year, and are now merely making somewhat better ones. In some fields, however,

our first examinations were lamentably bad. In most of
these fields we have learned to frame creditable or even
good examinations, but we shall sooner or later (I believe
soon) learn to make excellent examinations in all fields. I
blush with shame when I think of an examination we gave
in a certain field the first year, but I glow with pride when
I contemplate the examination in this same field given last
June, 1934.

Under our old plan some individual instructors and some
entire departments were habitually high markers, while
others were low markers. Phi Beta Kappa could be attained by a mediocre student who judiciously elected certain instructors and even certain departments and avoided
other instructors and departments. There was scant reliability in our marks. Our examinations now given are a
more searching and more nearly valid evaluation of a student's genuine attainments, and the official Board examination marks are much more reliable, than was true of
course examinations and marks under the old plan.

Though we had many excellent courses, well designed
and effectively taught, before the adoption of our New
Plan, we also had some courses that were a disgrace on the
scores of organization and presentation. Since early in the
design of the Plan we decided to abandon course credits and
course marks, and to rely upon comprehensive examinations open to any student at any time regardless of his
length of residence or his having pursued in residence only
part or no part of one or more of the year-courses offered
to assist students in preparation for the battery of comprehensive examinations, we decided that each year-course
should have a printed syllabus prepared by the faculty
members concerned. This was the first guaranty that
thought and care in impressive amounts must be given to

the organization of each course. A second guaranty to this same end, and at the same time a guaranty that serious study would be given to the selection and use of the most effective instructional methods, was inherent in the examination system adopted.

So seriously have the faculty members taken their obligations in the preparation of course syllabi that most of these syllabi have been revised each year to date. Most of the revisions of sections of the various syllabi (and in some instances an entire syllabus) have come as a result of experience in the administration of the courses, and particularly from the testing of results through our continuously studied and carefully administered examination system. The appearance of syllabi in cold type and the continuous critical study of results through the examinations have tended to smoke out defects and weaknesses in subject-matter selection and organization, and in the selection and use of instructional methods. We have developed in three years more significant improvements in the clear definition of educational objectives in each field, and in the selection of materials and their organization and presentation in courses, as a result of printed syllabi and our examination system, than would have come in a score of years without these stimuli.

CHAPTER VII

STUDENT-FACULTY RELATIONS AND REACTIONS—SIDELIGHTS

WHO ever heard of college Freshmen and Sophomores asking for the more frequent administration of searching, penetrating examinations? Who ever heard of junior-college students requesting that the library be kept open longer hours and that the privileges of book withdrawals be enlarged? Who ever heard of junior-college students asking for extra discussion-section meetings in a course for which they receive no course credit? Who ever heard of junior-college students writing long papers that are not required and for which no credit or course-mark premium is offered? Who ever heard of junior-college students asking for increased demonstration laboratory and laboratory-museum privileges when attendance is on the optional basis? Who ever heard of junior-college students daily discussing very earnestly the most fundamental questions in philosophy, literature, biology, astronomy, economics, political science, and sociology, at the dinner table and in the lounges of dormitories and clubs? Who ever heard of Freshmen, who have not failed one or more courses, spending most of the summer studying consistently, week after week, though not in summer school? Who ever heard of Freshmen taking large numbers of college books with them on a vacation at a lake in the northern woods? We have experienced each of these developments under the operation of our New Plan.

During the troublous days of the period immediately

following the American Revolution, one of the "fathers"—
a leading statesman—remarked: "It takes a long time to
make sovereigns out of subjects." Since the launching of
our New Plan, some of our leading "educational states-
men" have remarked: "We seem to have demonstrated
that young people of college age can be developed from
pupils into scholars much more rapidly than has been sup-
posed, if but given the opportunities and responsibilities
both appropriate and necessary for such development."

Among high-school and college educators greater emphasis, in rapidly increasing amounts, is being placed upon
substance as contrasted with forms. This is evidenced by
the very significant programs and activities of the Progressive Education Association's Commission on the Relation
of School and College, the Educational Records Bureau,
the Co-operative Test Service, the Study of the Relations
of Secondary and Higher Education in Pennsylvania, the
Every-Pupil Contest of the State University of Iowa in the
high schools of Iowa, the Committee on Revision of Standards of the Commission on Institutions of Higher Education of the North Central Association, the report on *Comprehensive Examinations in American Colleges* by Edward
S. Jones for the Association of American Colleges, and the
New Plan of the University of Chicago—to mention only
a few of the most outstanding of such programs and activities.

In the Pennsylvania Study, not a few instances were discovered such as the following: On a comprehensive objective examination given to Seniors, a young woman, about
to receive her degree *magna cum laude*, scored fifth from
the bottom in a class of forty-eight in her institution and
in the lowest 10 per cent for the state; after reviewing the

case the examiner at the institution reported that the girl
was an ambitious credit-hunter, extremely anxious to satisfy her teachers, and had received high marks term by term,
although his inspection showed that her courses were mainly those for which credit was notoriously easy to get; she
was tractable, of pleasant personality, very religious, and
apparently had put the faculty completely under a spell as
to the validity of her intellectual activities.

Under our old plan of measuring the student's progress
in terms of course credits and grade points based on course
marks—a plan still almost universally employed by the
colleges of this country—not a few students were elected
to Phi Beta Kappa at the University of Chicago because
they judiciously elected "snap" courses given by faculty
members who were notoriously "easy" or high markers,
and courses by some other faculty members who marked
not on genuine intellectual achievement alone but rather
more than less on student personality, character, and attitude—pleasantness of personality, faithfulness, promptness, neatness, and complete conformity in routine. Such
factors still enter too frequently and too prominently into
the award of high marks, and thus the award of the Phi
Beta Kappa key in too many colleges. I do not wish to be
understood as belittling the importance and value of a
pleasing personality, faithfulness, promptness, neatness,
and many other such personal traits. I merely raise the
question whether the evaluation of such traits and characteristics should be merged and confused with the evaluation of genuine intellectual attainment in the award of
course marks and Phi Beta Kappa. I believe that it is important to have the evaluation of such traits and characteristics of each student filed regularly by each of his instructors and entered in the student's personnel case history, but

distinct from, and not confused with, the record of the student's academic intellectual progress and attainments. We have endeavored to design and administer our New Plan at the University of Chicago in such a manner.[1]

Under the old plan an instructor in his classroom was literally monarch of all he surveyed. He was lord and master, because he was only infrequently, if at all, supervised by a superior officer, and because he held absolutely in his control the fate of his students in the power to dispense credits, marks, and grade points. Students had to attend his class regularly, had to study his whims and caprices, had to go through any meaningless routine he might prescribe, had generally to court his favor, and only rarely, even in a minor instance, dared offer in a most diplomatic manner the slightest criticism, if they were not to put their course credit and grade points in jeopardy.

Under the New Plan, with the award of credits, marks, and grade points taken away from the instructor, with the student free to attend class or absent himself at will, with courses offered solely with a view to assist the student in preparing himself for the demonstration of genuine educational attainment through the medium of comprehensive examinations, with the official Board examinations the only ones that count, and with these examinations scored by some one other than the instructor, it is evident that the traditional relationship between instructor and student is completely changed.

No longer confronted with any occasion, let alone any necessity, to court or fear an instructor, the student is in a position to criticize freely the objectives, content, organization, and methods of instruction of any course, and to request of an instructor more, or more effective methods of,

[1] See chapter viii, "Student Guidance and Personnel Work."

instruction that he thinks necessary or advisable in pursuit of his effort to attain the level of achievement he desires in the field with which he and the instructor are immediately concerned.

Members of the College Faculty were fully aware of all these implications or corollaries of the New Plan when they voted to adopt it. They welcomed this new and more wholesome relationship between student and instructor, realizing fully that each would have to devote more time and thoughtful effort to his duties as instructor than under the old plan. Group meetings of College faculty members in a common field for serious discussion of, and exchange of experiences with, different methods of instruction, in a search for the most effective method or combination of methods, were few and infrequent under the old plan, but are now regarded as a necessarily regular part of the successful administration of our instructional program and are numerous and frequent.

All Freshmen enter the College. The upper divisions and the professional schools begin their work at the senior-college level—some of the professional schools in the Junior year, and others in the Senior year. Our entering Freshman class numbers approximately 750 each year and is limited to that number because we have neither the staff nor the equipment to handle effectively a larger number.

Our entrance requirements are only very slightly prescriptive as to specific units and unit groups. We place much more importance upon the scholastic aptitude and the personal qualities of the applicant than upon specific units of credit and their distribution.[2] The great majority of our students enter by certificate. Our quality require-

[2] See chapter xii for a statement of our College entrance requirements.

ment is, roughly, graduation in the upper half of the class of a school of good standing.

Though we did not raise our entrance requirements, we hoped that the announcement of the New Plan would attract a larger number of superior students. This hope has been realized. We have had more applicants for admission than ever before from students who ranked in the top tenth of their graduating classes in excellent preparatory and high schools. During the last three years approximately 40 per cent of our entering Freshmen have ranked in the upper tenth of their graduating high-school classes, and approximately two-thirds in the highest quarter. Of the Freshmen who entered in 1934, one in every five ranked among the top four individuals in the scholastic ratings of his high-school graduating class. There are in the class 55 valedictorians, 37 salutatorians, and 30 who ranked third.

For many years we have given the American Council on Education Psychological Examination to all entering Freshmen. Our medians in terms of the national standard deviation and adjusted national medians for the years 1928–33, inclusive (the last three years of the old plan and the first three years of the New Plan), were .83, .83, .81, .98, 1.04, and 1.14, respectively. This means that our median gross score for 1933 was higher than the national adjusted median gross score by 1.14 per cent of the standard deviation of the national distribution of gross scores. The figure 1.14 for 1933 is a 38.5 per cent increase over the average of .823 for 1928–29–30, the last three years of the old plan. One standard deviation above the national mean represents a point below which 84.13 per cent, and above which 15.87 per cent, of America's college population is found in regard to its ability, as measured by the American Council Psychological Examination. Our median gross score for the class entering in the Autumn, 1934, jumped to 232.5, from 217.89 for 1933. At the time this is written, the national median is not available.

These objective evidences of superiority have pleased us; but we have been delighted to receive reports from instructors, from advisers, and from the physicians on our Health Service staff that our Freshmen of the last four years average higher as interesting and attractive personalities, and average better as specimens of humanity, than previous classes.

Under the old plan we maintained an Honor Commission, composed half of students and half of faculty members, to conduct hearings and impose penalties in cases of dishonorable conduct of students in course work or course examinations. During the three quarters of the regular academic year the Honor Commission heard approximately the number of cases typical of almost all student bodies the size of ours. These cases were also typical in character, involving the various forms of cheating in course examinations, plagiarism, copying large sections from other students' term papers and laboratory notebooks, etc.

In most such instances under the old plan the incentive to, and objective of, cheating was to get a better course mark than the student presumably otherwise would receive without devoting more effort. With the abolition of course credits and course marks awarded by instructors, the incentive to, and the objective of, such forms of cheating are removed. It is now impossible, in the pursuit of course work, for the student to cheat the instructor out of anything; if a student attempts to cheat an instructor, he succeeds only in cheating himself.

Since all tests, quizzes, papers, or examinations of any

type given in a course are solely for instructional purposes
and not for marking purposes, the possibility of a student
cheating the instructor through "cribbing" of any type has
been removed. All Board examinations (the only ones that
are officially recorded) are thoroughly proctored.

Since courses and course credits are not required, and
only the demonstration of achievement through Board examinations is required, students may or may not, as they
choose, attend classes, write the papers, prepare the notebooks, and take the weekly, monthly, or quarterly tests
that are suggested or administered in any course. The objective of each and every activity sponsored and conducted
by an instructor in any course is solely the education of the
student—the increase of his knowledge and the development of his powers and skills in the field of thought and
work to which the course is devoted. Student compliance
with suggestions or requests is not motivated by a desire to
satisfy or please the instructor in order to win from him a
credit and a favorable mark; student compliance is motivated solely by the knowledge that each course and the
various activities of each course are offered merely to assist
the student in his own education.

Early in the first year of the New Plan a paper was suggested in the Introductory Course in the Social Sciences.
It was announced that these papers would be carefully read
and criticized by the instructors and returned to the students. When one instructor read the papers handed in by
his students, he readily discovered that three papers were
almost identical. He knew enough of the abilities of the
three students to know that the paper was of a quality
higher than two of the students could have produced. Under the old plan the student who had permitted his paper
to be copied would have been summoned before the Honor

Commission for trial with the two who had copied. In this instance the instructor summoned the two to his office for a conference. The instructor explained that the sole object of written work by students was helpful criticism by the instructor in order to assist the student in the development of his power to think straight and to express his thoughts adequately and accurately. The instructor explained that he would discuss with its author the paper that these two students had copied, but not with them, because the author would profit materially thereby while they would not. There was no question of cheating the instructor; the two students had cheated themselves out of the opportunity to profit by a written exercise thoughtfully criticized for their benefit. The instructor, having also discovered that the two men were athletes anxious to be eligible for the University football team the following year, explained that he could have nothing to do with determining their eligibility except as they gave him every opportunity to assist them to educate themselves at least to the extent of satisfying the passing standard of the Board of Examinations in the comprehensive examination.

Similarly, the sole objective of the frequent papers written by students in the English composition course is the development of the power in the student to express himself with clarity and accuracy—the power to demonstrate to the satisfaction of the Board of Examinations on the English qualifying test that the student has developed acceptable and reliable habits of writing. It will profit the student nothing to trick the instructor through plagiarism into a belief that his ability to express himself with clarity and accuracy in written English is greater than it really is.

As soon as the first generation of students under the New Plan learned, as they did during the first year, that nothing could be gained, and much might be lost, by attempts to cheat or trick an instructor, they gave up the attempts. Wisdom of this sort is readily passed from one generation of students to the succeeding one, and it is now a rare instance in which a faculty member finds it necessary to explain this point to a student.

At the end of the first week of classes under the New Plan, a student came to the professor in charge of one of the new introductory general courses and said: "I have read the syllabus, noting the bibliographical citations, and believe that I am now adequately prepared for the examination in this field." "That's interesting," said the professor, "let's talk it over together." After half an hour the professor said, "I agree with you. It would be a boring repetition and waste of time for you to take this course. Go to your adviser and tell him that I recommend that you register for an advanced course. When the examination for the field of this course that you are dropping is offered, present yourself, and the chances are decidedly that you will pass it satisfactorily." He did. Such incidents have occurred frequently enough to be regarded now merely as a matter of course in the operation of the New Plan.

During the third week of the Autumn Quarter of the first year, 1931, when the professor in charge of the physical science general course was completing the discussion of one unit of work preparatory to beginning a new unit, one of the students, speaking for several of his fellow-students as well as for himself, asked: "How much of this material we have covered in this unit do we *have* to know?" The professor smiled and answered: "You don't seem to get the idea of the New Plan. As far as I am concerned, you don't *have* to know *anything*. I have no power to grant or deny you a course credit or a grade that counts on your degree. I and the entire instructional staff of this course are available to help you in every way we can to master as much of this field of thought as is possible in the time at your disposal. We are not here to crack the whip or hold a club over your head." Our students soon developed a realization and full appreciation of the changed relationships between student and instructor, and questions of this sort are now rarely asked.

In this same course, tests were given at frequent intervals during the first Autumn Quarter, not for credit purposes, but for instructional purposes, so that students and instructors might have indications regarding the progress made by the students toward mastery of the subject. Near the end of the term a group of students asked whether a final examination on all the work to date would be given. The professor in charge replied: "We shall let you decide. We are not required to have an examination on this part of our work at this time under the New Plan, though such was the requirement under the old plan. If you want such an examination now in preparation for the comprehensive examination, administered by the Board of Examinations, which you will have to pass to complete the college requirements, we shall be glad to give it." A poll of the class was taken, with the result that a large majority voted for a searching, difficult examination. Thus a class that early in the term asked how much they *had* to know, later in the term requested an examination in order that *they* might know how much they had achieved.

Though the official Board examinations are the only required examinations, it was agreed when the New Plan was adopted that reviews, tests, quizzes, and examinations of various types should be given at times and in amounts as needed to attain desired educational results, the need to be determined by faculty and student judgments in the light of experience as each course progressed. Interestingly enough, in not a few courses students have asked that examinations be given more frequently than the instructors thought necessary to acquaint both students and instructors adequately with the rate and degree of progress being made by the students. The tendency is to accede to student requests in such instances. In more than one instance at the end of the Autumn and Winter quarters, after several instructional tests have been given during the quarter upon the conclusion of logical units of work, it has been left to student vote to determine whether a final examination on the entire quarter's work should be given. In every such instance the students have asked for the examination, though they knew that the result would have no officially recorded effect upon their attainment of the junior-college certificate. They did know, however, that the examination papers would be carefully corrected and returned, and would thus serve as an excellent instructional aid in their endeavor to master as much of the field as possible in preparation for the official Board examination.

There are no regulations regarding attendance at classes by students. Under the old plan, with required attendance, most students seemed to think it necessary to take a standard number of "cuts" to preserve their self-respect. Class attendance on the voluntary basis under the New Plan has averaged almost exactly what it was under the old plan with attendance required. In some classes the attendance record has been higher, while in other instances lower, than under the old plan. Attendance under the New Plan seems to be in direct ratio with the extent to which the students think that the class period is profitable to them, while there was no such relationship under the old plan when a course credit was at stake. One of our faculty members gave simultaneously during the first year two sections of the same course, one section for New-Plan Freshmen and the other for old-plan Sophomores; he was one of our best instructors and used the same methods in both sections; he reported that the attendance record of the former class was better than that of the latter. A group of students, talking informally and not for publication, expressed their attitude as follows: "So many able and distinguished lecturers and instructors have been provided for the Freshman courses that we would no more think of 'cutting' a class than we would think of throwing away a ticket for a concert or the theater for which we had paid good money. If we 'cut,' we are sure to miss something of value to us for which we have paid a tuition fee; and the instructors are only interested in helping those who endeavor to help themselves." Students are visiting courses for which they are not registered, in addition to carrying a full program for which they are registered, more frequently than formerly.

In a course in which effective instruction can be given only with the intelligent and faithful participation of the students (for example, a laboratory course or an elementary course in a foreign language), the instructor may notify a student, whenever, through lack of interest, effort, adequate preparation, or ability, he has shown himself to be a hindrance to the progress of the majority, that henceforth he will be regarded merely as a visitor.

In the design of our New Plan we endeavored to give students greater encouragement, and, indeed, to confront them with an increased necessity, to do more independent work and to read more books with greater profit. But none of us dreamed that in so short a time Freshmen and Sophomores could be brought to read so much or so intelligently as soon proved to be true. At the opening of the Autumn Quarter of the first year we kept the College Library open from 8:00 A.M. to 10:00 P.M. During the first two weeks so few students used the Library in the evening that we decided to close the Library at 6:00 P.M. By the end of the fourth week we were besieged with requests from students to open the Library again in the evening. By this time they had come to realize the extent of their responsibilities and the amount of work necessary for them to make satisfactory progress in their own education. In answer to their request we announced that as a privilege to them we would keep the Library open until 10:00 P.M. as long as the number of patrons warranted the additional expense. In the first week of the second Autumn Quarter we were confronted with a library problem quite different from that of the first year: at the beginning of the first year the problem was to get the students started to using the Library; before the end of the first week of the second year the problem was to provide enough books and enough attendants to give adequate and prompt service to the library customers. Rush orders were sent by telegram for more books, and an already strained budget had to be revised to provide additional service. When several students were asked why they were reading so steadily early in the Autumn Quarter although the comprehensive examinations would not be faced until the following June, they replied: "We have been advised by students who were New Plan Freshmen last year to begin our reading at once and not to let it pile up or we would be hopelessly swamped by the end of the year." During the third year we had a daily circulation of over a thousand volumes of books used only in the humanities course and in the first- and second-year social science courses; and the reading in these volumes was in addition to rather heavy text assignments in one course and large amounts of indispensable readings in each of the other two courses in a set of several volumes rented to each student for the academic year. The College Library and the Rental Library are described in chapter ix.

Several members of the Faculty who in the second year had classes composed largely of second-year students reported with delight that these students showed a greater breadth and wealth of reading, of ideas, and of general intellectual background, as a result of their training in the new introductory general courses, than was true of any previous Sophomore class.

Though we offer none of the four introductory general courses and only parts of a few of the elective sequences in the Summer Quarter, during the summer of 1933 we had over a hundred students who, though not in residence (not registered for courses), came regularly each week to the College Library to withdraw books by the armful. Some of these students had failed one or more examinations in June and were preparing to take them again in September. A more significant group of considerable size, however, had passed a full quota of examinations in June and were "working up" new fields, without attending courses. Most of these students (from our best group) passed the examinations with distinction. One mother told me that, after observing that her son and two of his friends had worked faithfully on the physical science field during part of June and all of July and August, preparing to take the examination late in September without attending the course, she insisted that her son go with her to their camp in the northern woods for the first three weeks in September, prior to the examination. It was arranged that the two friends should join them two or three days later, after camp was put in order. She was astonished to observe, when she and her son met the two friends at the station many miles from camp, that the largest items of luggage were bundles of books brought in compliance with a conspiracy to avoid having their work interrupted by the vacation in unacademic surroundings.

———————

During the first year the Freshmen were extremely conscious that they were engaged in an experiment, and for some weeks their attitude was "Show me!" The Sophomores were continuing on the old plan and, either from an honest skepticism or from a sour-grapes attitude, tended to ridicule the Freshmen and the New Plan. And, it must be admitted, many students sensed that some instructors were none too sure of themselves as participants in the New Plan. The second year, however, the Sophomores, as "old timers" at the game, were a most wholesome influence in guiding the newcomers in the way they should go, and the Faculty was in a position to inspire confidence in a manner that was impossible the first year. Whatever the explanation, we were impressed with the celerity, eagerness, and effectiveness with which our Freshmen went to work in the opening week of the second Autumn Quarter.

Our New Plan was introduced with an entire entering Freshman class in September, 1931. During the first year only Freshmen were under the New Plan, and all students who had previously matriculated were given until August, 1935, to complete the requirements for the Bachelor's degree under the old plan. During the second year Freshmen and Sophomores were under the New Plan; in the third year the upper divisions received their first large group of New Plan students; and in the current June (1935) the first large group of students will complete the requirements for the Bachelor's degree under the New Plan. During each of these years from 1931 to 1935, inclusive, we have had a steadily decreasing number of old-plan "credit-chasers."

The following editorial appeared in the student paper (the *Daily Maroon*), January 3, 1935.

With the coming of the new year it is only fitting that some little time and space be devoted to a look at the academic calendar for the next four quarters. Such a look discloses a surprising number of possibilities.

The next two quarters will mark the passing of the last undergraduate survivors of the old plan. Although, for all practical purposes, the educational system which was so auspiciously inaugurated three and a half years ago is in complete dominance, the vestiges of the old are still present in a few Seniors who will no longer cloud the horizon of "progressive education" after June 11.

Most marked in our eyes is the difference in attitude of the Freshman of today as marked with the newcomer of 1931. Perhaps this is due to the fact that the "guinea pigs" were faced by mental handicaps which took some time to overcome. They cut classes for weeks at a time because of the freedom allowed them after rigorous high-school discipline. In short, the general attitude was, "How little work can I do and get away with it?" This mood changed after the first comprehensive examinations in June, 1932, and since that time there has been a subtle molding of interests and attitudes, until the present, when the incoming class surprised and is still surprising us all with a serious demeanor befitting a student of the University.

Several years ago fears were expressed to the effect that the University was becoming wholly a graduate institution. Indeed, although our graduate schools have reached a position second to none, our undergraduates are justifying their existence, and even carrying on respectable research projects.

Now all we have to do is laugh at, and thus ignore the "reds," and we shall be able to enjoy, from all indications, a successful and profitable year.

Of course, the terms "Freshman," "Sophomore," "Junior," and "Senior" are coming to have less and less significance since the time-serving element has been eliminated from requirements. Various students enter the upper divisions or professional schools after one quarter, one year, two years, three or even more years in the College; while various students qualify for the Bachelor's degree after one year or additional fractions of years up to a total of five, six, or even more years in the University. The tendency is becoming increasingly pronounced to classify students merely as "College students," "divisional students," and "professional-school students," without any additional appellation to designate length of time in residence.

In the conduct of the Introductory General Course in the Biological Sciences, which is designed primarily to serve the needs of students in regard to general education and only secondarily to give prerequisite training for future specialists, no manipulatory laboratory work on the part of the student is required. The object of the course is not to train botanists, or zoölogists, or physiologists, or bacteriologists, but is general education for Freshmen and Sophomores, at least three-fourths of whom will never pursue any more formalized instruction in biology. Many of the lectures are laboratory demonstration lectures, but the students who are not to pursue any further work in this field are not required to spend long hours in the laboratory developing skills and techniques they will never use. Those who desire to specialize in this field are given an intensive laboratory training in a second-year course.

Some of our faculty members protested against denying future biologists the privilege of laboratory experience in the first year. Hence we planned to provide laboratory contacts on a voluntary basis for members of the introductory class who requested it. By the end of the third week of the first year a number of students expressed a desire for more opportunity to observe laboratory phenomena than was provided in the lectures. The announcement was then made to the class that in answer to student requests laboratory demonstration exhibits would be arranged from week to week to illustrate further the work of the course as it progressed, and would be available at certain hours for all who desired to avail themselves of this opportunity. About half the class attended these exhibits during the remainder of the first year. Since the first year these special laboratory demonstration exhibits have been broadened in scope and improved in quality. On approximately two-thirds of the Monday and Tuesday afternoons throughout the year, special laboratory demonstration experiments and exhibits, arranged so that students individually and in small groups may have opportunity to examine, observe, and contemplate at close range and in an unhurried manner many illustrative phenomena, are provided on the voluntary basis. Each exhibit and demonstration is given in the graduate research laboratory of the department concerned. Though this not infrequently means, for the student, running all over the campus, locating buildings he has never before entered, climbing four flights of stairs in search of a particular laboratory, all at an inconvenient time, more than 70 per cent of the class regularly take advantage of these special offerings. These special demonstration exhibits are described in chapter ix.

The professor in charge of one of the three parts of the second-year biology course—a sequence in botany, zoölogy, and physiology devoted to intensive laboratory training—was very doubtful, when the New Plan was launched, concerning the wisdom of offering the Introductory General Course in the Biological Sciences without required laboratory work on the part of the student. Nevertheless, he agreed to participate in the introductory course and has given effective service as one of the lecturers and as a leader of two of the regular discussion sections. After experience with students in his part of the second-year sequence he reported that this class of Sophomores had successfully done a larger amount of more difficult work than he had ever dreamed could be expected from junior-college students. He had to alter his plans in mid-course, stiffening up both the quality and the quantity of experiments and problems. He explained this development on the following counts: though the class numbered so many students that it had to be divided into two large sections, those who enrolled in the course on the elective basis constituted a highly self-selected and excellently motivated group; the lectures, readings, discussion sections, and laboratory demonstrations and exhibits of the introductory course had given them thorough preparation for, and appreciation of the purposes and values of, laboratory training for further work in the field; they needed no further explanation of, or exhortation to, effective laboratory work and were eager to get at it.

A professor who plays an important rôle in the instructional program of another unit of this sequence reported as follows: "The students who have come on into the second-year biology sequence are, beyond argument, better prepared and more enthusiastic than any previous group. We have revamped our old-plan departmental introductory course as part of this New Plan junior-college sequence so that it is really more difficult than any one of the previous senior-college series, and yet the majority of students are thriving on it."

Toward the end of last Spring Quarter our supply of copies of the *Syllabus* for the Introductory General Course in the Biological Sciences was exhausted. We needed some copies immediately for students registered for the course in the Home-Study Department, for some students who wished to work independently during the summer, and for orders from other institutions. We did not wish to order a new printing from the plates of the current edition, because we were planning to publish a new edition during the summer. Placards were posted on bulletin boards offering a liberal price for used copies, and the clerks in the Rental Library asked each student when he returned his rental set for the course, after the comprehensive examination had been taken, whether he wished to sell his copy of the *Syllabus*. Under the old plan we had experienced no difficulty in purchasing used copies of textbooks when needed. In this instance we were astonished to find that only one copy of the *Syllabus* was offered for sale. Again and again a student stated that he wished to use his *Syllabus* for future reference and as a reading guide, even though he had passed the required examination.

In the introductory social science course a number of students expressed a desire to have an extra meeting each week for discussion of current national and international problems in the light of concepts and principles developed in the course. The professor in charge of the course said he would be glad to meet with all students so interested, and announced a place and time for the meeting. The attendance was surprisingly large, and the discussion by the students (with the professor acting merely as a moderator, willing to answer questions directed specifically to him) was stimulating and of remarkably high caliber. This extra-curriculum activity, entirely on the voluntary basis, continued to flourish throughout the first year and thereafter became a regular part of the course offerings sponsored by the course chairman for interested students on the voluntary basis.

During the winter of the first year the students in the humanities course were requested to write papers on projects selected by themselves and approved by a member of the instructional staff. Each project involved an intensive study of some exhibit in the Field Museum, in the Art Institute, or in the Oriental Institute, directly connected with the work of the course. The papers were carefully corrected and commented upon by the instructors with regard to content, organization, and presentation of ideas. The judgment of the instructional staff was that the papers were far better in quality than they had believed in the autumn it would be possible for the students to produce during their first year in college. At the end of the Winter Quarter a stiff, penetrating examination was given for instructional purposes. A large part of the examination was objective in character in order to eliminate subjective judgments of those who marked the papers. Each instructor registered a guess in advance as to what the average score of the class would be. When the papers were scored, the average was found to be 10 per cent above the highest guess of any instructor. One of the members of the staff said at the end of the Winter Quarter of the second year that the special-subject papers written by students averaged perceptibly higher in quality than the corresponding papers of the previous year.

A part of the ongoing program of the humanities general course is the organization of "special-interest" sections open to any student who has a burning desire to pursue the particular phase of the field announced for the particular special section farther than is provided by the regular program of the syllabus. These sections are in addition to the regularly scheduled discussion sections and are on the voluntary basis. Special-interest sections are offered in literature, in philosophy, in religion, and in fine arts. Each section is conducted by the member of the instructional staff best qualified and most interested in the particular phase of the work of the course to which the section is dedicated. Attendance is entirely voluntary, and the response has been most gratifying. During the third Autumn Quarter, when a member of the humanities staff announced the special-interest section for the field of literature, hoping to attract about twenty students, he was nonplussed when at the first meeting he found approximately a hundred students—twice as many as there were seats in the room. In spite of the fact that he gave them his assurance "as a gentleman and a scholar" that he would not attempt in any way to conduct the program of the section so that it would be of any direct assistance to any student in passing the humanities comprehensive examination, and in spite of the fact that he announced a qualifying examination to be given a week hence to eliminate those not genuinely in earnest in their expressed desire to pursue the study of literature solely for its own sake, he succeeded in cutting the number of the group no more than half. Even with a group too large for the plan of procedure originally contemplated, the program, as modified by necessity, attained excellent results.

One of the essay questions, to which sixty minutes were allotted in the June, 1933, humanities comprehensive examination, was the following: "Give a brief but adequate summary of the civilization of the Hellenistic period according to the plan suggested in the first diagram given you (in the syllabus); that is, sketch in first the political and economic background, then characterize successively the various forms of thought (philosophy, science, religion) and expression (literature, sculpture, painting, and architecture). You are expected to make general statements, but also to substantiate them by reference to definite names of persons and places, dates, works, and accomplishments. Try to spend at least ten minutes in marshaling your facts and planning your organization. Organization and presentation, as well as factual material, will be taken into consideration by the readers." After the examination papers were read and scored by the readers, some of the best and some of the poorest papers were read by two instructors in the Introductory General Course in the Humanities, merely for their own enlightenment on how students performed on the comprehensive examination in their field. These instructors agreed in the judgment that any one of three of the best answers written by Freshmen to the question quoted above could be substituted for chapters or sections on this topic in not a few widely used textbooks, with a resulting improvement of the textbooks in factual and thought content, organization, and literary style.

In the spring of the third year (1934), we found ourselves in the midst of a fervid, and in some quarters perfervid, debate over the relative importance of facts and ideas in various fields of intellectual endeavor. This debate was precipitated by a convocation address by President Hutchins the previous December, and drew the entire university community into participation. For three months the student paper, the *Daily Maroon*, ran an almost continuous series of editorials and communications, ringing the changes on the theme, to the extent that the factual and thought content and the instructional methods of courses and the comprehensive examinations of virtually every departmental and divisional field were searchingly and critically discussed. Even though many of the *Maroon* criticisms were unfounded in fact or unwarranted in basic concept, some were in point; and they brought forth a significant contribution to the intellectual life of the community because students and faculty alike devoted more critical thought in an articulate manner to all phases of the main project in hand—education—than the present writer has ever known to be true of any other college or university community in a generation.

One debate of this question of ideas versus facts, between two faculty members, arranged by an undergraduate group (self-started and self-propelled for the discussion of problems in biology), and scheduled originally in a classroom seating 350, had to be moved to Mandel Hall, seating 1,500, so great was the demand for tickets; and even this lecture hall was not half large enough to seat those who desired to hear the debate. Many small groups of students discussed the question for many hours. One such group—another self-started and self-propelled group—organized during the first year by students primarily interested in the social sciences, at one stage of their discussion asked a professor of physics to meet with them to discuss the inductive and the deductive methods of work as used by physical scientists, in order that these social science students might compare and contrast methods of work in the two fields. The professor of physics later reported that it was one of the most interesting and stimulating discussions in which he had ever been privileged to participate or to which he had ever listened.

Under the old plan the term "student activities" was applied to athletics, social affairs, dramatics, publications—activities in which only students were primarily concerned; the pursuit of knowledge and scholarship was regarded as a "faculty activity," one with which only faculty members were primarily concerned. Under the New Plan, with students attending classes voluntarily and not under compulsion, with students asking for examinations, with students asking to have the Library open longer hours, with students asking for more laboratory contacts, with students asking for extra discussion-group meetings, with students seeking more individual tutorial conferences with instructors than ever before in spite of, or because of, knowing that the instructor awards neither course credit nor grade points, it seems that the pursuit of knowledge and scholarship is becoming a major "student activity." Not all of the traditional "student activities" of the extra-curriculum variety are going to die a natural death in the face of this new competition for student time and interest, but there is evidence that some of them will die unless they can be revamped in character so that each will have something really worth while to contribute to the participants' educational experience. The extra-curriculum activities in best position to offer an educational appeal worthy of student interest and participation at the present time seem to be the University of Chicago Dramatic Association, the University of Chicago Symphony Orchestra, the University of Chicago Choir, the University of Chicago Chorus, and the student publications. The dramatic and musical organizations are doing really remarkable work of great educational value to participants and to the entire community.

Needless to say, not all our Freshmen have prospered educationally from the very beginning of their experience under the New Plan. During the Autumn Quarter of the first year approximately 50 per cent succeeded in getting well oriented into their new life with its new responsibilities and were happier, more exhilarated, and more enthusiastic than was true of so large a group under the old plan. During the Winter Quarter approximately 25 per cent more got satisfactorily adjusted and joined the ranks of the contented and enthusiastic. The Spring Quarter had to tell the story for the remaining 25 per cent, because at the end of the year those who had not been able to demonstrate that they could work with sufficient profit to themselves in the program we offer, either because of lack of ability or lack of proper motivation, would have to be denied the privilege of returning for further work next year, in fairness to themselves and to us. When the time of reckoning came, it was found that only approximately 5 per cent had to be told that they could not return for work in residence until they had demonstrated that they could, and would, profit thereby. A few of these individuals studied faithfully during the summer and reinstated themselves in September by passing one or more of the comprehensive examinations in which they had failed in June. Our academic mortality has been no greater under the New Plan than under the old plan, though there is no doubt that students have to work harder and more effectively than under the old plan in order to "make the grade" and "get by."

The percentage of the first year's Freshmen who returned the following autumn was larger than the percentage of returning Sophomores the year before. Since we know that the percentage of the first year's Freshmen who,

owing to the depression, were prevented by financial difficulties from returning the following autumn was larger
than in previous years, it would seem that more students
are satisfied with their educational progress under the New
Plan than under the old plan.

Each student who enters the University is given a fairly
thorough medical examination by the staff of our Health
Service. Further diagnosis and treatment are given as soon
as possible to each student whose first examination reveals
the need or advisability of such follow-up procedure. Each
Freshman, later in the year, has a health conference with a
staff physician, regardless of whether his first examination
indicated any need for such a conference. The conference
is of some length, and information is sought on every phase
of the student's living conditions and habits that may affect his physical or mental health. Dr. Dudley B. Reed,
Director of the Health Service, summarized for me in
April, 1934, some of the impressions of himself and members of his staff gained from these health conferences with
Freshmen, as follows:

. . . . As you know, we have had half-hour health conferences with
all Freshmen students during the last three years and we have been
particularly interested in certain changes in students' reactions toward
the University and the New Plan.

One of our questions to each student is: "Do you like the University
and the New Plan?" our interest being in his happiness and adjustment.
During the first year of the New Plan very many students replied that
they were uncertain about their feelings toward both University and
New Plan because they did not know what was expected of them and
did not know what reading they should be doing and also missed the
assurance of progress which was given by the high-school procedure to
which they had been accustomed. The second year there was much less
evidence of this sort of dissatisfaction and uncertainty, and this year
there has been still less. Almost all of the students to whom we have

put the above-mentioned question this year have made some such response as, "I like it very much," or "Yes, indeed!" or even "You bet your life!" In other words, this year we have met with almost universal enthusiastic approval. The few students who have not been enthusiastic have been those who had wished to go to some other institution or those who know what line they wish to follow and therefore feel that one of the general courses does not fit in with their plans. Sometimes it is one course and sometimes another. At any rate, it seems significant to me that there has been such an increasing enthusiastic appreciation of the University's educational plan, and I felt that you might be glad to have these observations passed on to you.

Incidentally, as I have told you by word of mouth, we feel that we are getting a much finer type of student in the main than we used to, our observations being based on evidences of personal hygiene as well as on those of alertness, intelligence, and good family training which appear in our contacts with students.

Under the old plan our faculty members were distressed by the disgracefully large proportion of students who seemed to be interested only in "beating the game." Each student had to accumulate the same number of course credits for a degree. Each course was too frequently regarded merely as one of a long series of little games, the object of each game being to beat the instructor out of a credit with a grade high enough to have it count as one of the mystic number required for a degree. Many a student seemed to think that if he could beat the game, acquire the necessary credits for a degree, and at the same time resist all efforts made on his behalf to have him acquire an education, the joke was on the institution. The students were not to blame for developing such an attitude; the system was responsible.

In the decade following the World War, students in steadily increasing numbers registered their disgust with the system. The development and inauguration of our New Plan was the result of student dissatisfaction as well as faculty dissatisfaction with the old plan. More and more frequently in recent years students said: "Don't ask us to be, and don't reward us for being, merely good sponges and parrots; don't tell us everything and don't do all our thinking for us; give us fewer petty tasks; give us more formidable and more significant objectives and goals; give us helpful guidance and assistance as we may need it, but give us also more freedom, independence, and responsibility for our own educational development."

Many of us have long held a belief which President Lowell of Harvard, shortly before his retirement, stated most aptly as follows: "Maturity is by no means wholly a matter of years; it depends much more on environment, and above all on responsibility. A youth who enters college at nineteen and is treated like a schoolboy matures less rapidly than one who enters at seventeen and is treated like a man." Our experience has done much to strengthen our belief in this basic point of departure.

Providing what we believe to be a conducive environment, and placing on the student what we believe to be an appropriately increased degree of responsibility, together with adequate provision for guidance and instructional assistance for each student to the extent of his need and desire, we have found that students are capable of maturing at a rate and to a degree above that of the presumption on which the old plan was administered. They not only assume increased responsibilities successfully, but they enjoy doing so. There has been a decided change for the better in motivation. The first year's Freshman class furnished the "guinea pigs" for an educational experiment that proved extremely exhilarating to those of us conducting the experiment and to the "guinea pigs" as well. Indeed, the "guinea pigs" so thrived under the experiment that our original faith in the soundness of the basic principles of the New Plan was converted into a conviction that we were on the right track. We began our second year with many of our fears and reservations eliminated, and with our enthusiasm strengthened by the satisfaction of having attained a degree of success even greater than we had dared hope would be possible. Most of the "doubting Thomases" among the College Faculty who had little faith in the New Plan when it was launched, after three years' experience and observation of results have become enthusiastic converts. Of course, there are some members of the upper-divisional faculties who still know little about the New Plan either in theory or in operation and still enjoy making disparaging remarks about it. But these same men, more often than not, know just as little, and make equally disparaging remarks, about any new development in any phase of life outside their own highly specialized field where their own intellectual sun rises and sets.

Since "the proof of the pudding is the eating," one may appropriately ask what the students think of the menu of courses and examinations served to them. Under our New Plan our students have greater respect for, and greater confidence in, the courses and the examinations; larger numbers of them are interested, exhilarated, and enthusiastic, are reading more and working harder, with verve and intelligent purpose, than was ever true of Freshmen and Sophomores under our old plan, which is still the prevailing plan in most institutions in this country.

Each June, in Convocation Week, the secretary of the Alumni Council stages for returning alumni a conference, with several sessions devoted to as many phases of the University's activities. At the sessions of the 1933 and 1934 conferences devoted to the College, he arranged to have several students discuss their experiences under, and their reactions to, the New Plan. Some of these students were Freshmen, some were Sophomores, some were men and some women, and some were from the Chicago area while others were from widely scattered states. Most of them were unknown to the Dean of the College prior to this occasion. They were selected with a view to typical representation of the College student body, and they were told merely that no one of them should speak more than ten minutes; they were told that they had complete freedom to say whatever they might choose on any phase of life and work in the College, and might be as pointedly critical as truthful exposition required. Some of the comments by these students are the following:

Indeed, I feel like a typical University of Chicago "New Plan" student. During the past three days I have been exposed to eighteen hours of comprehensive examinations—and believe me, they are real examinations!

The features of the New Plan that have been most significant to me have been impressed upon me as being significant only through discussion of education policies and practices as they are found in various colleges and universities with friends attending different institutions of higher learning. After discussing such matters with friends from several colleges and universities, I feel that the characteristics of our New Plan that have been most significant to me have been (1) the freedom of the plan, (2) the survey-course system, and (3) the opportunity for contact with outstanding men.

When I say I enjoy the freedom of the New Plan, I do not mean that I like freedom merely for the sake of freedom, for certainly no one need come to a university to be free. Not only have I enjoyed the social and general academic freedom, but I have particularly been benefited by the specific freedom from compulsory class attendance. When I first came to the University, I was handicapped by one of those smarting problems, a bad financial condition. Truly, the fact that I did not have to attend every class on my program made it possible for me to take advantage of odd jobs as they presented themselves and thereby work out my financial problem while going to college at the same time. Although I did not like to miss these classes, it was not a case of not liking to miss them; it was a case of missing some or not being able to attend any. Another way in which I found the absence of compulsory class attendance beneficial was in "cutting" classes that I knew would present material of a nature quite familiar to me. Instead of attending such classes I found it profitable either to study a more advanced phase of the subject presented in the classroom or to attend a lecture by some other professor on some other subject of which I knew very little.

The survey-course system has been keenly beneficial to me, not only by decidedly broadening my cultural outlook on life, but by making it possible for me to see new opportunities in fields that I feel certain I would not have stumbled upon had I attended a college presenting the conventional curriculum. Upon graduation from high school, I planned to follow civil engineering as my life-work, but somehow felt that my selection was not in accord with my deeper desires. Since attending lectures in the first- and second-year social science courses, I have become aware of opportunities in the new field of public administration, a field toward which my natural aptitudes lean much more heavily. In general, I believe the survey courses, if they do nothing more than assist a student to find his permanent place in the scheme of things, are invaluable. As I see it, the physical sciences course presents the relation of chemistry, physics, astronomy, geology, and mathematics to the processes of nature working not only throughout the earth but throughout the entire universe. The biological sciences course points out the evolutionary development of both the plant and animal kingdoms, to say nothing of a fine general treatment of human physiology. The humanities course presents a cultural development of man, the history of literature, science, arts, philosophy, religion, and institutions, from the time of prehistoric man to modern times. The social science course presents a picture of the development of economic, political, and sociological institutions, particularly emphasizing current developments. And, with such a panorama before one, certainly the selection of a field of life-work should be greatly facilitated. At least, I found it so.

The opportunity of hearing men who are not only outstanding on campus but really leaders in their fields on a national level has been very significant to me. Students in very few colleges and universities are privileged to hear such outstanding men as Doctors Carlson, Compton, Merriam, and others of equal standing. Even though I do not pretend to have understood all I have heard these men lecture about, I am confident that from listening to them speak and from talking to them after a lecture or group meeting, I have become more aware of the deeper and more worth-while things in life and have been inspired to go after them.

A new type of extra-curricular activity has arisen from the stimulus of the general courses and the contact with the Faculty that has been made possible under the New Plan. This contact with the faculty is possible because they are not in a position to give or withhold grades. In high school I would not have dreamed of going to a teacher of mine to talk over with him a particular aspect of the course I was interested in or to ask him for more material, because I always had the feeling that either he might think I was trying to impress him to get a good grade or, if he did not think so, some of the students might. Under the New Plan there is not a very sharp distinction between faculty members and students.

Now these new extra-curricular activities are quite different from the old cut-and-dried variety because they arise from, and are closely connected to, our studies. For instance, there was a conference at Druce Lake where about 35 students and from 15 to 20 faculty members spent a week-end during the winter discussing religion and its place in modern life and its application to intellectual activities. . . . . We had another conference in May on the general topic of "After College, What?" or the problems that face students when they leave the cloistered life. These conferences were not directly connected with our usual course of study at all, but were in response to a desire on the part of students to find out more about what the faculty thought and to get the results of their experiences.

Another interesting activity of this sort is the Social Science Parliament that a group of students in Social Sciences II started. After studying the machinery of the British government, these students decided to try to work it out. Dr. Staley was the king, and cabinets rose and fell over current problems. When we studied the French governmental system we changed the Parliament into a chamber of deputies.

Another activity that students have enjoyed thoroughly is a discussion group Mr. Gideonse has held on Thursday afternoons all year on current events. Here the students brought in problems that they had read about in the newspapers and would like to talk over—problems that could not be handled in the course, which, after all, is devoted to giving the students a background to enable them to handle these problems.

The biological sciences general course instituted honor discussion sections because of the desire of the students to explore questions that the general course did not have time to handle. Dr. Carlson, Dr. Coulter, Dr. Newman, Dr. Emerson, and others met with the students who were especially interested, and talked over modern developments in their various fields.

The same thing happened in the humanities group. Students who were particularly interested in literature, or philosophy, or art met with members of the staff to discuss their views on controversial problems brought up in that course. These various discussions are in no way part of the work of the course, that is, they are not prescribed as necessary; most of the work done by the students in these discussions is done purely because they are interested, and is really recreational. It is more of a recreation than the regular cut-and-dried student activities, which are now organized like business.

The physical science staff members have been delighted when students came to them and asked to see the problems they were handling in their laboratories; interested students were made welcome in the various labs, and all year they have enjoyed watching experiments being carried on. A group of about 10 students who were not majoring in physical science, but who were interested primarily in the social sciences division, went up to the Yerkes Observatory in May with about 10 of the physical science staff and spent a week-end.

Another group which is absolutely a student activity, which no faculty member ever has had anything to do with, is a group headed by two students; about 20 students meet every Friday afternoon at 3:30 and spend the rest of the afternoon with a member of the faculty discussing the problem he is especially interested in. Some of the men we have invited have been Professors Whitehead, Lemon, Ogburn, Gideonse, Wirth, Schlesinger, Carlson, T. V. Smith, and Frank Knight. The group is chiefly composed of Sophomores and Juniors who have had the general courses and are now specializing in their chosen field. But they want to continue the broad general education that was begun in the general courses. And so they invite these men and every week have had an entirely different type of individual and an entirely different subject. In that way they maintain an interest in all the various fields of intellectual activity on the campus.

This is a new type of activity on the campus—recreation closely tied up with studies. Studies thus are becoming so interesting that they are considered not a duty but a pleasure. We have been having a lot of fun studying.

———————

Although it may be considered by some too naïve to register enthusiasm, yet I can speak for many others besides myself when I say I am heartily enthusiastic about the Plan.

There has been quite a bit of discussion in recent years about educational objectives and ideals. I believe it is generally conceded that one of the greatest assets that could possibly be gained from a university experience would be the development of that unique human potentiality, ability to think. Education has tended too much in the past to be a pigeonholed variety, a course here and there to fulfil credits for a degree; or, if taken seriously, the course was still an isolated bit of knowledge not integrated into a useful whole. With our schedule of surveys covering all fields, we have a truer sense of a balanced whole. We have a broad picture in outline to which we can add all future knowledge and experience and have it always keep its proper proportions and relative values.

This balancing influence is especially good in cases where a person comes to school with a decided narrowing interest in one field. That type of person is apt to start his specializing immediately without seeing or realizing the possibilities of other fields. For other people, the great breadth of the material presented may make a choice more difficult, but it surely has more chance of being a wise choice. Instead of being put off till graduation time, this decision is stimulated early and can be made with greater insight.

Not only has the student viewed the scope of the fields of knowledge, but he has been stimulated to thought by various angles of presentation. For example, biological and social sciences often approach a subject from diametrically opposite views, such as the problem of heredity and environment. In other instances two fields may tend to emphasize a general principle and make it more impressive. It would be practically impossible, I believe, now for us to ever overlook in any problem the fact that there can be no gloriously simple solution, but that it is a matter of the interplay of many factors.

The stimulus of personal contacts can never be overemphasized. A pertinent comment was made by Mark Van Doren, of Columbia University, during his visit here a few weeks ago. He said that conversation and companionship with students and faculty are an invaluable part of a college education. We are privileged under the New Plan in having some of the most outstanding men as lecturers, supported by an exceptionally fine staff. These men make themselves more accessible than under the old system. A factor working toward greater faculty-student associations has been the arrangement of the College Library in Cobb. Opening off the reading-rooms are the offices of the College staff of the humanities and social sciences courses, where some of the Faculty are always available. With great informality students discuss their work and problems with the Faculty and frequently these contacts become an incentive to individual research projects which a student carries along through the year. The other division staffs have been equally considerate in arranging office hours elsewhere, although I do not believe it is quite as advantageous as using the central location of the College Library.

An illustration of some of these values of the New Plan is a group of students, Sophomores mainly, with their chief interest in the field of the social sciences. It is a group which entirely on its own initiative has met once a week and invited people like Professor Gideonse, Professor Knight, Dr. Carlson, Professor T. V. Smith, and Dean Gilkey to discuss informally around a table topics of interest, such as national and international politics and economics, religion as a social factor in our times, standards of values, socialized medicine, and the like. To my mind, this group represents a stimulation toward individual thinking, initiative which has been met admirably by the Faculty in willingness to co-operate, and broader interests than any former plan has made possible in two years.

———————

Although we all tend to idealize those adventures which lie before us, the New Plan has become a reality which has more than surpassed my optimistic expectations, although there have been some minor defects from my point of view.

To me, one of the most challenging aspects of the New Plan has been the student's chance for initiative and adjustment. For the entering Freshman, there has been the criticism that there is lack of authority and too much new freedom. As for this criticism, I must say that for those who want it, there is plenty of direction; but it is voluntary, and those with the initiative to succeed usually don't need it. The student is on his own; he is urged to depend upon himself more and more and to do his own thinking. However, for the individuals who do want advice and direction, one will find that the advisers, instructors, and professors are usually willing to aid the student become adjusted academically, and the University maintains a psychiatrist who helps any student in matters of personal social adjustment.

Now in speaking of the New Plan, there arises the question of whether or not the division of a general education into four general courses has been the most satisfactory one. At present we have the humanities, the social sciences, the physical sciences, and the biological sciences. It is my own personal reaction that a general education should not be 50 per cent science. One-half of our general education consists of the physical and biological sciences. On the other hand, such a large field as the humanities is crowded into one course. Now the theory behind the humanities course is excellent. But the practice is not. As you probably know, the course attempts to cover the history of man and mankind from earliest times through the present day. It includes the literature, art, music, architecture, religion, and philosophy of each period of history. It gives a broad sweep of history that is breath-taking in its scope. It is thrilling. It gives a picture of man's achievements in the field of thought and in the arts—but it covers none of these adequately and does none of them justice. It seems, then, that this course might well be divided into two distinct courses—one dealing with history alone, the other a pure humanistic course dealing with literature, thought, and the fine arts. Were this the case, there would be five general courses.[3]

One of the fine accomplishments of the New Plan is the fact that it has created a closer contact between professor and student. It is because all grades are based upon comprehensive examinations, that the

[3] It is interesting to know that similar suggestions have been made for each of the other fields by various students. A student who is, or who becomes, particularly interested in one of the four fields wants more of that field, feels that the field is worthy of more time in the programs of all students, and suggests that two year-courses, instead of one, in this field would be advisable. Perhaps this is good evidence that we have hit a fairly good balance in the present program, particularly since each student has leeway to the extent of two required and one optional year-course or year-sequence electives for pursuit of individual interests.—AUTHOR.

student can consult freely with the professor without fear of being accused of scheming for a good grade. And conversely, the professor is free from the responsibility of giving out grades. This is all handled by a Board of Examiners. And for this very reason, there can be the relationship of student and instructor united against the comprehensive examinations, rather than students united against the instructor, as formerly. Naturally, then, in my opinion, the New Plan has produced an ideal contact between professor and student.

But under the present system we have three lectures and one discussion group each week for each general course. Although this is admittedly a good organization and allows some individual expression and discussion, yet it is not perfect. Still better than this system, I think, would be the tutorial system of very small classes and individual conferences at regular specified times. This would allow for more intelligent expression and better discussion. I would advocate some such system because I have discovered that one learns a great deal more through discussion than he does by mere reading or listening to a lecture.[4]

I do want to say, though, that we have the finest professors possible for our lecturers. The list includes such stimulating personalities as Mr. Gideonse, Mr. Schevill, and numerous others. Authoritative information, coupled with a scintillating personality, makes a course worth while. I have found the social sciences course the most arousing of the general courses. In my opinion, this course has done more than any one other force in the New Plan to create intelligent discussion and thought concerning present-day and future economic, social, and political issues. Any course that accomplishes that is well worth while. This course has made me want to do individual investigation for my own information. It has shown that something is radically wrong with an order that allows one group to have everything and at the same time spreads unrest and open rebellion in a less privileged group. It has put petty thoughts of nationalism in the back seat, so to speak, and has made me think in terms of internationalism. Despite its inevitable faults, I cannot praise this course too highly.

Now I have spoken frankly and criticized freely in presenting a few

[4] Most of our general course chairmen and staff members favor having each discussion section meet twice a week, instead of once a week, as soon as the Administration may be able and willing to devote the necessary additional funds to the increase of the instructional staff to the extent that this would entail.— AUTHOR.

of my personal impressions and reactions, for it is only by criticism that any one or anything matures and is improved. Let it be known, however, that few persons exist under the New Plan who do not realize that they are working under an educational scheme which is more progressive than the curriculum in any other major institution. I am glad to say that I realize this fully and am proud to have it known that I am enthusiastic. This has been one of the greatest years of my life, and I look forward to an even more interesting future here at the University of Chicago. For the New Plan and the general courses and for what they have done for me, I am thoroughly grateful.

At the annual meeting of the alumni and "active" members of one of our national fraternity chapters, held late in the winter of the first year of operation of the New Plan, the student president of the undergraduate chapter analyzed the implications of the New Plan, as he saw them, for fraternities. I was told by an alumnus that this undergraduate speech made a deep impression upon all present. When I encountered the student a few days later, I asked him if he would give me the benefit of an opportunity to read his speech. He brought me his paper, to which he confessed he had devoted no little thought, and permitted me to have a copy made. Though both he and his fraternity should take pride in its publication, particularly in view of the manner in which the fraternity has risen to his challenge, I have deleted both the author's name and the name of the fraternity.

It has been the custom in the past at these gatherings, I am told, for the president of the chapter to rise and tell the assembled alumni of the campus achievements, the financial stability, and the general health of the chapter. This evening I shall do none of these things. I shall not tell you, for example, that our chapter contains among its members the student head marshal of the University, the president of the Dramatic Association, the editors of the *Daily Maroon* and the *Cap and Gown*. I shall not do this because I have a pessimistic message to impart.

This message concerns itself with the place of the fraternity in the

University following the reorganization of the University. My thesis is this: that we cannot long exist, possessed of a meaning and a purpose, if we remain as we are today.

The reorganization of the University has been regarded with a suspicious eye by fraternity alumni, who seem to feel that its inauguration bodes ill for the survival of their particular organization. If there are any of these suspicious alumni among you men, let me point out that the new educational plan was not pulled out of a hat by the Administration of this University; rather does it represent the trend in higher educational method of most of the better American universities today. The only reason that the University has adopted the plan in advance of its neighbors is that the University is an agressive institution unhampered by any tradition save that of its own excellence. If there is danger for undergraduate fraternities in the New Plan, this danger is not confined to our University, but is common to all, though elsewhere it may be less immediate.

There is danger for the fraternities in the New Plan, and the nature of this menace may best be seen by a consideration of the aims and method of the reorganization. In my opinion, the most important single aim of the reorganization is to raise the standard of college education. During the past few decades, our colleges and universities have been populated with the earnest seekers-after-truth who have always been the reason for the existence of higher education; but it has become necessary, at least in the undergraduate schools, to educate these men cheek by jowl with bond-salesmen-to-be, who have come to college because it is the thing to do, or because their fathers went, or because of the associations and contacts which they would make there. It is generally recognized today that the Bachelor's degree has merely a social value.

The University has determined to raise the standard of the Bachelor's degree—to separate the scholars from the play boys, if we may use this classification, as early as possible. This has been accomplished first by creating the College division, where a general education is dispensed to all comers; secondly, by removing the residence requirement for all degrees; and thirdly by merging the senior-college work for the Bachelor's degree with the graduate work for Master's and Doctor's degrees in the other four divisions of the University. A student in the College is a candidate for no degree; he is seeking the College Certificate of having satisfactorily completed a general education.

The net result of these changes, within a few years, will be that men who have come to the University merely because they have been graduated from high school and think that it would be amusing to go to college will pass through the College division and leave school, having been denied admission to the upper divisions. The graduate attitude—that detachment from undergraduate amusements and serious interest in things of the mind which may be observed in most successful graduate students—will descend upon the men working for their Bachelor's degree in the divisions. This, briefly, is a survey of the salient effects of the New Plan as I see them.

Now, how will these changes affect our fraternity? My answer is that we are offered a choice. Our first alternative is to continue along our present course. Let me pause here and outline briefly what our present course is.

The chapter is composed almost entirely of men who are good, healthy, human beings, in every way admirably normal. They have no ambition, once they have finished school, to pursue further any of their studies, or to maintain more than a semblance—if as much as a semblance—of interest in the things that they have presumably learned. Their conversation concerns itself with the-date-I-had-last-night and who-will-be-Big-Ten-champion, for most of their waking hours. A man of genuine intellectual interest and promise, cast into the midst of this group, is either seriously set back by following the common current of thought, discussion, and amusement, if we may dignify the activities of the chapter by terms as respectable as these—he is either set back or else he has the foresight and the judgment to leave the chapter, live elsewhere, and preserve his intellect unimpaired. The latter course, not by any means the honorable one, is nevertheless one which has been followed by several individuals since I have been a member of the chapter, and one for which I now think I see some small excuse.

Composed of men like this, the chapter is bound to become a fraternity in the College only; with a few exceptions, its members will leave the University either before or immediately after they have received the College Certificate. The College is designed so that the average student can complete his work therein in two years, and fraternities are no longer permitted to initiate men until they have been in college nearly a year. The end result is obvious: if ———, composed of the sort of men who now make up most of the chapter, will exist at all in five years, it will be, for all practical purposes, a one-year society. I do not think that I need dwell on the disadvantages of such a situation. This is the first alternative we are offered. If we accept it, the only thing which will make membership in ———— superior to residence in the new dormitories will be the fact that we wear badges and our house is more convenient to campus classes.

The second alternative, and the only other, is to make of the Chicago chapter of ———— the sort of society which ———— had in mind when he founded our fraternity. You remember that he said: "It was the contemplation of these and similar evils that first suggested to me the idea of establishing a society of a higher nature . . . . ; one that should combine all the advantages of a union for intellectual and literary purposes. . . . ." A society for intellectual and literary purposes is exactly what the Chicago chapter of ———— is not today; it is an eating-club, and a fine one.

As long as the University permitted men who were not scholars to stay in school for four years, allowed pledging in the first quarter of a man's residence here, and provided insufficient dormitory accommodations for out-of-town men, an eating-club could thrive and flourish here; but I tell you men quite sincerely that on the basis of my observation as an undergraduate, the day of the eating-club at the University is done. Signs of it are all about us; one fraternity has already shut up shop here, and more will follow this spring or next fall. We survive today as an apparently healthy eating-club merely because we have superior accommodations and a good reputation; we cannot long exist on our accommodations and our reputation in the face of the changing University scene.

I have painted a gloomy picture of the fraternity's prospects, but I am convinced that it is only by frankly considering the situation which exists today that we can insure our permanent reputation and prosperity. In the second alternative, there is hope for the fraternity; our present duty is to choose men who have definitely intellectual interests and are good bets to get into the divisions for our pledges, rather than men who are good bets for numerals in swimming, and to encourage and stimulate the growth of intellectual enthusiasm among the men of the chapter. The present atmosphere pervading the chapter is such that a man is ashamed to be caught thinking seriously on almost any subject; the ideal atmosphere is one where good honest amusements and mental endeavor would go hand in hand.

There are various means of attaining the ends necessary to the achievement of a union for intellectual and literary purposes, and I shall not bore you by considering them here. What I should like to point out is that our chapter stands at the crossroads, and that the path we choose depends not only on the efforts of the men in the chapter, but also on you, the alumni.

One of the excellent results of the New Plan has been the extent to which each faculty member has been continuously challenged to attain and maintain the maximum effectiveness of which he is capable as a teacher. The stimulus and challenge of a new and unique adventure have contributed most to this end to date. The maintenance of such remarkable effectiveness as teachers among so large a majority will depend in the long run, and, indeed, in the near future, upon the attitude and policy of the Administration in recognizing and rewarding successful teaching. Early in his administration President Hutchins stated his policy on this vital point: significant contributions in college education would receive recognition in promotions in rank and increases in salary comparable to the same form of recognition given for significant research scholarship at the graduate level. In so far as he has been able to do so in days of depression, he has kept faith with this promise. The real test will come if, as, and when, more resources become available; if, when that time comes, the College faculty members in considerable number who have made decidedly unique and effective contributions to college education do not receive a fair share of available rewards, the New Plan will suffer materially and precipitously in loss of effectiveness, because faculty members will then rightly conclude that they must, in justice to their families and themselves, devote their best efforts to research of the old orthodox type—the only type of activity that has won preferment in most institutions for a generation.

Our advice to all younger faculty members is to pursue some research activity in connection with their teaching; but, we have broadened the old definition of research to include, besides "pure scholarly research," research in course organization, in the preparation of significant course materials, and in the methods and practice of instruction. We have had some significant contributions in this newly recognized, by definition, area of research that have been duly rewarded, and many more that must be rewarded or production in this area will not continue to be so active. For a generation most university and college faculties have had within them possibilities for greatly increased effectiveness in instruction that have not been called forth because the prevailing system for promotion in rank and salary gave recognition almost solely to "pure scholarship" as testified by scholarly publications and consequent calls to other institutions.

Experience has demonstrated that a faculty member who is content to be merely a "good teacher" after a pattern already set, and does not bring to his teaching continuously renewed insight, verve, and enthusiasm derived from scholarly research or from instructional research, or from both, will soon cease to be a good teacher, because he soon is out of step with the procession, and hence out of date, and becomes stale and "soured" on the job. Of course, both types of researchers must keep abreast of the current scholarly advances in their fields through constant familiarity with current scholarly publications. But the man who continuously and critically restudies the content and organization of his courses, searches for the best materials, designs and publishes new instructional materials, experiments critically with new instructional methods and new combinations of methods, evaluates his results care-

fully, designs new examination materials for the more nearly valid and reliable measurement of results, and does all
of this in the light of a continuous re-examination of educational objectives—such a faculty member is worthy of official and material recognition, because he is making a significant contribution toward the attainment of one of the
professedly major purposes of a university,education, quite
as significant as a contribution toward the attainment of
the other major purpose of a university, the broadening of
the boundaries of knowledge.

Several significant pieces of evidence on faculty activities and reactions are presented in Appendix E.

CHAPTER VIII

STUDENT GUIDANCE AND
PERSONNEL WORK

W E HAD developed an excellent student-guidance program during the last half-dozen years of the old plan, and our experience in administering this guidance program furnished a significant contributing factor in the development of the New Plan. In designing our new program, however, it became evident that the need for the utmost effectiveness in student guidance would be even greater than under the old plan.

We believe that the administration of faculty affairs and of student guidance and personnel service can be conducted successfully only when thoroughly and harmoniously integrated with the daily instructional program for the attainment of chosen educational objectives. We follow this belief in practice, as witnessed by the fact that every one of us in faculty or student administrative work is a member of a department, a member of one or more faculties, and teaches at least part time. Thus we successfully avoid the numerous inconsistencies, cross-purposes, and friction, from which develop embarrassments and impediments for both faculty and students, that seem inevitable when a fifth wheel to the college cart is introduced in the form of an independent personnel department constituted of full-time professional "experts" who tend to become increasingly inept as their term of "disservice" progresses, because of continued lack of direct identification with, and participation in, the major educational program.

The Dean of Students in the College, appointed upon recommendation of the University Dean of Students with the approval of the Dean of the College, is in charge of the program for the guidance of College students. Faculty Advisers for students in the College are recommended for appointment by the Dean of Students in the College with the approval of the Dean of the College. The Dean of the College and the Dean of Students in the College necessarily work together constantly on many matters of administrative policy and practice, since at many points no sharp line can be drawn between their respective realms of administration—the interests of students and Faculty overlap and are inextricably intertwined at many points. The Dean of Students in the College is a member, and the Dean of the College is chairman, of the College Executive Committee and of the College Curriculum Committee.

There are eight Advisers of students in the College in addition to the Dean of Students in the College, who serves as Adviser for a group of students. Each Adviser is a member of a department and of the College Faculty, while some are also members of an upper-divisional faculty, and each teaches at least part time, while some teach full time and receive extra compensation for extra service as Adviser. Of the nine faculty members who serve as Advisers at the present time, two are instructors, five are assistant professors, one is an associate professor, and one is a professor of full rank. Four render service as Advisers as part of a normal full-time load that is a combination of teaching and administrative work. Each of the other five has a normal full-time program of teaching for "regular" salary and receives $1,000 additional a year (three-quarters) for the extra service as Adviser.

On the basis of their educational and vocational interests and ambitions, students are classified and distributed among the nine Advisers respectively as follows: (1) pre-medical students; (2) biological sciences students other than pre-medical students; (3) pre-legal students and social sciences students; (4) pre-business students and social sciences students; (5) humanities students; (6) humanities students; (7) physical sciences students; (8) physical sciences students and undecided students; and (9) undecided students. Thus, social sciences students may be assigned to either one of two Advisers; and the same is true of humanities students, physical sciences students, and undecided students.

Advisers are selected without regard to sex; the sole consideration in each instance is the prospective effectiveness of the person selected for the specific field in which he or she is to serve. The present Adviser for students interested primarily in the physical sciences, and presumably headed for the Division of the Physical Sciences, is a woman member of the Chemistry Department. No segregation of students on the basis of sex is made in their assignment to Advisers—each Adviser has both men and women advisees.

Advisers are selected with the greatest care on the scores of personality, judgment, temperament, and interest in this type of service. Ten years ago we thought it good policy to change Advisers frequently, in order to educate an ever increasing number of faculty members in administrative problems and in the character and extent of student interests and problems. Though it was advantageous for the Faculty to have as large a leaven as possible of members who had gained a broader view of the student side of the picture, this gain was found to be too much at the expense of student welfare. With Advisers serving for only a year or two, no one of them served long enough to reach the stage of most effective service. Any Adviser is sure to make many mistakes both of omission and commission during his first year, and still too many in his second year; he really begins to reach his true stride only in the third year and is still improving in his fifth year, if he has it in him to become thoroughly successful in this service.

Hence, our present policy, when approaching a faculty member regarding an appointment as Adviser, is to talk in terms of at least three years and an expressed hope of still longer service. Appointments are kept on the annual basis, however, with the possibility of discontinuance of reappointment, so that a change may be made in accordance with what seems best for all concerned. Since this service is not an extra load imposed without material recognition, but is paid for in extra compensation or in a reduction of other duties, enthusiasm and effectiveness can be expected and demanded—and actually are maintained. In some instances reappointments, though desired for the sake of the extra compensation, have not been made, because of ineffective service. Most Advisers serve from five to ten years.

Each Adviser devotes full time to his duties during Freshman Week, several hours a day during the first week of a quarter, and a minimum of eight hours a week through the remainder of the academic year. The Advisers have their offices in a suite of rooms adjoining the office of the Dean of Students in the College and have stenographic and secretarial service at their command. The Adviser's secretary always has readily at hand for him his appointment book and all records of all types for all of his students. When an Adviser reports to his office for a series of student conferences, he finds on his desk a copy of his schedule for the day and all records or memoranda accumulated to date

problem, he endeavors, usually successfully, to arrange for the student a conference with the best person available for the needed assistance.

Each Adviser endeavors to be, and endeavors to have each of his students regard him as being, a guide, counselor, and friend, but not a policeman or nursemaid. An Adviser is always ready to give a student all the advice he may need or desire, but will then let the student disregard the advice and make his own mistakes in his own way if he chooses to do so. Since a memorandum of each conference is kept on file, if a student disregards advice and gets into difficulties as a result, responsibility can be placed where it belongs. For example, if an Adviser finds that a student is devoting too much of his time and energies to extra-curriculum activities, and advises him to discontinue some of them, the student may even take on more such activities if he chooses to do so. We have no eligibility rules or "point" regulations for participation in "student activities"—a student may hang himself, academically, by the extra-curriculum activity method if he chooses to do so. However, we have few difficulties of this sort, because our academic program is of such a character and is conducted in such a manner that it can meet successfully the competition of extra-curriculum activities without official regulations.

The Advisers never ask their students such pointed questions as how they like this or that course or faculty member unless requested to do so by the faculty member or the chairman of the department concerned. It is a function of an Adviser, however, to find out how a student is progressing in his work, and whether he is interested and satisfied with what he is accomplishing. In discussing these points students not infrequently volunteer information or opinions that are of significance regarding course content, organization, and presentation, including pointed comments on the effectiveness of faculty members as lecturers or teachers. Little attention is paid to isolated or scattered comments; but when a significant number of students comment favorably or unfavorably about a certain course or faculty member, the comments are considered significant and are relayed to the Dean of the College directly or through the Dean of Students in the College.

Many of our personnel records are made on 6×4-inch cards or on 6×8-inch sheets that are folded to 6×4-inch size for filing. The records of each student are filed in a heavy folder, with the following form printed on one side of one-half of the folder:

Name _____

University Address _____ Tel. No. _____

Parent or Guardian _____

Address _____ Tel. No. _____

High School_____ Transferred to_____

Rank in Graduating Class_____

Psychol. Exam. Percentile Rank_____ Date_____

Reading Test: Rate_____ Remarks_____

        Comprehension_____

Personality Score_____

Adviser_____

Date_____

The following forms explain themselves.

The University of Chicago   **Adviser's Record of Student Conference**

STUDENT _____ Date _____ Adviser _____

PROBLEM DISCUSSED	√	VOLUNTARY	SUMMONED
Program of Studies		Comment and Recommendation	
Change of Registration			
Unsatisfactory Progress			
Choice of Field of Specialization			
Comprehensive Examinations			
Choice of Vocation			
Outside Work			
Campus Activities			
Health			
Study Conditions			
Study Habits			
Worry			
Scholarships			
Campus Friendships			
Commuting			

The University of Chicago

PERSONNEL RECORD

Student...Date..

University address..

    Home..............., Rooming house..............., Fraternity..............., University hall...............

Meals (check ⅓, ⅔, ¾): Home..............., Fraternity or club..............., Cafeteria or restaurant...........

How many *hours per week* do you spend:

    In study?...

    In classroom and laboratory?..

    In travel to and from Campus?...

    In employment for self-support? (give type of employment)...................................

Name all University organizations and activities in which you participate; indicate the *hours per week* given to each:

....
....
....
....
....

(OVER)

Name all organizations and activities outside of the University (church, orchestra, lodge, tennis, dancing, etc.) in which you participate; indicate *hours per week* given to each:

....
....
....
....

Suggest below activities on the Campus in which you would like to participate:

....
....
....

How do you spend your summer?...

....

....

What vocation do you plan to enter?...

....

....

The University of Chicago   **STUDENT'S ANALYSIS BLANK**

NAME..DATE...

FACTORS AFFECTING ACADEMIC SUCCESS—In order that advisory officers may be more fully informed concerning the conditions which aid or hinder you in your academic work, you are requested to check (✓) the statements in this form which describe your situation most accurately.

Health—Indicate the degree to which good health is an advantage or poor health is a handicap to you in your work.	I enjoy excellent health.	I think my health is above average.	Neither exceptionally good nor unusually bad.	Might be better.	I am in poor health.
Study Conditions—What is the character of your study conditions?	Excellent in every way.	Generally free from distraction.	Not especially good or bad.	Could be better.	Very distracting.
Campus Activities—Do you participate in such a large number of activities that they tend to interfere with your work? Or, could you devote more time to campus affairs if you had an opportunity?	I am not interested and do not participate in any activity.	I am interested but do not participate because of lack of opportunity.	I am in a few activities but they do not affect the time given to my regular work.	I engage in numerous activities and am giving considerable time to them.	My activities program is very heavy.
Use of Time—Do you so plan your time as to make the best possible use of it?	I budget my time regularly.	I follow a definite program but do not budget my time.	I have no systematic program nor do I waste much time.	I am not using my time to the best advantage.	I do not use my time well at all.

(OVER)

Outside Work—To what extent is outside work for self-support affecting your University work?	I am doing none.	I work only occasionally. No interference with University work.	I work regularly for self-support. Am able to keep up in University work.	I am working too much to be able to do my best in the University.	Outside work interferes seriously with my University work.
Choice of Career—Is the quality of your work affected by your decision or indecision with reference to a career?	I am inspired to do my best by my definite choice of a career.	Uncertain as to my career. Am encouraged in my work by several possible choices.	I give no thought to a career in connection with my University work.	My indecision interferes with my University work.	I am so undecided that I can't keep up interest in my work.
Study Habits—Do you have well-organized methods of study?	Well organized and effective.	Generally good. Sometimes at a loss as to how to proceed.	I give little thought to my method of study.	I do not know how to proceed to get the most out of my courses.	I am failing because I do not know how to study.
Worry and Nervousness—Do you find yourself handicapped by worry concerning your work or personal problems?	I never worry.	I am seldom worried enough to affect my University work.	I worry somewhat but as a rule my work is not seriously affected.	My work is seriously affected at times by worry.	I am unable to do satisfactory work because I am constantly worried.
Commuting—Does commuting in any way interfere with your academic work?	Not at all.	Not enough to be noted.	Occasionally but not seriously.	I am handicapped because I commute.	My work suffers seriously.
Student Friendships—Do your student friendships influence your academic success?	They are an aid.	Sometimes helpful.	Neither a help nor a hindrance.	They interfere at times.	Make it difficult for me to do good work.

The University of Chicago

INSTRUCTOR'S PERSONNEL REPORT

STUDENT...

COURSE..

Please write in the space below or indicate in the check list on the reverse side (or both), your estimate of the ability, habits of work, achievement, personality, and physical condition of this student. Also indicate any special handicap which in your opinion may affect his work.

Instructor's signature...

Date...

(OVER)

INTELLECTUAL ABILITY	Very limited in ability	Slower than the average	Average	Alert, above average	Keen, superior
INTEREST AND ZEAL	Unresponsive	Usually indifferent	Studious and generally responsive	Energetic and enthusiastic	Craves scholarly work
SOCIAL ADJUSTMENT	Tends to be anti-social	Self-centered	Fairly well adjusted	Co-operative, considerate of others	Strongly altruistic
ADEQUACY OF EDUCATIONAL BACKGROUND	Poorly prepared	Lacks in certain fields	Satisfactory	Better than average	Excellent both in tool subjects and content subjects
COMMAND OF ENGLISH	Very poor	Improvement is necessary	Satisfactory	Very good	Excellent mastery
PERFORMANCE IN COURSE	Unsatisfactory	Work poor in quality	Satisfactory	Work is better than average	Work is superior
HABITS OF WORK	Haphazard, careless, unresponsive to suggestions	Below average in accuracy, thoroughness, and organization; requires much supervision	Usually effective; needs some supervision	Accurate, punctual, thorough, well organized	Excellent in every respect; works well independently
PERSONAL TRAITS	Repellent	Weak and colorless; neither attractive nor repellent	Average; well-balanced	Well-balanced; attractive	Superior in emotional balance and personal attractiveness

Before the instructor's personnel report blanks are sent to faculty members, the name of the student and the course are entered on each blank in the office of the Dean of Students. A letter is always sent to each faculty member with the personnel report blanks that he is asked to fill out for his students. This letter is re-written from time to time to make it most useful. The following paragraphs from a recent form of this letter explain themselves.

The "Personnel Reports" are being sent to instructors with the special request that they be returned by the end of the quarter, perferably before quarterly quiz papers have been read and marked. If the reports are made before quarterly quiz papers are read, the instructor will be able to record more accurately the impression which he has gained of the student through class contact and personal conference. The early return of the reports will, moreover, prevent the accumulation of a large amount of work at the end of the quarter. . . . .

These reports are found to be very helpful; they are used regularly by Advisers in the College and by other administrative officers. The comments and opinions of instructors are regarded as confidential information and are used with discretion. The reports should be returned to the Office of the Dean of Students in the College. Upon request from any of you at any time, the Dean of College Students will be glad to transmit any information in hand concerning any one of your students.

We assure you of our appreciation of your co-operation and of our desire to co-operate with you in the best interest of the student.

The letter is signed by both the Dean of the College and the Dean of Students in the College.

In Freshman Week each student fills out a vocational-interest schedule. The returns last autumn (1934) showed that 63.1 per cent had made a vocational decision, 36.9 per cent had not made a vocational decision, and 40.1 per cent expressed a desire for vocational counseling. Toward the end of October a letter is sent by the Executive Secretary of the Board of Vocational Guidance and Placement to each Freshman who has indicated a desire for vocational counseling. The letter dated October 25, 1934, contained the following:

According to our information, you are interested in extending your knowledge of opportunities in various vocational fields. To assist you to do this, a series of lecture conferences has been arranged for the Autumn Quarter, concerning vocations for which special training is offered at the University of Chicago. In each case, the speaker will be a person who is thoroughly conversant with his subject. We cordially invite you to attend all of the lectures, and urge you not to allow a prejudice against any particular field to deter you from hearing the address concerning it. The schedule of lectures is as follows:

Time	Subject	Speaker
October 30, 3:30	Social Service Administration	Dean Edith Abbott
November 6, 3:30	Education	Prof. W. S. Gray
November 13, 3:30	Ministry	Dean S. J. Case
November 20, 3:30	Law	Dean H. A. Bigelow
November 27, 3:30	Medicine	Dr. Joseph Miller
December 4, 3:30	Business	Dean W. H. Spencer

The lectures will be given in Room 108, Haskell Hall, School of Business, with the exception of the lecture on Medicine, November 27, which will be given in Room 117, Pathology Building.

It is not our intention to decide upon a vocation for you. The objective of this project is to assist you to make an intelligent choice early enough in your college life so that you can prepare yourself for the requirements of the field you plan to enter. We hope that you will take advantage of this opportunity.

A second letter, reminding the student of the opportunities offered, is sent a week or ten days later. The Executive Secretary of the Board of Vocational Guidance and Placement, who is also an Adviser in the College for vocationally "undecided" students, has prepared and made available in mimeographed form some "Suggestions to Those Who Desire Vocational Counseling" that are given to students in individual conferences. These suggestions include references to several books on the subject that are available in the bookroom of the offices of the Board of

Vocational Guidance and Placement. Thus, much is done to assist the student, who desires to do so, "to find himself."

As I write these pages, I have before me the accumulated personnel data for each of six students who last June completed two years of residence work. Two of these students attained an exceptionally high average on the seven Board examinations for the College Certificate and the Associate in Arts title, and each of them, while doing so, anticipated some of his upper divisional requirements; two made a "C" average; and of the remaining two, one barely passed with a straight "D" record and was advised not to attempt work in an upper division, while the other has barely passed approximately two-thirds of the College requirements and will need another year to complete the remaining requirements, if capable of doing so, which seems doubtful. Of the six, three live in Chicago or suburbs, one is from Omaha, Nebraska, one from Dallas, Texas, and one from Minneapolis, Minnesota.

To print here all of the personnel data of various types in hand for these six students would require literally dozens of pages. Though I do not know personally any one of the six, I feel that I have gained, from the data accumulated from many sources in the course of two years, a fairly complete and accurate picture of each as a person, as a personality, as a student, as a citizen in the College community, and that I have a reasonable basis for rendering sound advice concerning what each should or should not attempt in further educational or vocational pursuits in the immediate future.

For each student there is, in the first instance, his application for admission to the University, with accompanying materials, containing: a photograph; data concerning family background; complete record of work pursued in high school or preparatory school; ratings by the principal and several teachers on personality, personal characteristics, and scholastic aptitude; several personal and confidential letters; an autobiography; financial status; and educational and vocational interests and ambitions.

For each of these students there are in his personnel folder at least twenty-five separate items, and in some instances as many as fifty, accumulated since his appearance at the University. These include: the cumulative record of courses pursued, with quarterly evaluations of the student's progress by each instructor, and a record of the reports from comprehensive examinations taken; percentile rank on all aptitude and placement tests; reports of our Health Service medical examination and health conferences; reports of each interview by his Adviser; several personnel record cards and student's analysis blanks filled out by the student at the time of conferences with his Adviser; and numerous instructors' quarterly personnel reports.

Some instructors prefer to write paragraphs on the personnel reports, some prefer to use the analysis check list, while others do both. Some instructors give only a few meager reports of little value, while some give very complete and extremely valuable reports for all their students. On the whole, it may honestly be said that we get excellent co-operation with these reports from the majority of the members of the instructional staff of all ranks. In the main, the instructors who use the check list on the personnel report show that they have done it thoughtfully and with discriminative insight. Those who write paragraphs generally show that they have made a more complete analysis and diagnosis of the student than the check list can reflect.

Some typical comments from many instructors on the six students (three men and three women) whose personnel folders happen at the present writing to be on my desk are given below in random order, in order to prevent identification of any one of the six (most of whom are still in the University), to avoid the possibility of causing personal embarrassment. A naïve reader might amuse himself by endeavoring to sort and group these comments into six patterns. Though in each of two or three instances the personnel folder, with its various data, presents a clear-cut and consistent pattern, in each of the other instances it does not do so, because a student may do well in one field and poorly in another, may work faithfully in one field and neglect another, may start poorly and then improve materially, may start well and then slump, may make an excellent impression on one instructor and a poor impression on another instructor, or may have a personality that "clicks" with one instructor while he may be unable to work congenially with another instructor (which may be as significant a comment on the instructor as on the student). The reader would be further handicapped in this "matching" game by the fact that complete data are not furnished for any one of the six students; not all of the written comments are given, because of lack of space, and at least half of the instructors' reports were made by use of the analytical check list and are not here presented.

Some of the typical comments of instructors on the personnel reports are given herewith merely to indicate one type of data available for Advisers in their conferences with their advisees.

Strangely enough, Mr. ——— has been fairly regular in class attendance. Otherwise he would classify neatly as a thoroughly bad student. He is decidedly below average in intellectual ability. and is apparently unaware of it. He is haphazard, careless, and lazy in his work habits, and during two quarters of work with me has shown amazingly little improvement. He has turned in very little written work. On such tests as I have given, he has turned out below average.

Has worked hard but still has difficulties with the subject matter.

Good student, very pleasant; has difficulties but overcomes them.

An excellent student in every respect. A keen mind, a thoughtful attitude, real intellectual curiosity, initiative, though rather quiet and unobtrusive in manner. He does consistent work of the highest caliber. Very fine personality as well.

One of the finest chaps I have ever taught. Fine personality plus intellectual ability.

Miss ——— keeps up her remarkable work. I am hoping she will earn a scholarship on her record, for she needs the money badly. Personally, she is a funny, appreciative, easy-going girl who is not gifted with an over amount of beauty. But somehow I think her personal appearance will never handicap her—she has such a good-natured personality, and such ability.

Is apt to ask unnecessary questions to attract attention; otherwise O.K.

A failing student in English as the result of poor background, poor high-school training, and, I gather, a centering of interest in scientific fields. Does not seem unintelligent, but can do extraordinarily badly. Did little work for me.

Seems much more interested in extra-curriculum activities and social affairs than in acquiring an education, and hence will not do well in this institution unless he acquires a genuine educational interest and a new viewpoint. Probably should have gone to a college more of the "country-club" type.

I don't know what to make of this girl. For one thing, she has the idea she can write and that writing is the only thing that counts. Another thing, she believes that inspiration is the guide to knowledge—she blows hot and then cold continually. But when all is said and done, I rather doubt if she is capable enough to pass her work here. She can't read intelligently, and she can't think logically. She certainly has no reason for feeling she has any special talent.

A very able student. He entered the class late, but easily made up the work and ranks among the best students. Fine chap in every way.

Exceptionally capable. Should make a high-grade scientist. Has been invited to the Honor Section on the basis of the high quality of his work. His penmanship is an almost undecipherable scrawl.

Intelligent and industrious. Learns easily but needs to think more for herself; too fond of memorizing.

An excellent student whose work all year has been outstanding. She is serious-minded, industrious, and eager to learn. She is much more mature than most young folk her age. She has a pleasant, rather jovial personality. Her physical condition is apparently very good.

L—— never came to class the first quarter, but he has attended with fair regularity this quarter. His work is uninspired, on the lean side of average. I don't think he works very hard. I don't think, however, that he has any unusual abilities. As a student, he is average and un-animated. He is a rather nice-appearing fellow, but without any force.

Suggest that he make use of my office conference hours.

She is a very nice young lady, but with certain fixed ideas. She is interested in writing—but no expository writing—she wants to create. Perhaps she can create (she certainly has intelligence), but her perform-ance in class (irregular as it was) was mediocre. She should, for safety's sake, do more of the assigned work.

Miss ——— has done unsatisfactory work this quarter. She is so retiring I have been unable to find out anything about her.

A student of average ability whose work all quarter was distinctly good. He seems to be very serious-minded and industrious. He is rather quiet and uncommunicative, participating only rarely in the class dis-cussions. His physical condition is apparently good.

Does very uneven work—some of it very good. Needs to strive for more sustained effort.

———————————

An earnest student of no more than average ability, who plugs steadily along to the terminus.

———————————

Miss ——— wrote the highest exam written in the humanities course this quarter. I'm not quite sure I believe she is the best in the class, but she is certainly one of the best. She has the robust mind and manner of a man. She is an honest-to-goodness person. And yet this quarter has not been a very happy one for her. She has been lonesome and very sick at times. I wish some one would take care of her socially.

———————————

A competent, though not a brilliant student. She has been handicapped this fall by illness.

———————————

Rather colorless in class but has had good training and background.

———————————

Very good student; quiet, but very intelligent. Writes fairly well. Pleasant personality. She came to see me at office conference hours a few times. Wants criticism of her work. Will improve. Deserves encouragement.

———————————

He can do moderately good work; does not go beyond requirements, and fell off from these in the latter half of the course.

———————————

I know nothing about this student.

———————————

Careless, not much interested.

———————————

He is one of the best students in the class on all scores.

———————————

An outstanding student—regular in attendance and willing to work.

———————————

An excellent student who does not hesitate to criticize teaching methods, examinations, etc. Because of financial necessity she is more concerned about getting a scholarship than an education, but she is quite bright and will acquire the latter in spite of her emphasis on comprehensive examination grades.

———————————

Possesses an excellent mind; would rank high in any group. Believe she is improving each quarter.

The following comments are typical of the reports of student conferences as made by Advisers; they are presented to illustrate some of the various types of students and student problems the Advisers encounter, and to illustrate the manner in which an Adviser functions.

The New Plan "overwhelmed" her at first. She is planning her work more effectively now and enjoys her work very much.

Chemistry satisfactory up to course exam, which he flunked flat. Didn't work on the English composition course, and flunked the test; didn't like it at first, but likes it now.

Asked questions about available scholarships. Wanted to see her personnel reports, "if that's being done." (Second request this year.) Naturally the request was refused, though I endeavored to give her appropriate advice in the light of these reports, without betraying instructors' confidence in us. Believe she is better adjusted emotionally than she was in the Autumn Quarter.

Plump, ambitious girl with a few shattered illusions. Didn't make the social success she expected, and is having some difficulty adjusting herself to the new order of things. Courses going well for her.

Gave advice on law and the foreign service as possibilities for him. We agreed to have another conference after he reads some references I gave him.

Is planning to take the physical science examination on the basis of independent study, and I encouraged him to go ahead with this plan.

Have urged M—— to report to the Health Service for a conference. Have reported this to Dr. Reed with the suggestion that he interview the student with a view to determining whether the student should see our psychiatrist.

Though he is doing well in ———— (course) as shown by instructional tests and examinations in the course, he thoroughly dislikes the instructor and says that if he cannot change to another section with another instructor he will drop the course. Since I have encountered several similar reactions from excellent, as well as poor, students, I have changed his section.

Will complete the College requirements in less than two years and is planning intelligently his program in the Humanities Division. Will likely take his Bachelor's degree in three years or less and pursue graduate work for Ph.D.

K—— has an excellent mind and could do distinguished work if not handicapped so severely by the struggle for self-support through odd jobs. Have arranged for a loan from the student loan funds and have enlisted the co-operation of the Placement Bureau in an effort to secure steady part-time employment.

Reports that, though not doing well in ———— (course), the fault is his and not that of the instructor, about whom he is enthusiastic. It is interesting that students of all types are enthusiastic about the work of this instructor. Am reporting this to the Dean.

Though W—— is not attending his classes regularly, and probably will receive some "R" reports, he is working in an intelligent fashion and will probably pass his comprehensive examinations with high marks. Though not a conformist, he seems to be an effective independent worker and should be encouraged to work in his own way. Though he would have been unhappy under the old plan, because conformity to routine chafes him, the New Plan enables him to work happily and effectively, appealing to instructors for assistance as he needs it.

B—— was at first too much impressed with the "freedom" of the New Plan, and not enough aware of the responsibilities. Has fortunately awakened to the latter in time to save himself scholastically, and the lesson learned this way has been learned effectively.

This student, though discouraged and unhappy during the first two quarters, is now happy and well adjusted because, he says, he has at last learned, for the first time in his life, how to work effectively.

Seems to be flighty and without serious purpose of any kind. Have advised her that if she is not willing to make the effort to find a vital interest she had better withdraw from the University.

Believe C—— is working too hard for physical and mental welfare; have advised a check-up by the Health Service.

Routine conference—no problems. Thoroughly wholesome, normal, average student.

Summoned for conference upon recommendation of Health Service to drop a course; not physically able to carry full program. Asked her to come back for a conference in about a month.

Referred her to the School of Social Service Administration for advice regarding the advisability of her preparing for work in this field.

Does not budget the use of his time, has poor study habits, and spends too much time in "bull" sessions and bridge games. Have tried to impress upon him that, if he cannot or will not change his habits, he will surely fail his comprehensives, and, what is more important, will fail to attain anything worthy of being called an education.

CHAPTER IX

SPECIAL INSTRUCTIONAL *MATÉRIEL*—LIBRARIES, MUSEUMS, LABORATORY DEMONSTRATION EXHIBITS, SOCIAL SCIENCE FIELD TRIPS, TALKING MOTION PICTURES

OUR instructional personnel soon saw that the new courses called for new instructional *matériel*. Since our students were to be expected to read different varieties and different combinations of books in much greater quantities than under the old-plan organization, the necessary books, reading-room facilities, and faculty-student conference rooms must be provided. Since two new natural science courses were to be offered without required laboratory work on the part of the student, the best possible substitutes, such as laboratory museums and laboratory demonstration exhibits, and talking motion pictures, should be developed and used as effectively as possible for purposes of general education. Since, in the study of the social sciences, it was seen to be desirable to give students (even junior-college students) opportunities for personal observation of the actual operation of social, economic, and political principles and phenomena, appropriate field trips (hitherto provided only at higher study levels) should be organized. To meet all these needs, numerous members of our staff devoted much time and critical study, and showed considerable ingenuity. The results of their efforts are presented here with the thought that they may be of interest to others with similar problems.

THE COLLEGE LIBRARY

Just as the comprehensive examinations must follow, rather than precondition or determine, the curriculum, so must the library. As M. Llewellyn Raney, Director of the University of Chicago Libraries, who has consistently given with genuine interest the most effective co-operation in our attempts to cope successfully with our College library problems, has so aptly put it: "The ideal way, then, to establish book standards for junior colleges (for there will be many, not one) is, first, to get the college clearly committed to a philosophy; then, to give the philosophy the personification of instructors; to plot it in a curriculum; and finally, to stage the plot with books. Needless to add, a dozen books pertinent are worth more than a thousand misfits, and whoever in any degree at any juncture does the fitting is truly *librarius*. The play's the thing!"[1] We have followed precisely this sequence of successive steps in the design and administration of our New Plan.

As soon as our new syllabi for College courses were prepared, with copious bibliographical citations of two categories—indispensable readings and recommended optional readings—it became clear that we must purchase at once several thousand volumes and must provide the necessary accompanying reading-room space and delivery service. A special College Library, something we had not had before, seemed to be imperative.

Thanks to a liberal grant from the Carnegie Corporation, the purchase of the necessary books was made possible. To house them and to provide reading-room space and delivery service, the north end of the third floor of Cobb Hall, a building containing classrooms and several adminis-

---

[1] "Junior College and Its Books," *Library Journal*, February 15, 1934.

trative offices, was converted into a makeshift College Library. Two small rooms, behind a delivery desk that was constructed in the corridor, house the books: one room for the reserved (indispensable) books, and the other for the optional books. One large and three small classrooms were converted into reading-rooms. A door from one end of the large reading-room opens into a suite of three small offices occupied by the staff of the Introductory General Course in the Social Sciences, and a door from the other end of this reading-room opens into a similar suite of offices occupied by the staff of the Introductory General Course in the Humanities. The office of the staff of Social Sciences II is next door to the entrance to the College Library.

Since the humanities course and the two social science courses depend less upon the Rental Library and less upon museum and laboratory demonstration exhibits, and more upon the College Library, than do the natural science courses, to meet the needs of their students, it has proved particularly desirable to have the offices of the staff members of the humanities and social science courses adjoining (really a part of) the College Library. These staff members distribute their office hours for conferences so that there is at least one staff member available in each office through many hours of each day. When a student encounters something in his reading that is not clear, he can step from the reading-room into a conference room for assistance. When, in a conference with a student, an instructor wishes to refer to a syllabus reference, he can step into the Library and get the book. There is no doubt that student-faculty contacts and conferences are much more numerous and effective with the present juxtaposition of reading-rooms and offices than would be the case if they were separated by the distance between two buildings or even by a flight of stairs.

Though it was originally planned to house the books for all College courses in the College Library, it was early discovered that our space limits in the rooms taken over for this purpose were inadequate for delivery service and for readers. Hence the books for most of the elective sequence or departmental courses had to be transferred to the respective departmental libraries.

Besides the syllabi, textbooks, and rental sets, which the students are presumed to supply themselves, for the four introductory general courses, there are about 75 other indispensable titles and approximately 675 optional titles which the University provides in the College Library. For the sequence and departmental courses, similarly, the students are expected to procure syllabi, textbooks, and an occasional rental set, while the University provides, in single or multiple copies, a total of approximately 1,300 titles. Thus the grand total provided by the University, not including syllabi, textbooks, and rental volumes, is approximately only 2,000 titles. These are distributed among the four fields approximately as follows: 160 titles in the physical sciences, 190 in the biological sciences, 500 in the social sciences, and 1,200 in the humanities. The number of copies per title ranges from 1 to 95, and the total number approximates 12,000.

The small number of titles is explained by two facts: first, each title was carefully selected for a specific purpose in a carefully designed program of offerings; second, though the College Library has its own *Encyclopaedia Britannica* and a few other reference books, College students are expected to use the general library and the departmental libraries, in adjoining quadrangles, for other reference works and periodicals.

A striking characteristic of the books cited in the indispensable and recommended optional reading lists in the various syllabi is the recent date of publication of the majority. Of the books on the shelves when the courses were offered for the second time in the Autumn Quarter, 1932, 20 per cent had been published since January 1, 1931; 30 per cent within three years; 45.4 per cent within four years; 53.1 per cent within five years; 78.7 per cent within a decade; and only 15 per cent were published prior to 1920. The modal year of books used in the academic year 1932–33 was 1930. Twenty-seven of the 69 indispensable titles in the two social science courses, offered first in the Autumn Quarter, 1931, were issued after January 1, 1931.[2]

Our book-circulation statistics show that the New Plan has effected two significant changes in the reading habits of our junior-college students: they are doing an unprecedented amount of reading, and their reading is distributed remarkably uniformly through the successive weeks of the academic year. Under the old plan no instructor dared conduct a course on the assumption that junior-college students could, or would, read as much as our students are now doing; and what reading the students did, under the old plan, was seasonal, with obvious peaks centering around term-paper and examination requirements.

The current status can best be shown by the circulation statistics for the humanities course and the two social sciences courses. Though the amount that students read

[2] More detailed accounts of our library equipment and service for College students have been presented in the following articles: "The New College Plan at the University of Chicago and Its Library," by M. Llewellyn Raney, in the *Library Journal*, March 1, 1934; and "Some Implications in the New Plan of the University of Chicago for College Libraries," by Augustus Frederick Kuhlman, in the *Library Quarterly*, January, 1933. Mr. Kuhlman has been of great assistance in expediting book purchases and in providing adequate service by attendants.

in these courses in the first year of the New Plan was beyond anything known under the old plan, the number of book withdrawals has gone up each successive year in spite of the fact that the tendency on the part of the course chairmen has been to reduce the number of pages of "indispensable" reading, since the amount so labeled the first year was unreasonably large. It should be kept in mind that the circulation figures quoted below are only for books in the College Library; this reading is in addition to the syllabi, texts, and rental sets of several volumes.

During the academic year 1931–32 the average number of book withdrawals per registrant in these three courses was 67.82; for 1932–33 it was 76.94; for 1933–34 it was 79.96; and for the Autumn Quarter, 1934, it was 29.76, indicating 89.28 for the year. During the Autumn Quarter, 1934, the 1,598 registrants in these three courses (717 in Humanities, 649 in Social Sciences I, and 232 in Social Sciences II) were responsible for a total of 47,562 book withdrawals. Excluding the first and the last of the twelve weeks of the quarter, that were not regular full-schedule weeks, the weekly circulation for the other ten weeks averaged 4,248 withdrawals, ranging from 3,258 for the ninth week, which included Thanksgiving Day, to 5,178 for the third week. The average per registrant per week was 2.7. The total withdrawals of volumes containing "indispensable" reading assignments was 44,968, an average of 28.14 per registrant, while the withdrawals of recommended "optional" volumes was only 2,594, an average of 1.63 per registrant. The relatively small usage of the optional volumes is readily explained by the fact that the indispensable readings are so large in amount that they command most of a student's available time.

The 1934–35 requirements, though lighter than in previous years, are 4,224 pages for the year in the Humanities course, 7,894 pages in Social Sciences I, and 6,063 pages in Social Sciences II. While the policy in the Humanities course this year is to have the students read fewer books than previously, but read them more intensively, the social sciences courses include two distinct types of works: some that are to be read intensively, as one expects to read a text, and others that are to be read cursorily, as one reads a newspaper, merely for the sake of general impressions.

For the circulation figures quoted above, I am indebted to Frederick Kuhlman, Associate Director of Libraries. Mr. Kuhlman has also made a careful canvass of the reasons for the selection of certain books by faculty members to attain specific objectives of various types in the several College courses, and the reasons for discontinuing the use of some of them, after one or two or three years, and for substituting others that, in the light of experience, were judged to be more appropriate. Since the introductory general courses were distinctly new adventures, no satisfactory texts were available, and the selection of the best combination of books of various types, to serve best in each course the attainment of newly determined and distinct objectives, required the exercise of the most severely critical judgment of many minds. The wonder is that more selections, that experience would soon show to be mistakes, were not made.

The library of Burton Court, of the College Residence Halls for Men, is constituted of one or more copies of the books in the College Library supplemented with recreational material, including 25 periodicals and 5 newspapers. This library is designed to serve student needs and enjoyment and is under the management of our Graduate Library School for use as a laboratory for the study of student tastes and the testing of technique, for the stimulation of student reading.

Another one of our special library ventures for College students, the pioneer of them all, is the College Modern Language Library, housed on the fourth floor of Cobb Hall, surrounded by classrooms and staff members' offices. This special library was started in a modest way in 1923, grew slowly but steadily in proportions and in significance, and under the New Plan has been greatly improved in books, space, and equipment. Before our New Plan was adopted, Professor Otto F. Bond and Professor Peter Hagboldt had produced remarkable results through the development of new techniques, and the production of new teaching materials, in elementary French and Spanish, and in German, respectively. The inauguration of the New Plan emphasized the importance of their work and gave added incentive for the further development of their programs.

To Professor Bond and Professor Hagboldt we owe very largely the development of a series of texts and instructional materials originally published by the University of Chicago Press, recently taken over by D. C. Heath and Company on a co-operative basis. The Heath-Chicago Language Series includes, besides the French Series edited by Professor Otto F. Bond, the Spanish Series edited by Professor Bond and Professor Carlos Castillo, and the German Series edited by Professor Peter Hagboldt, an Italian Series edited by Professor Walter L. Bullock and a Latin Series edited by Mima Maxey, all of the University of Chicago.

While vocabulary, grammar, composition, and oral and aural training receive due attention, these are all incidental to, and are considered primarily as contributory to, the development of reading ability, which is the primary objective of the elementary courses. An analysis of the extensive reading records of 541 beginning students in French who went consecutively through three quarters, an academic year, during the years 1927–32, inclusive, shows the following: 1,054 titles were read by various ones of the 541 students; a total of 769,093 pages were read; the quarter distribution norm was 13 per cent in the first quarter, 38 per cent in the second quarter, and 49 per cent in the third quarter, with a ratio of 1:3:4; the yearly average of the entire group was 2,141 pages; the averages for each of the three quarters were respectively 287 pages, 798 pages, and 1,056 pages; the distributions between fiction and nonfiction pages were 80.4 per cent and 19.6 per cent, respectively; between authors of fiction and authors of nonfiction works, 33.5 per cent and 66.5 per cent, respectively; between fiction titles and non-fiction titles, 59 per cent and 41 per cent, respectively. Equally significant results were attained in German. The non-fiction works ranged in fields as numerous as the departments in the University offering work at the undergraduate level.[3]

[3] Professor H. C. Morrison in his book *The Practice of Teaching in the Secondary School* (1926) concluded that of the two primary objectives of foreign-language study—speaking and reading—only reading can be attained; that for many students the reading course is all that is essential or desirable; that the reading course is *the* foreign-language contribution to general education; and that all forms of class work must focus on the attainment of this one objective. In the report written for the *Modern Foreign Language Study* (1929) Professor Algernon Coleman indicates the following desiderata: (1) reaching the reading stage as early as possible; (2) reading material to consist of simple graded and articulated texts "written down" in word range in accordance with standard word lists and idiom counts, and consisting of cultural, as well as literary, matter; (3) early, continuous, abundant outside reading; (4) carefully constructed work books and suitable testing instruments. We are conducting our elementary courses in modern foreign languages in accordance with this recommendation. In his book

Such remarkable results could not have been obtained by the instructional staff without the special College Modern Language Library so conveniently located that students can step immediately from the classroom to the Library, frequently with the instructor accompanying them to assist them in the selection of books either to be read in the reading-room or to be withdrawn. Besides books, there are in these rooms displays, sales talks, a bulletin-board clipping service maintained in part by students, and reading lists; newspapers and periodicals; pictures, posters, announcements of foreign-language radio programs, plays, cinema plays, lectures, meetings of foreign-language clubs, etc.; and, in a special inner room, audition instruments with phonograph records of folk songs, anecdotes, literary selections, and drill passages.

THE RENTAL LIBRARY

In view of the amount of reading, the various types of reading in various types of books, and the number of volumes that were necessary for the several new College courses under the New Plan, we saw that all needs could not be met by student purchases and the College Library. We could not ask the student to make more than a reasonable investment in textbooks for any one course, and, even with a generous grant from the Carnegie Corporation, we could not provide enough copies of each of the indispensable volumes to serve all students adequately. Furthermore, in each of several courses, it was seen that it would be advisable for each student to have in his pos-

---

Modern Languages and Their Teaching (1931) Robert D. Cole, after making a thorough survey of the teaching of modern foreign languages in the United States and Canada, concluded that the outstanding experiments with reading courses had been directed by Professor Otto F. Bond, of the University of Chicago.

session for study and frequent reference throughout each course several particularly chosen volumes. In each of these courses the number of these volumes represented an investment that it would be unreasonable to ask the student to make; and, even if we had money available for sufficient duplicate copies at the reserved-book desk in the College Library, it would be necessary, for satisfactory results, for the student to have these specially selected volumes in his possession for the duration of the course, because the need for any one of them was likely to arise at times when it would be inconvenient or impossible for the student to go to the College Library. The appropriate answer seemed to be the Rental Library.

Fortunately, we had been experimenting increasingly successfully with a rental library for several years before the New Plan was launched. In 1913, in order to provide the student with his required-reading volumes in one of the period courses in English literature so that the reading might be done under the best possible conditions, and to reduce the demand for these copies from the reserved-book desk, a few sets of several volumes were purchased by the University Library and rented to students in the course. The plan met with such favor with both students and faculty that requests were made that additional sets be made available for this course and for other courses. Over a period of fifteen years approximately 30,000 volumes were purchased and made available through the Rental Library as a branch of the University Library.

In the summer of 1929 the Rental Library was transferred to the Bookstore. When the New Plan was launched in 1931, the stock of the Rental Library was doubled to approximately 61,000 volumes. Though the rates of rentals were not raised when the Bookstore took over this service, the staff and hours were increased, and the enterprise was put on a self-sustaining but non-profit basis. The average life of volumes in the Rental Library is five years, and hence the rental fees are set so that a book will be paid for by the time it is worn out. In fixing the fees, however, a slight margin must be allowed to provide each year for the substitution in some rental sets of currently published new books that are much better for the purpose of the course than older books purchased so recently that they have not had time to pay for themselves in the Rental Library. Though faculty members are asked to give careful and judicious consideration in the selection of titles for rental books, and are told of the necessity that the Rental Library be self-sustaining, we are always ready to co-operate with a faculty member in the best interest of his students when the unforeseen publication of a new book puts out of date a recently purchased volume even in a rental set of which we have several hundred duplicates.

Of the 61,000 volumes in the Rental Library, the majority are rented in sets on the yearly or quarterly basis, a few volumes are rented individually on the quarterly basis, many more are rented on the daily basis, while for some foreign-language courses we have what is called the "flat-rate" rental plan. The Rental Library has 1,703 sets rented on the yearly basis, and 844 sets rented on the quarterly basis, making a total of 2,547 sets. Virtually all of the yearly sets are in circulation throughout the Autumn, Winter, and Spring quarters. Of the quarterly sets, only part of them are in demand each quarter, because some of the courses are offered during only one quarter of the academic year. The average circulation of quarterly sets is 250 sets. The average circulation of volumes on the daily rental basis is 150. The average quarterly circulation of about

40 titles available on the single-volume quarterly basis is 200. The average number of "flat-rate" rental cards for foreign-language courses in circulation each quarter is 250; this means that each student pays one dollar a quarter for an unlimited number of withdrawals during the quarter with a limit of one volume at a time—the student may change volumes each day, or even twice a day if he chooses to do so. In French we have 5,426 volumes; in German, 2,270 volumes; and in Spanish, 1,009 volumes. As the student progresses each quarter in the mastery of a foreign language, the number of titles he is qualified and expected to read increases rapidly.

For the Introductory General Course in the Biological Sciences the rental set includes 10 volumes that would represent an investment of $26.00 for the student if he purchased them, but are available to him for the academic year for a rental of $7.50. The rental set for the Introductory General Course in the Physical Sciences includes 11 volumes, that cost $38.25 and rent for $9.00 for the year. For Social Sciences I a rental set of 9 volumes, costing $22.75, is available at $7.50 per year. The set for Social Sciences II numbers 7 volumes, worth $19.00, that rent for $6.00 per year. Since not infrequently two or three students share the same rental set, the cost to each student is proportionately reduced and we do not have to stock as many sets for each course as there are registered students. We have 450 sets for the biological sciences course, 435 for the physical sciences course, 405 for Social Sciences I, and 150 for Social Sciences II. For the Introductory General Course in the Humanities so many titles are used for the indispensable reading during the year that we found it impracticable to provide rental sets; we endeavor to meet the demand as far as possible at the reserved-book desk in the College Library, but provide a supply of most of these titles in the Rental Library on the daily rental basis for students who wish to keep the books longer than the reserved-book circulation rules permit. Rental sets of from 2 to 8 volumes are provided for each of nine of the departmental courses in the College, and sets of various sizes are provided for several upper divisional courses.

No deposits are required from students who rent these sets; but proper identification must be given, such as the receipt for the current tuition fee, and the rental fee is collected in advance. If a student loses a book or mutilates it unreasonably, he is required to replace it, or pay the retail price of a new copy. A very small percentage of our stock is lost or stolen. Out of a collection of 61,000 volumes, our loss averages only about 15 copies a year, for most of which we are reimbursed. If a student has been given a deferred date for payment of his rental fee and then does not meet his obligation, or if he fails to return the books, the amount of indebtedness is reported to the University Bursar and the student is debarred from examinations and is refused a transcript of credit until settlement is made and his record cleared. We have very few such instances.

Textbooks that the student is expected to purchase for various courses (kept at a reasonable figure for each course) are not, as a rule, available through the Rental Library. It so happens, however, that a title used as a reference or required-reading volume in one course may be a required textbook in another course. If the former course is not given during the same quarter that the latter course is offered, the copies of the textbook for the latter course are taken from the rental sets for the former course and are available for students on the rental plan.

If available in the latest edition, we purchase used books

for the Rental Library; however, since most of the books purchased for the Rental Library are recent publications, few used copies are obtainable. If possible, we purchase inexpensive reprints. We have paper-covered editions rebound.

When new books are purchased for the Rental Library, they are catalogued and placed on the shelf immediately. Catalogue cards in sufficient numbers are inserted in the files of the general and departmental libraries of the University so that all students and all employees in the various departments may know what titles are available in the Rental Library.

Including all required texts and rental sets, the average necessary expenditure per student for the two College years is approximately $50.00. Though from one viewpoint it may be argued that the existence of a rental-library system is a confession by the College that it is not meeting its obligations to its students in library service, this is only partially true. Our Rental Library gives a type of service that is educationally valuable, that a college library cannot be expected to provide without fee, that is worth to the student even more than it costs him, and that keeps his total expenditures for books much below what they would necessarily be without the rental opportunities, even with the most generous regular library service.

In general it may be said that our Rental Library meets excellently a real need in a manner greatly appreciated by both students and faculty. The extent of this need could, and should, be somewhat reduced if we had adequate funds for library book purchases and service. No small part of the success of our Rental Library, even to the extent that we may frankly admit that it is a temporary solution of a library problem that should be met by the University in the library budget, is due to the helpful co-operation of Mr. Frederick H. Tracht, Manager of the Bookstore, who runs the Rental Library with a view to meeting promptly and efficiently the educational needs of students and faculty; though he is responsible for seeing that the Rental Library is self-sustaining, he does not expect it to show a profit. Of course the University has had repeatedly to make loans of no small size to the Rental Library for book purchases, but these loans are always repaid in a reasonable length of time.

Our library experience since the inauguration of the New Plan leads to the following conclusions:

1. Junior-college students can be led to read on an unprecedented scale.

2. With books playing a major rôle that is precisely integrated with the course syllabi and with the comprehensive examinations conducted on such a large scale, it is necessary that all students in the large general-course classes be given access to the same material. Large classes combined with heavy reading demands means multiple copies on a large scale. Costs for adequate library service are large, and we have not as yet met our obligations completely.

3. Since so many of the essential books are recent publications, the library should be kept up to date. It seems that ideally most of the collection should be replaced every seven years, and a large part every four or five years. This is particularly true of the social science field, where we are now using books purchased only three years ago that next year will be replaced by others more recently published and better suited to our purpose, if the relatively small number of necessary dollars are made available for this purpose.

4. There must be flexibility of mind among instructional

staff and librarians if the necessity of changing books is to be recognized frequently and promptly enough to produce the best educational results: academic ruts must not be allowed to develop.

5. Many inadequacies of books that are now available have been discovered at many points in our new program. The only corrective here is the writing of new books to meet new needs. Three such books have been published, others are about to be published, and still others will be published in succeeding years.

6. College library circulation has long been known to be a delicate, sensitive flower, that may very easily be withered by bungling at any one of several points. There must be the closest co-operation between administrative officers, instructional staff, and library staff, in order to develop and maintain reading morale; mismanagement in regard to a single essential title, through lack of united team play between these three essential members of the service team, may seriously stunt or deform the growth of the flower. Our New Plan, however, seems to have produced a hardy growth of the plant from which this flower blooms. Under the old plan, when students encountered difficulties, in getting access to books, through lack of co-operation by the various university staff members, they would soon lose interest and would refuse to make serious efforts to get books in the face of difficulties. Now, however, our students regard intelligent reading guidance, an adequate supply of books, and efficient library service, as their rights; if there is bungling at any one of these points, the students protest vigorously. Our instructional staff and our library staff have co-operated magnificently. Our greatest handicaps have come from inadequate and poorly designed library space, and from lack of sufficient funds for book

purchases. The President's Office has expressed a readiness to meet these needs as soon as the necessary funds may be made available.

THE PHYSICS MUSEUM[4]

The development of a museum as an auxiliary instructional device in the field of physics came as a result of our decision to offer an introductory general course in the physical sciences for general education rather than for the training of specialists. Since the course was to be offered without individual manipulatory laboratory work on the part of the student, some other means of bringing students into direct contact with phenomena must be devised. It was argued that one might as well try to interpret literature to students who had never read any books as to try to teach science to those who never had experienced any conscious contact with the phenomena that comprise its source material. In physics, especially, it seemed clear that the conventional laboratory method could not be used; and yet the part of the new general course dealing with this subject would leave no lasting impression without some type of laboratory contacts. Our attempt to solve this problem took the form of student museums of physics, chemistry, and geology, now in existence as an integral part of the course offerings.

It now seems quite likely that the museum of chemistry, which has been expensive and very difficult to administer, will be replaced by a suitable series of talking motion pictures. Through the courtesy and co-operation of Dr. Philip Fox, Director of the Adler Planetarium and Astro-

---

[4] I am indebted to Professor Harvey B. Lemon for most of the material on this topic. He has described this museum and its operation at greater length in his article in the *American Physics Teacher*, February, 1934.

nomical Museum, special demonstration lectures are given in the Planetarium for the students in our physical sciences general course. Students are advised also to attend several other times the free public lectures regularly given there and to study and inspect carefully the exhibits and photographs in the corridors of the Planetarium building. Geological processes are illustrated in demonstrative models in the building that houses our Department of Geology. The more important of these models are (*a*) a deformable stream table, an apparatus to duplicate in the laboratory the major processes of running water; and (*b*) a pressure box, a machine in which artificial strata are deformed to simulate the folding and the faulting of rocks in the earth's crust. The special Physics Museum is our most imposing venture in this type of instructional device in the field of the physical sciences.

Each student in the course has for continuous reference during the year a detailed syllabus of the subject matter of the entire course, and a rental set, procured through the Rental Library of the Bookstore, composed of eleven volumes (textbooks and reference works) dealing with the various sciences. The rental volumes for physics are of the type best described as intermediate between descriptive high-school and analytic college texts. One of these volumes, *From Galileo to Cosmic Rays*, was specially written by Professor Harvey B. Lemon for this course. In addition, in the College Library multiple copies of many other books are available, some of a popular nature, others more advanced, and some historical. Lectures are given regularly three times a week in a room specially equipped for demonstration lectures.

In the course syllabus the following suggestions for the use of the museums are offered.

At intervals extending over considerable periods during the year and appropriately chosen to coincide with the lectures dealing with the same subject matter, the museums of physics, chemistry, and geology will be open several hours daily with attendants in charge to supervise apparatus and to answer questions. Members of the faculty associated with the course will also usually be present for consultation and comments.

Since first-hand contact with the source material of the course is to be had only in these places, the student is advised to utilize these facilities to the utmost and therein to do as much of his studying as possible on the topics presented. The illustrations accompanying this syllabus are from museum exhibits, and continual references to them are found in the text. When the museums are open, students may come and go at their own convenience without any formal supervision. Familiarity with museum materials, quite as much as with that given in lectures, discussion groups, and reference texts, will be assumed in the formulation of the comprehensive examinations on the course.

Since there were no known precedents for guidance in our Physics Museum venture, the co-operation of the staff of the newly organized Museum of Science and Industry of the city of Chicago was sought and readily obtained. This museum possessed detailed plans for a very extensive museum of physics; and these plans in their topical outline showed, upon examination, possibilities for integration with the syllabus of the general course in the physical sciences. Members of the staff of the Museum of Science and Industry assisted our staff materially in drawing plans for the layout of space in our Physics Museum, and to them we also owe the loan of about one-half of the present equipment and assistance in its installation and maintenance. The remaining experiments and exhibits were assembled from the existing resources of the laboratories of the University.

It should be kept in mind that the Physics Museum is only a small part of a comprehensive and elaborate organization for the course. Its unique character among all museums springs from this fact. Although it has many visitors from among special groups of the general public and is under continual increasing demands from the outside, its entire *raison d'être* is to be found in the needs of our particular problems of instruction, and its major value lies in what it can contribute to the special needs of the curriculum of general education in the College.

The museum is housed in temporary and entirely inadequate quarters, the chief disadvantage of which is a rather remote location from the other activities of the students in the course. As was previously stated, the equipment is partly borrowed from another organization and partly assembled from apparatus which in turn has been borrowed from other University laboratories. It has been operated for nearly two years without a budget of its own—indeed at almost negligible cost—and the installation cost was not unreasonably large.

The museum has about three thousand square feet of floor space; this is divided into three rooms and part of a wide corridor to which the rooms open on either side. Being interior rooms in a one-story structure, the rooms are sky-lit and windowless, and hence ideal for exhibition purposes. The wall area for charts, etc., and the lineal footage available for experiments have been greatly increased by the installation of temporary partitions which create circuitous paths and impose a definite direction of circulation upon the visitor.

The three rooms house a total of 125 experiments and exhibits, the majority of which are either self-operating or student-operated by means of push buttons or similar easily manipulated devices.[5] In each sequence of subjects

[5] A list of the exhibits in the Physics Museum, as found in the current (fourth) edition of the course syllabus, is given in Appendix F.

in any field the attempt is made to lead the visitor from the most simple and elementary aspects through a sequence of increasing complexity to one or two experiments of the utmost refinement and precision.

The manner in which exhibits are mounted for display is very simple. Unlike many other types of museum display, there is no need for stagelike settings or lighting, or for large exhibits, since the number of visitors at any time before any given exhibit is never more than two or three. Narrow tables are built in around the walls and along each side of the six-foot partitions that divide the rooms. These are covered with a heavy gray-green floor linoleum and make, with the brown-stained woodwork, a quiet and inconspicuous appearance.

The necessary electric, gas, compressed-air, and water outlets and small sinks sunk in the table tops were of course planned after the layout of experiments was complete. Wall charts cover nearly all of the space behind the tables; the planning and execution of them required fully as much time and effort as did the exhibits themselves. Typewritten placards framed under glass go with each exhibit. These provide a concise explanation of the phenomena shown, their relation to the other exhibits by cross-reference, and any necessary directions for operation or instructions as to what should be observed. Cautions which must be observed are printed in red, and students are drilled to read and study them before attempting to manipulate the exhibit. Since the student visitors to this museum are also in frequent attendance at lectures, it is a relatively simple matter to inculcate in their minds the proper attitude with respect to the museum's use.

Because of increased familiarity of both staff and students with the needs of the new curriculum and increasing experience in handling it, the museum played a much greater part in the students' experiences during the second and third years than it did during the first. This is obvious to any careful observer who watches the way in which many students are using the museum more and more after the manner in which they would use a reference library. Many of them obviously come prepared to devote themselves to a certain experiment or to some small group of related ones, with respect to which they have already informed themselves somewhat. They come armed with the Syllabus, and often with reference texts, which are consulted together with the printed directions and explanations of the experiments, before any manipulations are made. Of course there is still a considerable amount of undesigned roaming about, but much of it frequently terminates in a focus of interest and real study.

The continuous presence of an attendant, preferably one in each room, is absolutely necessary. An inoperative experiment is regarded as an intolerable event, the one unforgivable fault on the part of an assistant. His first duty is to see that everything works before the doors open. But he is also there to help students clear up points regarding experiments and the general principles which they involve. His rôle is precisely that of a good laboratory instructor, who has eyes everywhere, who drops a word here or there if there is difficulty, who asks a leading question to stimulate thought and interest if it flags, but who never indulges in full and detailed lectures and explanations.

During the Autumn Quarter, 1934, three-fourths of the students in the physical sciences general course averaged four visits per student to the Physics Museum; approximately one-fourth did not visit the Museum even once. Two students made sixteen visits each. A study of the correlation between the grades on examinations and the records of attendance at the Museum shows that those who study the exhibits receive the higher grades. This is explained by the fact that the better students are the ones who most frequently visit the Museum, and also by the fact that purposeful attendance facilitates an understanding of the principles demonstrated by the exhibits.

After three years' experimental trial the Physics Museum has assumed a sufficiently effective and necessary place in connection with the general course so that recognition of the importance of its place in the University has resulted. A policy, not only of maintaining it, but of improving the present obvious defects in housing and location and of ultimately providing a budget for maintenance, has been assured as soon as circumstances permit. It is also intended to make it independent of the Museum of Science and Industry, its foster-parent, cordial and kindly as this association has been. Furthermore, although the sister physical sciences of astronomy, chemistry, and geology, possibly even mathematics, face quite different problems in museum development and maintenance—some of them much more difficult—there has arisen out of the present venture a real desire on the part of several men in these fields to attempt similar enterprises for the purpose of instruction.

BIOLOGICAL SCIENCES LABORATORY DEMONSTRATION EXHIBITS[6]

Equally significant and equally unique in their development as instructional aids are the laboratory demonstration exhibits prepared from week to week for students in the Introductory General Course in the Biological Sciences.

[6] I am indebted to Professor M. C. Coulter, chairman of the Introductory General Course in the Biological Sciences, for most of the material on this topic.

The considerations that made necessary the development of this type of instructional device for this course were much the same as those that were responsible for the development of the Physics Museum. While the exhibits in the Physics Museum are continuously assembled in one place and hence bulk impressively large, the biological sciences exhibits would make even a greater impression in size and significance if they could be assembled all at one time in a biological museum. This is impossible, however, because of the nature of the materials used and because of the character of many of the demonstration experiments that can be performed only by experts.

Each student in the Introductory General Course in the Biological Sciences has in his possession throughout the year a detailed printed syllabus and a rental set of ten volumes obtained through the Rental Library. Dependent upon the subject under discussion, several of the lecturers make liberal use of lantern slides. Occasionally these slides are interjected at several points in the lecture; more often, however, five or six minutes of lantern slides are shown at the end of the lecture as a résumé as well as for clarification. Some of the lecturers use laboratory demonstrations with apparatus that has been devised so that the main course of the experiment can be followed by students sitting at some distance. There is opportunity and need for considerable extension of this policy. At the present time many of the demonstrations are such small-scale affairs that it is not feasible to conduct them in the general lecture; in consequence they are necessarily moved over into the laboratory exhibits. With more equipment and ingenuity (the latter is available whenever the necessary money may be provided for the former), we could undoubtedly modify some of these small-scale demonstrations into large-scale affairs so that they could be conducted effectively in the lecture.

On five or six occasions during the year-course, approximately forty-minute programs of educational movies are provided outside the regular class period. With attendance on the voluntary basis, approximately 75 per cent of the class attend and have expressed their satisfaction with the programs. Though as yet we have produced no films specifically for our own course, the chairman of the course and some of his colleagues have examined scores of those that have been produced elsewhere for other purposes; and we have bought or rented enough to provide for the programs thought to be most desirable. The decided majority of educational films that have to date been produced in the field of biology are not quite suitable for our purpose, since they are more appropriate for high-school and popular audiences. Our selection has been based upon two criteria: (1) adjustment to the intellectual level of our students; (2) adjustment to the content of our course—for it is our plan to reinforce the course with the movies, rather than merely to provide popular entertainment. The course staff members feel that educational movies represent a very promising lead; and they propose to extend the use of them, both along the lines already being followed and by producing films of our own, as has been done in the physical sciences field.

On approximately two-thirds of the Monday and Tuesday afternoons throughout the year, from one to four o'clock on each of the two afternoons, special laboratory demonstration exhibits are arranged for members of this course. The demonstration for each week is arranged in the particular one of the various biological departmental laboratories that is best equipped for the subject matter of that week in the general course. Students are not co-erced to attend this laboratory. It is made clear to them that attendance is not a necessary part of their prepara-tion for the comprehensive examination. It is merely stated that in the interests of general education attendance at the optional laboratory is very much worth while. Ap-proximately 70 per cent of the students attend—some regularly and others periodically—and the majority are enthusiastic over the educational values of the demonstra-tions and exhibits.

In the laboratory the students do no individual work; but they have an opportunity to see specimens of all sorts, both macroscopic and microscopic, already prepared and set up for their convenience; also to see, and to listen to explanations of, demonstration experiments conducted for them by laboratory instructors and assistants. Since large numbers must be accommodated, the displays are usually arranged on the cafeteria principle—a steady stream of students moving from one item to the next in a designated sequence. Usually it takes a student about forty minutes to see the entire exhibit for the week. The exhibit is con-tinuous through the two three-hour periods each week, with a view to accommodating students who have differ-ent schedules, and to reducing the number present at any one time.

We have abundant evidence that in conducting these laboratory demonstrations we are doing something really significant in education. More than once it has been re-marked by adult visitors to some of our laboratory demon-strators that a half-hour of this type of experience is more valuable to the average student for general education than a month of old-fashioned laboratory work.

The schedule for these laboratory demonstration exhibits for the current year, indicating the number of different exhibits through a corresponding number of weeks in each of nine of the fourteen subdivisions of the course is as follows: "Plant Kingdom," 2; "Invertebrates," 4; "Vertebrates," 2; "Anthropology," 1; "Embryology," 1; "The Cell," 2; "Physiology," 7; "Bacteriology," 1; "Heredity," 1.

The gross outline of the main content of a series of seven exhibits in physiology, a detailed outline of a single exhibit in embryology, and a detailed outline of a single exhibit in bacteriology, are given in Appendix G.

SOCIAL SCIENCE FIELD TRIPS

For the Introductory General Course in the Study of Contemporary Society (Social Sciences I), the city of Chicago provides many "laboratory demonstration exhibits" for the study of current economic, political, and social phenomena and problems. In each quarter of the academic year various members of the course staff organize and conduct from three to five trips as extra or supplementary curriculum activities for students in the course, on the voluntary basis. For some of these trips the number of students that can be taken is necessarily limited to the fifty who are most interested, while on other trips as many as two hundred can be, and are, accommodated. Through these trips theory and readings are checked with a face-to-face meeting with the city. All members of the staff and a majority of the students agree that these trips contribute significant educational values to their study of this field.

Some of the purposes and results of these trips are indicated in the following excerpts from some informal reports by staff members to the Dean on some of the trips conducted last year.

Watching at the polls during the Primary of last spring was perhaps the most effective field trip, inasmuch as 250 students turned out for it. It was very enthusiastically done by the students; at a meeting to exchange impressions and findings of watching the polls about 60 students turned up and discussed for three hours what they noticed in the way of election irregularities.

———

About 160 students visited ——— (one of the large meat-packing plants at the Stock Yards). The management had arranged to have a guide for each group of twenty; and at the end of the trip through the plant, which took about two hours, an executive of the company spent an hour with us in the auditorium, discussing questions which had arisen as a result of the plant visit. The students had an unusual opportunity to observe a very high degree of specialization of tasks, and the apparently brutalizing character of some, which made a deep impression; to see government inspectors at work; to see a highly diversified industry as far as products are concerned; and to have explained the far-flung extent of markets in relation to buying raw materials and selling finished products. Many questions were asked which showed a deep interest in wages, hours, and working conditions, and in problems of management in relation to purchasing raw materials, control of production, development of markets both domestic and foreign, determination of selling prices, influence of tariffs, and other subjects which form part of the content of the first quarter's work. One student remarked the next day, "There's hardly any question relating to the economics part of our course which that trip through ——— did not bring up!"

———

The trip which about 100 students took through the ——— Works was also interesting. Here the effects of the depression were more obvious—whole parts of the works closed down, idle machinery, a general blight over everything. In the ——— works we saw an excellent example of the kind of mechanization which results in "technological unemployment." Huge machines were turning out tons of ——— with a minimum of human supervision. In one great room only four or five people were used to guide about forty tremendous machines. A trip through the foundry showed the students some of the dirtier and heavier work of the plant, the greater accident hazards, etc.

———

The Federal Reserve Bank authorities were most kind in planning for about a hundred students an interesting and enlightening trip. We sat on the platform in the clearing house, watching messengers with their satchels scurrying in and out and watching the checkers at their nerve-racking task. Later on, when silence was no longer enjoined, the students had an opportunity to ask questions, and they more than availed themselves of this opportunity. Some guides assigned to us took us into the vaults and showed us the huge safety devices provided to guard the gold bullion and the various forms of money. Counterfeit-detectors were shuffling huge trays of coins in some barred "cells" and in others examining paper money for counterfeits. After the trip through all the departments, including large rooms full of clerical workers, we went to the Board of Directors' room, where some of the bank officers answered the many questions left in the students' minds.

The visits to the Board of Trade and the Stock Exchange furnished much excitement to the 75 students who took this trip. We saw in the "Pit," at the former, men acting like wild monkeys, scrambling over each other, gesticulating in finger sign language, oblivious of everything but the attainment of speed in their transactions. A guide took us up to the inspection department to show how the various grades of grain are determined, how the grain is deposited in the elevators, and so on. The Stock Exchange guides took us down to the floor of the Exchange at noon when the riot was over and the members had departed, and explained to us the technique of posting prices, of flashing the news to other centers, of getting news of the New York and San Francisco exchanges within 15 seconds of its dispatching, etc. The way the students crowded around guides and asked questions here, as in all the other places we have visited, was sufficient proof of the worth-whileness of the trips. For weeks afterward they discussed various questions concerning them with discussion leaders.

This trip to the ——— Steel Works was planned to give the students an idea of the operations involved in one of the heavy engineering industries, the isolation of the individual worker or small group of workers in relation to their fellows, the degree of skill required for the various operations, the working conditions, including heat and various hazards, the combination of raw materials and the manipulation of them in making steel. No explanation of processes was offered either prior to or subsequent to the trip through the plant, and partly because of poor guides and partly due to noise very few students heard satisfactory explanations of what they saw. About forty students went on this trip, which involved a long bus ride.

A few superior students with more than ordinarily inquiring minds asked me to let them visit a "scientific management" plant. In Chicago we have the ——— plant where surgical dressings and adhesive plaster are manufactured. Mr. ———, who has been a member of the Taylor Society for many years and has installed scientific management in his plants in the East and South, bought this Chicago plant a couple of years ago and is gradually installing scientific management there. We therefore had a good opportunity to see a plant with the proper routing and distribution of work through centralized control, selection and assignment of personnel on a reasoned basis, job analysis, functionalized foremanship, rates set by time study and analysis and synthesis of elements in the operations, and various other phases of scientific management either installed or being installed.

The students who availed themselves of the trip to the United States Customs House were impressed by the high degree of skill and intelligence shown by the federal customs inspectors who were specialists in their fields, for example, in textiles, in metal ornaments, in real and fake antiques, etc.

About eighty students went to the Field Museum on a trip conducted under the leadership of Professor Fay-Cooper Cole. This expedition, devoted to a study of aboriginal American cultures, helped make clear the course materials dealing with various aspects of culture and its study.

About one hundred and twenty-five students attended a faculty-conducted bus trip entitled "A Panoramic View of What the Sight-Seer Does Not See of Chicago." On this tour, which lasted about two and a half hours, it was possible to point out the markedly different types of areas that make up a large city. An appreciation was gained of the physical and social structure of the city ranging from the location and significance of means of communication and transportation, manufacturing, wholesale and retail establishments, the wastelands of the city, and parks and playgrounds, to the different cultural areas and population types, including immigrant areas of first, second and third settlement, the Negro district, Chinatown, etc.

A trip was conducted to the Near West Side which about forty students attended. Our walk through this area included stops at the Clearing House for Unemployed Men, a shelter house, a colony of homeless men in improvised shelters built in a vacant lot, the Unemployed Council Headquarters, and Hull-House. At all stops talks were given on the nature and scope of the work of the various organizations by those in charge. At Hull-House, after a talk by Jane Addams, the group was guided through the settlement.

Another of our trips included visits to the Chicago Plan Commission, where a lecture was delivered by Mr. Taylor, on "The Planning of the City," and to representative departments of the city government including the Department of Public Works, the Bureau of Engineering, the Health Department, the Fire Protection and Fire Alarm Service, and the Traffic Division. In each instance an official explained the work of his department.

Besides the regularly scheduled trips I took several small groups for informal visits to the Museum of Science and Industry.

In the issue of the *Daily Maroon* (the student paper) for October 9, 1934, under the headline "Social Sciences I Schedules Field Trip to Western Electric," appeared the following:

Continuing a policy of several years' standing, the Social Sciences Department in the College will again offer a series of field trips to interesting spots in the city in connection with the work in the Social Sciences I general course. The first trip of the autumn quarter will be a visit to the Hawthorne plant of the Western Electric Company on Tuesday, October 16.

The purpose of this excursion will be to furnish an example of the minute division of labor characteristic of modern industry, which is a part of the subject matter for the first quarter of the course. The trip will be limited to the first 50 students who sign their names on the notice posted outside Cobb 304. They will be shown through the plant with one guide for each group of eight.

Students are to meet at gate No. 1 of the Western Electric building at two o'clock. Directions for reaching the plant via the south side "L" are included in the notice in Cobb Hall.

Another type of device used by the social sciences staff that plays a rôle comparable in part to the laboratory demonstration exhibits of the natural science fields is reflected in the following excerpt from a report by the chairman:

. . . . I would also like to stress the very real significance of the bulletin boards, in the reading-room near the door to our suite of offices, which we used last year, but are using to an increasing extent this year for a critical comparison and annotation of current significant items in the news, cartoons, etc. We have plenty of evidence that this has been of genuine educational significance.

THE NEW-PLAN TALKING MOTION PICTURES

During a period of several years prior to the launching of our New Plan, Erpi Picture Consultants, Incorporated, New York City, had experimented in the development of educational talking motion pictures with gratifying results. They had found satisfactory short subjects in several fields through assistance from scholars in several universities. Shortly before the announcement of our New Plan they had concluded that the major problems of production on the mechanical side had been solved to the point that they were ready for a comprehensive educational program of integrated scenarios. When our New Plan was announced for inauguration in September, 1931, they asked that copies of the syllabi for our four introductory general courses be sent to them as soon as available. An examination of these syllabi led to the conclusion that our program met their needs even beyond their fondest hopes. Conferences were arranged, and a contract for production was signed. Our staff members were to write the scenarios and serve as production directors on the educational side, while Erpi Picture Consultants were to be responsible for production on the technical and mechanical side.

As the work of organizing the introductory general courses progressed, careful consideration was given to the selection of the best combination of methods for the most effective presentation that was possible. When the development and use of the talking motion picture was suggested by Erpi Picture Consultants, it was decided to experiment with this medium as an integral part of instruction in the new general courses. We decided that each film to be produced should be designed to meet a precise need growing out of an actual instructional situation. In no one of the four large fields would we attempt to produce a series of talking pictures that would constitute a complete course. We did not think of the films as a substitute for the instructor or for material already available, but merely as additional classroom material for the greater effectiveness and ease of teaching and learning.

Our original and present plan calls for the production of eighty talking pictures, twenty in each of the four divisional fields—the biological sciences, the humanities, the physical sciences, and the social sciences. It was decided to begin production in the field of the physical sciences, and six films have been completed and are now in use. Professors Harvey B. Lemon and Herman I. Schlesinger, who edited the syllabus for the introductory general course, wrote the scenarios and supervised the production of these pictures. The titles of the pictures now in use are "The Molecular Theory of Matter," "Oxidation and Reduction," "Energy and Its Transformation," "Electrostatics," "Sound Waves and Their Sources," and "Fundamentals of Acoustics." Six more are now in process of production. Tentative subjects for additional films in the physical sciences series are the following: velocity of light, matter and force, heat and work, interference of light, spectroscopy, electromagnetism, chemical equilibrium, velocity of chemical reactions, electricity and matter, atomic structure as related to chemical reaction, electrochemistry, carbon and its compounds, composition of the atmosphere, the solar system, time and the calendar, eclipses of the sun and moon, the changing surfaces of the earth, beneath the earth's surface, and weather and forecasting.

Many of the advantages that it was hoped would accrue from the production and use of such films have actually been attained. For example, the time and energy of instructor and students that can be saved on one topic through the use of a film can be devoted to the better mastery of another topic or to an additional topic; thus the course content can be enlarged and, in many instances, with increased effectiveness. In some instances a single film can present in ten minutes a demonstration of scientific theories and processes ordinarily requiring the use of a large amount of expensive apparatus and six to nine hours of laboratory preparation, demonstration, and lecture. Natural processes requiring days, weeks, months, and years can be portrayed vividly and accurately through time-lapse or slow-motion pictures which make visible movements imperceptible to the human eye. By using animated drawings, many forms of experiments may be clarified by focusing the attention of the student upon the important processes involved; this is particularly true of pictures dealing with electrical phenomena and sound waves. The size of the motion picture on the screen makes possible the focusing of the attention of a large class upon important details which in a lecture demonstration would be lost to all but the fortunate few within close view of the instructor's demonstration desk.

Demonstration experiments with delicate and costly laboratory equipment and of a type that depends for its success upon ideal atmospheric conditions can be recorded on film and shown to students at times when most needed in the course program, regardless of the state of the weather. A telescopic lens brings distant objects prominently upon the screen. The microscopic lens enlarges minute living and moving organisms to the size best adapted for study and shows actual physical changes taking place. X-ray photography makes possible the observation and demonstration of processes within opaque objects. Sound amplification can often be used so that inaudible sounds can be clearly heard.

In the selection of materials to be presented by our new talking pictures the subject matter that can be adequately presented by textbooks or blackboards is eliminated. The pictures endeavor to present significant processes rather than merely popular or spectacular features. For each of the pictures a printed *Guide* or handbook is available that contains discussion leads, references, bibliographies, a list of the demonstrations to be shown, the synchronized lecture that accompanies the picture, and all the materials necessary for the student to prepare himself to gain the maximum benefit from the first showing of the film. The following suggestions to instructors and students are quoted from one of the *Study Guides:*

In order to derive the greatest advantage from the film, the student should become thoroughly familiar with the introduction and the objectives before the film is shown.

Previous to the initial showing, it is desirable to discuss the objectives and their relation to the study. After the picture has been shown, phenomena observed in specific scenes should be recalled and consideration given to the significance of those scenes to the sequences of which they were a part. The sequences of the picture also should be compared with each other; for instance, the similarity between the phenomena associated with the burning of phosphorus and with the corrosion of iron may be developed. Such an analysis prepares the student more intelligently to view the picture the second time and gives him the proper foundation for beginning the development of the subject.

This may be an opportune time to discuss topics not treated by the film; to relate individual scenes to what the student has already learned about chemistry; to select specific problems to be studied, and to associate phenomena portrayed by the film with the student's every-day experience. The second showing should be given after progress has been made with classroom and laboratory work and need for the showing is evidenced.

Before the second showing, the student may find it helpful to prepare a list of unanswered questions or problems which were suggested by the first showing or which have arisen in subsequent study. The second projection of the film will undoubtedly answer many of these questions and will provoke additional questions and suggest further activities. At its conclusion, discussion will bring out the significance which certain scenes have for the activities in which the students are engaged. This will allow him to redirect his efforts and to seek assistance if necessary. It likewise will indicate what elements he should study during subsequent showings of the film.

It is believed that a minimum of three showings is desirable to secure the best use of the film. The third showing should bring to a focus the student's ideas about oxidation and reduction, and should add meaning to the activities which he has carried on during the study. As with the other showings, the student may note questions and should review the objectives. Group discussion following the third showing should bring to a successful conclusion the study of the subject and should aid the student in preparing for whatever tests are to be undertaken.

Though in some of the films several dramatic illustrations and applications of principles and processes, that it would otherwise be impossible to bring into the classroom, are included, it should be kept in mind that the subjects for the pictures in this series were not chosen because of their spectacular or dramatic possibilities. Each subject is chosen because of its usefulness in our Introductory General Course in the Physical Sciences. "The Molecular Theory" was chosen because it illustrates the use of experimental devices impossible of reproduction in the classroom, because it is particularly adapted to demonstrate the value of animation, and because most of the apparatus takes considerable time to set up. "Oxidation and Reduction" was selected for filming because it illustrates quite different advantages. Most of the apparatus is quite simple and was used (aside from its appropriateness) to show that much of the lecturer's time can be saved even in such cases, and that even for simple apparatus the moving picture has the advantage of bringing to every student in the room equal opportunity for seeing every detail. A second important point was to show that practical applications of scientific subject matter can be more vividly portrayed in less time by the moving picture than in other ways.

Last year a controlled experiment was conducted with two groups of students in the Introductory General Course in the Physical Sciences, to determine whether the use of these talking motion pictures had any demonstrable effect. "The Molecular Theory of Matter" film was shown to 212 students in a morning section, supplemented by lecture and lecture demonstrations. At an afternoon section on the same day, the lecture and lecture demonstrations were given by the same lecturer to 170 students, but without the film. The material presented and the manner of presentation, except for the motion picture, were substantially the same for the two sections. Three days later tests, carefully equated for difficulty, were given to both groups. The tests were fifteen minutes in length, were of the objective form, and were designed to cover the subject as outlined in the syllabus; they were not based on the film, though the film presentation covered essentially the same subject matter.

The same procedure was followed for the film "Electrostatics," except that the experimental (picture) group and the control group were reversed. The section that saw the film "The Molecular Theory of Matter" did not see "Electrostatics," and vice versa. This counterbalanced order was expected to correct for any difference in the average ability of the two groups.

The report of the examiner, Mr. M. W. Richardson, shows that in each instance there was a difference in the average scores of the two groups that is statistically significant in favor of the group that had seen the talking motion picture.

At the meeting of the American Association of Physics Teachers in Pittsburgh, December 27, 1934, Professor C. J. Lapp, of the State University of Iowa, gave a report on the experimental use of the two films "Molecular Theory of Matter" and "Electrostatics," with two sections of a course in elementary physics, under controlled conditions. In one experiment the "Electrostatics" film was shown twice to one section in a single class period. During the intermission between the two showings, the instructor commented on the picture and urged attention to certain details at the second showing. To the other section the film was not shown, but a carefully prepared demonstration lecture of fifty minutes was given, covering as nearly as possible the same material as the film and using almost identical equipment and experiments. The lecture was so carefully prepared that members of the class declared it superior to the regular performance of the same lecturer. In this and the other experiments, tests, which were carefully prepared, administered, and scored, showed results that were statistically significant in favor of the use of the films.

Our use of these pictures to date has not been extensive enough to warrant the drawing of large conclusions with certainty. Results to date do show, however, that this supplementary instructional medium has possibilities that warrant the expenditure of the no small amounts of genius, energy, time, and money that the further development of our program in this area will demand.

CHAPTER X

EXAMINATION RESULTS

MANY persons have rightly observed that the keystone of our New Plan is the examination system: our educational arch will stand firmly, will sway uncertainly, or will fall, depending upon the degree of success attained in the construction and administration of the examinations, since the award of the College Certificate is based entirely on the results of these examinations.

At the time our New Plan was publicly announced, I was serving as a member of the Board of Review of the Commission on Higher Education, of the North Central Association of Colleges and Secondary Schools. The Board of Review is primarily responsible for the enforcement of the accrediting standards, since the Association looks to the Board for recommendations to grant or to deny to institutions places on the accredited list. As a member of the Board I shared in the work of inspecting institutions and sat through the hearings and the long executive sessions.

One night, in the wee hours of a new day, just after we had voted that a certain institution should be stricken from the accredited list, a fellow-member of the Board turned to me and said with a smile, though perhaps somewhat in earnest: "When you get this new plan of yours in operation we'll have *you* up here on the carpet in answer to *quo warranto* proceedings. We can't let you throw our standards to the winds without allowing other institutions to do likewise. You are setting a dangerous precedent that will give some of the would-be 'diploma mills' just the opportunity they want."

I replied in effect as follows: "The present standards of this Association are stated almost solely in terms of the mechanics and forms of education. It is demanded that each institution meet certain minimum requirements in regard to financial income and stability, plant, equipment, number of volumes in the library, faculty training in terms of time spent in graduate schools, and student entrance requirements and graduation requirements in terms of time-serving. From no accredited institution do we have evidence other than that the student is exposed for a standard length of time to an environment that is presumed to produce an educational result of significance. We have no accurate or reliable evidence regarding the educational product—the sole *raison d'être* of the whole system.

"We believe that when your inspectors visit us, at the University of Chicago, after the New Plan has been in operation two years, we shall be able to present to them evidence regarding the educational attainments of the student that are of much greater significance than the impedimenta of the educational process. We shall be able to show for each student: a syllabus, usually of considerable length, for each course he has pursued; a fairly complete case history of educational guidance and personnel records; a copy of each of seven six-hour examinations that the student has been required to write; the examination papers that he actually has written under supervised conditions; and his score and percentile rank in each examination. We believe that data of this type are of far more significance than the type you are now getting and acting upon for accrediting purposes."

At the time of this friendly *badinage* in the Board of Review a new committee on the revision of standards was being set up by the Commission on Higher Education in response to a widespread feeling among members of the Association that the old standards had outlived their usefulness. Last April (1934) this committee made a most significant report that included a set of recommendations for new standards stated primarily in terms of the quality of performance in the light of the stated educational objectives of each institution. The framing and adoption of these new accrediting standards constitute the most important forward step taken by the Association in a generation.

We believe that the College of the University of Chicago now has its house in order, ready for a rigorous inspection by the North Central Association under the new standards for higher institutions.

Though the comprehensive examinations and their rôles were discussed in an earlier chapter, an appreciation of the extent to which they are really "comprehensive" at the junior-college level can be attained only by a careful study of several of them, preferably an entire battery of seven. It is impossible, within the space limits of these pages, to print enough sample questions to give anything approaching an adequate impression of even a single examination. The remaining pages of this chapter will be devoted to an analysis of some of the data from examination results.

At my request (and partially at the expense of my budget), Mr. W. F. Cramer, of the Registrar's Office, supervised the compilation of a considerable amount of statistical data for several specific studies of the results of examinations and the progress of students under the New Plan. These tabulations include the records of all New-Plan Freshmen who entered the College from the opening of the Autumn Quarter, 1931, to the Spring Quarter, 1934, inclusive, and carry their records to October 1, 1934, including the results of the examinations given in September, 1934. The records of students who entered with three or more courses of recognized college work, and of students who transferred to the New Plan after completing three or more courses under the old plan (357 students), are not included in any of the tabulations here cited, since I wish to present the results for students who have been solely and entirely New Plan college students.

The records of 2,109 students were included. Of these students, 110 were dismissed for unsatisfactory work and have not been reinstated; 421 voluntarily withdrew before they had qualified for the College Certificate; 719 have been in residence less than six quarters (two academic years); 203 have been in residence six or more quarters but have not qualified for the College Certificate; 656 have completed the College requirements.

A passing grade in each of seven examinations is required for the College Certificate. A passing average for the seven examinations is not sufficient. Transmuting the official Board examination grades of A, B, C, D, and F (with D passing), into 4, 3, 2, 1, and 0, respectively, grade averages can be computed and used for comparative studies of examination results and of the relative progress made by various students.

At the time this study was made (December, 1934), there were, for the 2,109 students, a total of 9,931 officially recorded Board examination grades distributed as follows: A, 1,099 (11.07 per cent); B, 1,987 (20.01 per cent); C, 4,071 (40.99 per cent); D, 1,751 (17.63 per cent); F, 1,023 (10.30 per cent). This group of students wrote more than 9,931 examinations, since the total number of failures by all students on all examinations was 1,880. Of these 1,880 F grades, 857 (45.59 per cent) were subsequently raised to passing grades by repeated examinations, and a few passing grades were raised to higher passing grades by repeated examinations. The average of all recorded passing grades is 2.27, with 2 representing C. The average of all recorded grades, including the F grades, is 2.04. The average number of failures per student is 0.891. The average number of failures per student per examination is 0.189.

Out of approximately nine thousand passing examinations included in this study, there were only 33 instances (0.38 of 1 per cent) of students repeating an examination to raise their grades after having received passing grades. Approximately three-fourths of these students succeeded in raising their grades. About half of the students in this group were pre-medical students who endeavored to better their chances for admission to medical school by raising their grade on the biological sciences general examination. In only one instance did a student who repeated an examination to better a previous grade of D receive a grade of F. His previous passing grade of D is still his officially recorded grade, in accordance with our official policy in such instances, since we wish the student to have all possibility of gain with nothing to lose.

An analysis was made of the records of those students who have failed to complete the College requirements because of failure to pass one or two of the examinations, to determine whether these one or two failures tend to be on one or a few specific examinations. Ninety-four students who have been in residence six or more quarters have taken the seven examinations required for the College Certificate but have not as yet succeeded in attaining a passing grade in each of the seven examinations. The percentage of failing students in this group in each of the five specifically required examinations is: biological sciences, 5.32;

humanities, 6.38; physical sciences, 12.77; social sciences, 10.54; and English composition, 21.28.

The high percentage of failures in the English qualifying examination in this study is due in large part to the character of both the course and the examination during the first year, and to some extent in the second year. Since both the course and the examination have been materially improved, in the third and fourth years, the percentage of failures among those who have pursued the course faithfully is now running lower and is in line with the results in other fields. Another explanation is found in the fact that, since the grades on the English qualifying examination were not included in the determination of honors and scholarship awards during the first two years, students were more inclined to "take a chance" on the English qualifying examination without serious and extended preparation than was true of the other examinations. This held true to the extent of a second, third, or even a fourth attempt at an examination previously failed, as is shown by the fact that this group of 94 students wrote 158 examinations—74 passing examinations and 84 (53.16 per cent) failing examinations—on the English qualifying examination. For the biological sciences examination the data for the group of 94 are 89 examinations passed and 13 (12.76 per cent) failed; for humanities, 88 examinations passed and 16 (15.38 per cent) failed; for physical sciences, 82 examinations passed and 26 (24.08 per cent) failed; and for social sciences, 84 examinations passed and 25 (22.94 per cent) failed.

Of these 94 students the largest number who took one of the approximately thirty elective sequences and the corresponding examination was 39 in Social Sciences II; the next in order was 24 in Biological Sciences II, and 24 in

Geography 101, 102, 103; the numbers of students in the other sequences dropped rapidly from this point, down to only a few or even only one in a given sequence. The number of students passing, the number of students failing, the number of examinations passed, and the number of examinations failed, respectively, were: for Social Sciences II, 26, 13, 26, and 18; for Biological Sciences II, 19, 5, 19, and 9; for the geography sequence, 13, 11, 13, and 16. Where the number of examinations failed is larger than the number of failing students, the explanation is found in the fact that some students failed the examination for the same sequence more than once.

This study was made to show particularly whether any one of the five specifically required examinations was proving to be an impassable barrier to an unreasonably large group of students. The data indicate that this is not true—that no one of the four required general course examinations is relatively unreasonably difficult for a significant number or percentage of students.

An analysis was made of the records of those students who barely satisfied the College requirements with D grades in most of their examinations, to determine whether a significant number received high grades in one or two examinations, and, if so, whether these high grades tended to be on one or a few specific examinations. Forty-six instances were found of students who received D grades in four or more of the seven required examinations. If each student had passed each examination the first time he took it, there would have been 7 times 46, or 322, examinations. Since several students had to take one or more examinations more than once to attain a passing grade, there were 412 examinations, with grade distributions as follows: A, 1; B, 11; C, 103; D, 211; and F, 86, with an average of 1.39 (with D or 1, passing), exclusive of the 86 F grades.

Interestingly enough, the 1 A grade and 5 of the 11 B grades were in the English qualifying examination, and this may be accounted for by the low validity and reliability of that examination during the first year, and to only a somewhat lesser extent in the second year. The other 6 B grades were distributed among six of the elective sequence examinations, three of them in foreign-language examinations.

This analysis seems to show that no one of the four required general course examinations is unreasonably easy for low-grade students or for generally low-level performers.

Within this group of 46 students there were 4 instances of students who attempted an examination without having registered for any part of the corresponding course, 4 who attempted an examination after having been in the corresponding course only one quarter; 18 were registered for two quarters; 277 for three quarters; 9 for four quarters; 6 for five quarters; and 4 for six quarters. The average quarters of registration in corresponding courses for the entire group was 2.98, with 3 normal. These low-level performers, who barely met the passing standard, averaged only the amount of time in residence expected of average students to attain approximately average results.

An analysis of the records of students who passed the College requirements with honors was made to determine whether a significant number had received high grades in most of their examinations but low grades in one or two examinations, and, if so, whether these low grades tended to be on one or a few specific examinations. Honors are awarded to not more than the highest 15 per cent (14.3 per cent, actually, to date) of the students completing the requirements for the College Certificate, selected on the basis of their performance in the comprehensive examinations. There were 94 students in this group who received the College Certificate with honors whose records were studied. If each student had passed each examination the first time he took it, and if no student had repeated an examination to raise his grade, there would have been 658 examinations. The group wrote 693 examinations (675 passing and 18 failing examinations), with passing-grade distributions as follows: A, 427 (63.26 per cent); B, 203 (30.07 per cent); C, 39 (5.79 per cent); D, 6 (0.88 per cent). The average was 3.56, with 4.00 representing A and 3.00 representing B.

The 18 F grades and 5 of the 6 D grades were in the English qualifying examination. Here again, the explanation is found in the status of the English composition course and the English qualifying examination during the first two years. There was not a single D or F grade in any one of the examinations on the fields of the four introductory general courses. This shows that no one of these fields has proved unreasonably difficult of mastery for any of the superior students in this study.

There were 66 instances in this group in which a passing grade was attained without registration for any part of the corresponding course; 23 instances after one quarter of registration in the course; 59 after two quarters; 526 after three quarters; and 1 after four quarters. The average registration was for 2.55 quarters per course, with 3.00 normal.

One hundred and eighteen students took more than two academic years (six quarters) to complete the College requirements: 41 took seven quarters; 18 took eight quarters; 50 took nine quarters; 7 took ten quarters; and 2 took eleven quarters. The average passing grade in all examinations for each of these five groups was 2.31, 2.33, 1.88, 1.59, and 2.00, respectively, with 1.00 passing; while the number of failures per student on all examinations per group were 1.17, 1.50, 2.48, 1.43, and 0.50, respectively. This indicates that the first two groups were composed, on the whole, of fairly good students, while no group was dominated by barely passing students.

This is further indicated by the fact that, while completing the College requirements, and for valid educational reasons in many instances, these five groups of students respectively anticipated upper divisional requirements to the extent of the following number of quarter courses per student: 5.56, 9.06, 8.86, 10.00, and 9.00. Since, at the upper divisional level, three courses per quarter is the normal full-time load, the first group, at the time they completed the College requirements, averaged 2.56 quarter courses per student ahead of the normal schedule of four years for the Bachelor's degree; the second group averaged 3.06 quarter courses ahead of schedule; the third, fourth, and fifth groups were behind schedule 0.14, 2.00, and 6.00 quarter courses per student, respectively.

Of the students who took seven quarters to complete the College requirements, one had, in addition, completed satisfactorily 12 upper-divisional quarter-courses and was a full year ahead of schedule for the Bachelor's degree; four had completed 10 upper-divisional quarter-courses; two had completed 9; three had completed 7; seven had completed 6; etc. Of the students who took nine quarters (a full academic year above normal) to complete the College requirements, one had, in addition, completed satisfactorily 14 upper-divisional quarter-courses and was almost two quarters ahead of schedule for the Bachelor's degree; two had completed 13, two, 12; four, 11, three, 10; eight, 9; etc.

Of the group that took seven quarters to complete the College requirements, three were awarded honors; of those who took eight quarters, two earned honors; of those who took nine quarters, three earned honors; and of those who took ten quarters, one was awarded honors.

Among those who took longer than the customary six quarters to complete the College requirements, and did not at the same time pursue enough upper-divisional courses to keep up to the normal time schedule of four years for the Bachelor's degree, several were forced to register for less than a full program during some quarters because of poor health or part-time employment for self-support.

Thus, the fact that a student may not complete all of the College requirements until after he has been in residence more than two academic years does not necessarily mean that he is a low-grade student or that he is destined to take more than four years for the attainment of the Bachelor's degree; he may actually be ahead of the normal schedule, as was true of approximately half of the students in this group, and he may be distinctly a high-grade student.

Of the 656 students who had completed the College requirements at the time this study was made, 8 had been in residence three quarters at the time they completed the College requirements; 6, four quarters; 20, five quarters; 504, six quarters; 41, seven quarters; 18, eight quarters; 50, nine quarters; 7, ten quarters; and 2, eleven quarters. The average per student was 6.32 quarters. As has been shown, this does not mean that the average student was one-third (0.32) of a quarter behind schedule, because so many of those who took more than six quarters to complete the College requirements were simultaneously anticipating some upper-divisional requirements and will take the Bachelor's degree in the customary four years or in less than four years.

Thirty-four students completed the College requirements in less than six quarters (two academic years) of residence. The average grade per student in all examinations taken by this group, including 18 failures in the English qualifying examination and 3 failures in elective sequence examinations, was 2.52, or B—. There were 46 instances of examinations in which students had not registered for any part of a corresponding course, 22 instances in which a student was in the course only one quarter, 67 instances of two quarters, 103 instances of three quarters, and 3 instances of five quarters. The average number of quarters of registration in corresponding courses per student per examination was 1.99, with 3.00 normal. There were 44 A examinations, 73 B's, 89 C's, 35 D's. This shows, as would be expected, that the students who complete the College requirements in less than normal time are high-quality students. Several of these students also anticipated some upper-divisional requirements while completing College requirements in less than two years.

Fourteen students who completed the College requirements in two or more calendar years were in residence less than two full academic years. Of these 14 students, 1 was in residence only three quarters, 5 were in residence four quarters, and 8 were in residence five quarters. For financial or other personal reasons these students were forced to drop out of residence periodically.

Though most students attend courses through the entire academic year before taking the corresponding examinations, in the first calendar year that examinations were offered (June, 1932, to June, 1933, inclusive), 131 students took examinations after having attended corresponding courses only two of the three quarters, 62 after attending only one quarter, and 78 without attending at all. The average of these 271 students was 2.31, while the average of all taking the examinations was 1.90. The letter-grade proportions for the 271 students who took examinations before completing the customary three quarters of the course were: A, 14 per cent; B, 30 per cent; C, 36 per cent; D, 12 per cent; and F, 8 per cent. The proportions for the entire group taking examinations were A, 9 per cent; B, 18 per cent; C, 41 per cent; D, 18 per cent; and F, 14 per cent.

The proportion of high grades, A and B, was much higher for those students who took examinations without registering for the course or after only one quarter's attendance than for those who attended the full three quarters. The proportion of failures in the faster group was only half the proportion of failures of the entire group. Thus, the students who take examinations with less than the customary amount of instruction receive the better grades. This fact might be used as the basis for a "wise crack" to the effect that a student would do better on the examinations if he did not attend the corresponding courses, or, that by taking a course a student lowers his chances for a high mark on the examination on that field. The facts merely show, however, that the superior students are taking advantage of the opportunities offered under the New Plan. The important result is not merely that students may save time by completing the junior-college requirements in less than two years, and the Bachelor's degree requirements in less than four years, though this is a factor of real significance in some instances; but the important result is that students are encouraged to work "on their own" and are saved from perfunctory and routine repetition or boring and unnecessary review and are encouraged always to be engaged in work that challenges their capacity to the utmost.

In the June, 1933, examination period, 1,961 comprehensive examinations were written on the four general course fields. Of these 1,961 examination papers, 188 (9.6 per cent) were scored A; 345 (17.6 per cent), B; 883 (45 per cent), C; 318 (16.2 per cent), D; and 227 (11.6 per cent), F. In the September, 1933, examination period, 272 comprehensive examinations were written on the four general course fields. Of the 60 students who took an examination without registering for any part of the corresponding course, 26.7 per cent wrote A examinations, 46.7 per cent wrote A or B examinations, and 10 per cent wrote F examinations. Of the 99 students who took an examination after attending the corresponding course less than the customary three quarters (two or less than two of the three quarters), 17.2 per cent wrote A examinations, 36.4 per cent wrote A or B examinations, and 14.1 per cent wrote F examinations. Of the 173 students who took the examinations after attending the entire corresponding course, 1.7 per cent wrote A examinations, 6.4 per cent wrote A or B examinations, and 39.3 per cent wrote F examinations. Of the total 272 students, the 60 students first mentioned (22 per cent) wrote 80 per cent of the A examinations, 60 per cent of the A and B examinations, and only 7.3 per cent of the F examinations.

The group of students customarily taking these examinations in June, immediately following the completion of the corresponding courses offered to assist students in their preparation for the comprehensive examinations, may be regarded as typical. Though a few good students postpone taking one or more examinations until the following September, in order to have additional time to devote to preparation in the hope of writing better examinations, as many poor students do likewise. The group of students taking the examinations in September is atypical, because heavily weighted with two types of students: (1) some of our best students, who have passed a full quota of examinations in June and use the summer months for independent study in fields in which they take examinations without attending the corresponding courses; and (2) some of our poorest students, who have failed one or more examinations in June and take them a second time in September.

A special analysis of the records of the entire group of students in this study was made to discover the number of times some students repeat an examination in an endeavor to attain a passing grade, and with what success.

Of the students included in this study, 1,586 had taken the biological sciences general examination. On their first attempt, 181 made a grade of A; 291, B; 689, C; 232, D; and 193, F. Of the 193 who failed on the first attempt, 89 took the examination a second time, with the result that 2 made A; 17, C; 26, D; and 44 received a second F. Of these 44, 15 took the examination a third time, with the result that 1 made A; 2, C; 2, D; and 10, F again. Of these 10, 2 took the examination a fourth time and 1 received a grade of D, while the other received still another F.

A total of 1,352 students had taken the humanities examination. On their first attempt, 134 received a grade of A; 251, B; 613, C; 195, D; and 159, F. Of the 159 who failed on the first attempt, 66 took the examination a second time, with the result that 2 made B; 12, C; 22, D; and 30, F. Of the 30 who failed twice, 13 took the examination a third time, with the result that 1 made B; 1, C; 2, D; and 9, F. Of the 9 who failed three times, 5 took the examination a fourth time, with the result that 3 made C; 1, D; and 1, F.

A total of 1,113 students had taken the physical sciences examination. On their first attempt, 134 received a grade of A; 217, B; 449, C; 199, D; and 114, F. Of the 114 who failed the first time that they took the examination, 50 took the examination a second time, with the result that 1 made A; 7, C; 25, D; and 17, F. Of these 17, 6 took the examination a third time and 1 received a grade of C; 2, D; and 3, F.

A total of 1,482 students had taken the social sciences general examination. On their first attempt, 173 made A; 250, B; 660, C; 203, D; and 196, F. Of these 196, 85 repeated the examination, and 1 made B; 15, C; 26, D; and 43, F. Of the 43, 17 took the examination a third time, and 2 made C; 6, D; and 9, F. Of the 9, 2 had taken the examination a fourth time when this study was made, and 1 received a grade of D while the other one received another F.

A total of 1,767 students had taken the English qualifying examination. On their first attempt, 146 made A; 349, B; 482, C; 207, D; and 583, F. Of the 583 failing students, 402 took the examination a second time, with the following results: 11 made A; 62, B; 124, C; 63, D; and 142, F. Of these 142 students, 98 took the examination a third time, and 8 made A; 6, B; 27, C; 23, D; and 34, F. Of the 34 students, 24 took the examination a fourth time, and 1 made A; 3, B; 5, C; 5, D; and 10, F. Of these 10 students, 6 hardy souls braved the examination a fifth time, with the result that 3 made C; 1, D; and 2 received a fifth F.

It is interesting to note the number of instances in which a student who had failed an examination one or more times succeeded in attaining an A grade in a subsequent examination in the same field. This happened four times in the four general course fields, twenty times in the English qualifying examination, and not once in the various sequence examinations. Again the explanation in the case of the English qualifying examination is found in the low validity and reliability of this examination during the first two years. Though nothing comparable to the tutoring school run so successfully and profitably by the "Widow" at Harvard, before the tutorial and comprehensive examination system was introduced there, has developed here, and probably cannot be profitably developed, a few graduate students in a few fields have done some very successful tutoring of a few habitually low-performing, though frequently not low-caliber, students; this may be the explanation of some of the instances in which students who had made F grades later raised these grades well above the passing mark.

On all of the elective sequence examinations, out of a total of 2,631 grades there were 359 grades of F. To the date of this study, 85 examinations had been taken a second time, with 40 second F grades; and 18 examinations had been taken a third time, and in 5 instances a third F was received.

Item analyses of Board examinations are made periodically. For example, a report on a complete item analysis of the June, 1933, physical sciences examination, including several hundred items, made by the examiner for that field, Mr. M. W. Richardson, includes the following:

The purpose of the analysis was to determine whether individual items would discriminate between the best and poorest students. Accordingly, the 75 highest and the 75 lowest students of the 374 taking the examination were used as the reference groups. An item is said to be discriminating when a higher percentage of good students than poor students answer it correctly. (It is understood, of course, that a non-discriminating item might be legitimately used, if perfectly in line with course objectives. The failure to discriminate might mean that the point was so well understood by all students that practically none failed to answer the item correctly. However, non-discriminating items are dead weight from the standpoint of measurement.)

Since the differences in percentages of upper and lower groups passing the item have to be interpreted in terms of the difficulty of the item, a complete study of the difficulty of all items was made.

In interpreting the summary two points should be considered: (1)

We have been rather severe in assigning items to Class D (non-discriminating). (2) While all divisible parts of the examination are called "items," they were by no means of equal weight in the examination.

Examination booklets are attached with results of analysis. A key is given on the front cover of the booklet. . . . . A means high discrimination; B, good discrimination; C, low but positive discrimination; D, poor item (in red); Dn, non-discriminating; De, too easy; Dd, too difficult. Colors: Blue means difficult; Green, average difficulty; Brown, easy.

The booklet for the morning period, three hours, contained 23 pages, divided into 14 parts; the booklet for the afternoon period, three hours, contained 11 pages, divided into 8 parts. In the analysis report several tables are given showing the classification of items according to the foregoing key by the subject groups: chemistry, physics, astronomy, mathematics, geology, and geography. A summary table for the objective parts of the examination shows high discrimination, 28.1 per cent; discriminating, 49.4 per cent; low discrimination, 10.7 per cent; poor items, 11.8 per cent, with each of the first three of these classifications further broken up into three groups characterized as "difficult," "of moderate difficulty," and "easy," and the poor items further classified as "no discrimination," "too easy," and "too difficult." The Pearson correlations of the various subject parts with the total objective portion were computed and ranged from $.75 \pm .02$ for mathematics to $.91 \pm .01$ for physics. The reliability coefficient of the objective portion of the examination was found to be $r = .95$. The correlation between the objective and essay scores was $r = .77$. Correcting this correlation for attenuation, it becomes approximately .90, and this suggests a high community of function tested by the two forms; but further research into this matter is being pursued.

Some supplementary reports on examinations and tables showing examination results are presented in Appendix H.

CHAPTER XI

THE FOUR-YEAR COLLEGE—INCLUDING THE LAST TWO YEARS OF HIGH SCHOOL AND THE FIRST TWO YEARS OF COLLEGE

IN THE Elementary School of the Laboratory Schools of the University of Chicago, the eight grades were reduced to seven in 1913. The six-five plan was instituted in 1919 by making the seventh grade of the elementary school the sub-Freshman class of the high school. The fact that the University High School has always admitted pupils who have finished the University Elementary School, and pupils from other elementary schools who have completed eight grades of work, make possible a comparison of a group of graduates of the high school who have had, exclusive of kindergarten, eleven years of school training with a group who have had twelve years. Mr. John C. Mayfield, after making such a comparison, drew the conclusion that "the shorter University Elementary School course enables pupils to graduate from the University High School at an earlier age and fits them as successfully for a high-school career as do eight-year elementary schools." Since virtually all graduates of the University High School continue their education in some higher institution, criticism of the eleven-grade plan in this school cannot be made as successfully as against such a plan in a school whose graduates are thrust out to seek employment a year younger than graduates of twelve-grade systems.

As early as 1918–19 superior students in the University High School were permitted to take certain junior-college courses offered in the high school for credit in the University toward the Bachelor's degree. The first courses so organized and offered were in English. By 1922–23 the list of courses had been extended to include junior-college history, mathematics, French, and economics. During that year, 68 high-school Seniors earned a total of 157 quarter courses of college credit, or 523 semester-hours, an average of 7.7 semester-hours per student, in addition to high-school graduation requirements. In this way certain students were saving more than the one year represented in the difference between a twelve-grade and an eleven-grade plan of organization.

A few high schools have already begun to guide their students preparing for admission to the University of Chicago, not only so that they may meet our admission requirements, but that they may also anticipate some of our junior-college requirements, and by examinations at admission, or shortly thereafter, satisfy some of these requirements. This we encourage the high schools and their better students to do. In the three years of the operation of the plan we have enough evidence to show that, in the near future, many of our best students, having been wisely guided through their high-school courses, will earn our junior-college certificate in one year or even less than a year in the College, progress at once into the upper divisions of their choice, and there in turn save more time in ratio with the degree of their superiority. Thus, we encourage a student always to be engaged in work that challenges to the fullest his capacity for attainment.

In January, 1933, the Board of Trustees approved a resolution adopted by the University Senate upon recommendation by President Hutchins: "That the work of the College in general education be extended by removing the

last two years of the University High School from the jurisdiction of the Division of the Social Sciences and the School
and Department of Education and incorporating them in
the College program." The considerations that led to this
proposal for a new college administrative and educational
unit in the University of Chicago, including the last two
years of high school and the first two years of college, were
of two categories: (1) those considerations growing out of
the present conditions and trends in the field of secondary
education throughout the country; and (2) those considerations growing out of our experience in the design and administration of our new college (junior-college) plan.

We have learned increasingly in recent years that the
problems of senior high schools and junior colleges are at
many points common, and cannot be solved felicitously
when the two institutional staffs are separated, not only
institutionally, but also in the prevailing organization of
regional and national associations, in which each group is
too much inclined to pass the buck to the other group,
along with some uncomplimentary epithets.

The six-three-three-two plan of organization, the "two"
being a separate junior-college unit, does not seem to be
proving entirely satisfactory, because a separate two-year
unit is an unsatisfactory one, and because the prevailing
tendency seems to be for the separate junior college to become either merely two more years of high school or a poor
copy of the junior-college program of the local state university.

In limiting the term "college" to a new junior-college
program, and in merging the senior-college program with
the programs of the graduate and professional schools, calling students above the junior-college level "divisional" or
"professional-school" students, we acted upon our belief

that four years of the old type of college program is an unnecessary and wasteful preliminary to "higher" education
of the tone and tempo of graduate and professional schools
requiring the Bachelor's degree for admission; and that a
new junior-college program, properly designed and effectively administered, can serve more adequately the needs
of students in regard to general education and can bridge
more successfully the gap between "secondary" (high-
school) education and truly "higher" (university) education.

The junior-college years, as the capping-stone of the period of secondary education, should also serve as a transition period between secondary and higher education—a
transition that can be made instantly by only a few students, even in an institution with an admission system
more highly selective than ours. If the junior-college period is merely a continuation of high-school performance, it
fails; or, if it is a truly university performance, it is likely
to fail. We have endeavored to design our College program so as to bridge the gap successfully. Instead of per-
mitting the tone and tempo of high-school performance to
reach up and control the junior-college program, we have
insisted that the tone and tempo of university performance
must be pushed down into the junior-college program, there
to meet the high-school influence, to remold it, and to
dominate it, as the student progresses in his appreciation
of what his status must be, as a scholar, if he is to enter one
of the upper divisions or professional schools.

It seemed to many of us that, in view of the extent to
which we had shown that this influence from above can be
made to dominate the junior-college area, the time had
come to carry the experiment down somewhat lower, into
the senior high school area, and thus to begin the gap-

bridging period between secondary and higher education two years earlier. This, distinctly, was the proposal: to push the college influence, through control, down into the high-school area—and not to push the high-school influence up into the college area.

Success of the plan would seem to point to a six-(three or four)-(three or four) arrangement, with the student spending six years in elementary school, three or four years (as he may need or desire) in high school, and three or four years (as he may need or desire) in college, at which time his institutional training—designed primarily to serve his needs in regard to general education—would be completed. He could then, with adequate preparation, proceed to specialized work in a real university program in arts, literature, and science, or in professional education, if he so desired.

Under the new legislation, members of the High-School Faculty who teach in the last two years in the high school are members of the College Faculty, just as any university faculty member who teaches in the College is a member of the College Faculty. The College Curriculum Committee now includes, within its personnel and jurisdiction, instructional staff members and the program of studies of the last two years in the High School and the first two years in the College. For the first time in the history of the institution, staff members, of what in the past were regarded and handled as two distinct areas, but are now regarded and dealt with as a single area, are working earnestly and continuously on the solution of common problems.

In the *School Review* for September, 1933, Mr. Arthur K. Loomis, Principal of the University High School, who is also Associate Dean of the College under the new organization, has described "The New Curriculum of the University High School of the University of Chicago." The major features of the new curriculum include new integrations of subjects, changes in grade placement of subjects, new provisions for individual differences, and changes in requirements.

The new integrations of subjects are three in number: (1) social sciences, humanities, and oral and written language; (2) science and mathematics; and (3) fine and practical arts.

Changes in the grade placement and time allotment of subjects involve ancient, medieval, and modern history, economic society, American political institutions, art and music appreciation, grammar, algebra, geometry, and beginning work in a foreign language.

An important change in providing for individual differences is the policy of recognizing achievement, wherever and whenever attained, by excusing from class attendance those pupils who have demonstrated such achievement for any unit in any course. In all courses, pupils who care to do so are encouraged to work ahead of schedule, if their work in other courses is satisfactory. This arrangement makes it possible to complete two years' work in one year in one or more subjects. The purpose is to keep the more capable pupils working up to capacity at all times, instead of allowing them to mark time, and so to develop habits of idleness, while they wait for the slower ones to catch up. Adequate provision is also made for pupils who are in need of remedial work in the tool subjects—spelling, handwriting, reading, language usage, and arithmetic.

Before the adoption of the new curriculum 50 per cent of the work for a high-school diploma was prescribed; but under the New Plan about 75 per cent of the amount needed to satisfy the minimum requirements for graduation is prescribed. All courses in the sub-Freshman and Freshman years are required; in the Sophomore year, there are three required courses and two electives; in the Junior year and in the Senior year, there are two required courses and three electives. The endeavor was made to have the required courses of the five years furnish a respectable minimum of general education necessary for intelligent citizenship in the modern world.

All of these changes originated in the High School Faculty. As soon as the senior high school and junior-college faculties were combined into a single faculty, in January, 1933, the new College Curriculum Committee, with many sub-committees, composed of both senior high school and junior-college faculty members, gave long and careful consideration to an excellent curriculum report already prepared by the high-school faculty. The present courses are the result of co-operative work of the two faculty groups. Henceforth, the program of the last two years of high school and the first two years of college will be a co-operative enterprise of a single faculty. In the current year the members of the joint curriculum committee, organized into several sub-committees, are devoting much time to a consideration of many problems involved in an appropriate integration of the program of studies through these four years.

In the faculty legislation setting up the new four-year unit, provision was made for the enrolment of qualified high-school Seniors in College courses *with* College students and not in special sections. Pupils who carry College courses successfully in the Senior year in high school receive credit toward graduation from high school and, at the same time, by passing the comprehensive examinations required in the College, receive credit toward the College

Certificate. Thus, it is possible for a qualified student to substitute a College program for the last year of the High School program, and to earn the junior-college certificate in one additional year or less. This experiment is being conducted with the consent of the North Central Association.

It is contemplated that, as soon as satisfactory examinations can be framed, the progress of the High School student toward the attainment of a high-school diploma will be measured in terms of comprehensive achievement examinations, rather than in terms of course credit, just as is now the practice in measuring the progress of a College student toward the attainment of the junior-college certificate.

For the present, the last two years of the High School are called, as heretofore, the Junior and Senior years of the High School. Classes continue to meet in the same buildings and under the same teachers as formerly. The present legislation, however, gives complete freedom for the placing of student and faculty personnel in the program of the last two years of high school and the first two years of college, wherever they should be placed for the best possible attainment of desired educational objectives.

During the three academic years 1929 to 1932, the yearly average number of students in the last two years of University High School was 230; the average number of graduates was 111; the average number of graduates entering the University of Chicago was 45, or 41 per cent; the average number of graduates entering other institutions was 57, or 52 per cent; the average number of graduates not continuing in a higher institution was 9, or 7 per cent.

Approximately 750 students enter our College as Freshmen each year. Approximately 6 per cent of our Freshmen come from University High School, and approximately 94 per cent come from other schools. Since 93 per cent of the graduates of University High School enter the University of Chicago or some other institution, University High School serves as a college preparatory school for the great majority of its students. It seems, therefore, that the program of the last two years of University High School should be designed to serve primarily the needs of those who continue the pursuit of education in college rather than for the few who do not enter college.

Since only 41 per cent of the graduates of University High School enter the College of the University of Chicago, while 52 per cent enter other institutions, the program of the last two years of University High School should be designed to serve the needs of those who enter other institutions as well as those who enter the University of Chicago. It seems that during the next few years the number of students who may be expected to pursue a continuous program in the University of Chicago, through the last two years of high school and the first two years of college, will be relatively small. As our new four-year program at this level progresses, this number may materially increase.

Though at some indefinite time in the future, when we may have a majority of students who pursue a continuous program through what is now the last two years of high school and the first two years of college, it may be advisable to frame a continuous and completely integrated program for a consolidated four-year unit, it would seem inadvisable to attempt to do so at the present time. In the light of the current status of student personnel and what would seem to be the prospect for the immediate future, it seems appropriate to attempt merely to develop as much co-ordination and integration of the two-year programs as is possible and advisable. This in itself will be a significant improvement of the past situation and is the appropriate first step in the development of a consolidated four-year program as rapidly as may be wisely done in the light of experience and changes in student personnel.

In *The Six-Four-Four Plan of School Organization in Pasadena, California*, a report by William Martin Proctor, professor of education, Stanford University, acting as director of research studies for the Pasadena public-school system for 1931–32, published in 1933, the author writes on pages 163 and 164:

Sometimes it is claimed that the best reason for a six-three-three-two set-up is that a four-year unit is too long and violates the principle of homogeneity. A study of this problem was made by a statistical expert who studied the age, height, and weight data for 14,000 children in Pasadena, Ventura, Riverside, and the Menlo School and Junior College. He found that in physical maturity there is an apparent break between the sixth and seventh grades; between the seventh and fourteenth grades there are several small breaks which might be made the basis for the separation of groups of grades into two units, or three. One of these smaller breaks is between the ninth and tenth and the other between the tenth and eleventh. Between the twelfth and thirteenth grades, where the traditional break between high school and the two year types of junior college is made, he found no break at all. The index of alienation between these two grades was the smallest of any from the fifth through the fourteenth. There was evidence that physical maturity was reached between the tenth and eleventh grades, and that therefore the group in grades eleven, twelve, thirteen, and fourteen is physically and mentally mature. There is thus no greater violation of homogeneity in grouping these four years together than in grouping grades nine to twelve, or thirteen to sixteen in one institution. A four-year junior high school admittedly has a wider span of maturity than a three-year junior high school. However, there are two thousand six-year junior-senior high schools in the country. Reports from many of these six-year high schools are to the effect that they experience no serious difficulties on account of lack of homogeneity. The actual educational and social advantages found in the two Pasadena four-year units in addition to the outcomes of the homogeneity study seem to outweigh the theoretical disadvantages, if any, of lack of homogeneity.

Walter Crosby Eells, professor of education, Stanford University, and editor-in-chief of the *Junior College Journal*, says that the study carried out by Dr. Herbert Popenoe, and cited by Proctor, dealt only with the age, height, and weight of the pupils studied. At that time Popenoe was interested in devising a method for investigating social and educational maturity and homogeneity. He felt it was impossible at first to secure reliable measures of personality, social development, etc. Therefore, in order to make use of data the nature and reliability of which was unquestioned, he decided to use age, height, and weight. This was with the understanding that it meant nothing in itself, but was merely for the development of a technique which he hoped might later be applicable to the question of social homogeneity, the question which he was especially interested in studying as director of research at the Menlo Junior College. It seemed obvious to Popenoe and to Eells and to all others interested in the study that nothing could be proved by such data concerning the real question at issue. It is still the opinion of Eells that conclusions concerning social maturity drawn from data on height and weight are drawn almost, if not entirely, from irrelevant data.

Eells, in his book on *The Junior College*, published in 1931, beginning on page 714, discusses at length the difficulty of too great variety in age and interests of students in the four-year junior college. He points out that "the college Sophomore is much more mature, can be given greater independence, does not require such rigid restrictions, is on a different social plane, and constitutes a very different disciplinary problem from the high-school Junior." He cites statements of some critical observers of experiments that "senior-high and college students do not mix well," or that though a three-year institution including high-school Seniors and college Freshmen and Sophomores might operate satisfactorily, the inclusion of high-school Juniors in the same institution with the three classes above is a mistake unless the high-school Juniors are handled separately and are subjected to special regulations on many scores. He quotes one thoughtful observer as follows:

I have had the opportunity of watching a combination of the last two years of high school and the first two years of college fail quite miserably. The buildings, equipment, faculty, situation, and other conditions usually making for success were possessed in their finest and most modern forms, but the spirit of the high school college was deadening. The high-school students disliked being with older students, and the dignity of the college students was decidedly offended by the combination.

If and when we may secure a special building for our four-year junior college, it is clear that, in the design of the building and in the administration of the curriculum and the extra-curriculum activities, particular attention will have to be given to problems that grow out of the lack of complete social homogeneity in a student group composed of those in the last two years of high school and the first two years of college.

CHAPTER XII

SUMMARY OF PRINCIPAL FEATURES OF THE NEW COLLEGE PLAN

MANY of the points listed in this summary have been presented at various places in the preceding chapters, but some others appear only in this summary.

ADMINISTRATIVE ORGANIZATION

The work of the University in Arts, Literature, and Science is organized in five divisions: the College—a lower division for the junior-college program[1]—and the four upper Divisions of the Biological Sciences, the Humanities, the Physical Sciences, and the Social Sciences.

All Freshmen enter the College. The upper divisions and the professional schools begin their work at the senior-college level. We have limited the term "College" to our new junior-college program and have merged the senior-college program with the programs of the upper divisions and professional schools, calling students above the junior-college level either divisional or professional-school students.

Departments in the Division of the Biological Sciences: Anatomy, Botany, Home Economics, Hygiene and Bacteriology, Medicine, Obstetrics and Gynecology, Pathology, Pediatrics, Physiological Chemistry and Pharmacology, Physiology, Psychology, Surgery, and Zoölogy.

Departments in the Division of the Humanities: Art, Comparative Religion, Greek Language and Literature,

---

[1] See chapter xi for a discussion of our new Four-Year College organization, including the last two years of high school and the first two years of college.

English Language and Literature, Germanic Languages and Literatures, History, Latin Language and Literature, Linguistics, Music, New Testament and Early Christian Literature, Oriental Languages and Literatures, Philosophy, and Romance Languages and Literatures.

Departments in the Division of the Physical Sciences: Astronomy and Astrophysics, Chemistry, Geography, Geology and Paleontology, Mathematics, Military Science and Tactics, and Physics.

Departments in the Division of the Social Sciences: Anthropology, Economics, Education, Geography, History, Political Science, and Sociology.

The University has the following professional schools: the School of Business, the Divinity School, the Graduate Library School, the Law School, the School of Social Service Administration, Rush Medical College, and the School of Medicine of the Division of the Biological Sciences.

All Bachelor's, Master's, and Doctor's degrees are awarded by the four upper divisions and the professional schools.

The College Faculty consists of approximately one hundred and sixty members, most of whom are also members of the faculty of one of the upper divisions. While the College is a separate administrative unit with all the freedom needed for effective management of its own program, it is so closely knit into the upper divisions that it has at its command all of the educational resources of the entire University. Many departmental chairmen and professors who are scholars of international renown are interested participants in College instruction.

The Dean of the College prepares the docket for, and presides at, College faculty meetings; serves as chairman of the College Curriculum Committee and of the College Executive Committee; represents the College on the Board of Examinations; is responsible for the preparation and printing of the course syllabi; is responsible for the character, amount, and quality of college instruction; recommends persons to the President for appointment in the College Faculty; recommends faculty members for promotion in rank and increases in salary; is responsible for the preparation of copy for the College *Announcements* and the quarterly time schedules; prepares and administers the College budget.

The Dean of Students in the College is responsible for supervising the student guidance program administered by eight Advisers and himself. Each Adviser has approximately eighty Freshmen and as many Sophomores and devotes a minimum of eight hours a week to individual conferences with students by appointment in the suite of offices of the Dean of Students.

ENTRANCE REQUIREMENTS

Our entrance requirements in terms of high-school units are only slightly prescribed. Twelve senior high school units (the tenth, eleventh, and twelfth years) are required, including one major (3 units) and two minors (2 units each), or four minors (2 units each) selected from groups (*a*) to (*e*), with only one of the minors (2 units) in English specifically required: (*a*) English, (*b*) a language other than English, (*c*) social sciences, (*d*) mathematics, (*e*) biological and physical sciences. The four or five additional units may be selected from any senior high school subjects accepted by an accredited school on its diploma.

In administering our entrance requirements we place much more importance upon the scholastic aptitude and the personal qualities of the applicant than upon specific units of credit and their distribution. The great majority of our students enter by certificate. Our quality requirement is graduation in the upper half of the class of a school of good standing.

Our entering Freshman class numbers approximately seven hundred and fifty each year and is limited to that number because we have neither the staff nor equipment to handle effectively a larger number.

COLLEGE REQUIREMENTS

The requirements of the College for the junior-college certificate and the Associate in Arts title are stated solely in terms of seven comprehensive examinations designed to test primarily general education.

Course credits and course marks that count for anything in the attainment of the junior-college certificate and the Associate in Arts title have been abolished. The old lock-step, time-serving, routine requirements in terms of course credits and grade points have been abolished.

For the junior-college certificate and the Associate in Arts title five of the seven comprehensive examinations are specifically required of all students in the following fields: English composition, the biological sciences, the humanities, the physical sciences, and the social sciences. The two additional examinations are elective and may be selected from any two of the following departmental or divisional fields, each examination covering the work of a year-course or sequence of three quarter-courses: Art, Biology II (a three-quarter sequence in botany, zoölogy, and physiology, with emphasis on laboratory training), Chemistry, English literature, French, Geography, Geology, Geology and Astronomy, German, Greek, Italian, Latin, Mathematics,

Military Science, Music, Philosophy, Physics, Social Sciences II (a year-course, comprising economics, political science, and sociology, with the Introductory General Course in the Social Sciences, or its equivalent, a prerequisite), and Spanish.

The specific foreign-language and mathematics requirements for the College Certificate are met by nearly all our students at entrance, though not required for entrance. Two entrance units in a foreign language (or a passing grade in an equivalent Board examination) and two entrance units in mathematics (or a passing grade in an equivalent Board examination) are required for the College Certificate. A student who, because of failure to offer two units in a foreign language or two units in mathematics, is required to pass the equivalent Board examination in either or both subjects, must do so in addition to passing the seven required examinations.

A student who offers two entrance units in each of two foreign languages may use the two units in one of the languages to meet the College foreign-language requirement, and may offer the examination on the first-year College course in the other language as an elective sequence for the College Certificate without taking the sequence in residence in the College, even though he used two units in this language for entrance requirements.

A student who offers four entrance units in a single foreign language may use two of the units to meet the College foreign-language requirement, and may offer the examination on the second-year College course in the same language as an elective sequence for the College Certificate without taking the course in residence in the College, even though he used all four units in this language for entrance requirements.

COLLEGE COURSES AND STUDENT PROGRAMS

A carefully prepared syllabus, with appropriate biblio-graphical citations, for each course offered in the College is available in printed form for each student, through the University of Chicago Bookstore.

Four new courses, a year-course in each of four large fields of thought—the biological sciences, the humanities, the physical sciences, and the social sciences—have been specially designed to serve general-education needs, with a wide variety of instructional methods carefully selected and proportionated in the light of educational objectives to be attained.

Approximately 15 per cent of the entering Freshmen are advised, on the basis of a placement test, that they do not need the course in English composition. They are advised to take the English composition qualifying examination when offered in November. Most of them pass the exam-ination. The few who fail are advised to attend the course the remainder of the year and take the examination again the following May, or to take the course the following year.

The normal program for a student in the College is three or four courses in each of the Autumn, Winter, and Spring quarters. The program of each student in his first year includes a combination of general courses and sequence courses that seems advisable in the light of his ability and interests. The normal program for the first and second years comprises two general courses and one or two se-quence courses each year. Each course is organized to re-quire of the average student a total of ten hours each week, including the classroom periods.

Since four courses at a time constitute a full program, and since only seven examinations are required, a superior student has the opportunity in the two college years to anticipate two or more courses to meet upper divisional requirements while completing the college requirements; an average student can anticipate at least one divisional course, if he desires to do so; a below-average student may carry three courses the first year and four courses the second year, or, if he elects four courses the first year and fails one examination, he has an opportunity to repeat the course the second year without loss of time.

Superior students are not held to the level of performance of the average student. In many of the College courses special honor sections are organized for students who show that they can progress more rapidly and penetrate more deeply into a subject than the average student.

In many courses special review sections are organized for students who have difficulty in maintaining the rate of progress set by the majority of the class.

A uniform number of class hours is not specified for each course, as the amount of formal instruction and the amount of independent study are determined by the subject matter. In each course the number of lectures, recitation periods, small group discussions, individual consultations, and the amount of written and laboratory work are determined by the objectives of the course. Most courses meet four times a week. Thus, a student carrying four courses (a full program for the average and better-than-average students) spends sixteen hours a week in classes.

All college courses, offered to assist students in preparing themselves for comprehensive examinations, are year-courses or year-sequences. College students are registered in the autumn for the entire year. This means that the quarter system is of little significance to college students. A superior student may enter the college at any time during the academic year after the opening of the Autumn

Quarter, register for less than a full program, make up the work he has missed in the courses he elects, and take the appropriate examinations in June.

THE COMPREHENSIVE EXAMINATIONS

The Board of Examinations is a legislative body consisting of eleven members of the University faculty: one member from the College, one from each of the four upper divisions, one from each professional school using the comprehensive examinations, and three members appointed by the President. The University Examiner is chairman of the Board.

The policies determined by the Board of Examinations are carried into effect, under the direction of the Chief Examiner (who is recommended for appointment by the University Examiner), by a technical staff of four examiners, one representing the field of each of the four upper divisions of the University.

Nearly all Board examinations for the College Certificate are given at least twice a year. It is the desire of the Board that the examinations be given as often as once every quarter whenever there is sufficient demand to warrant the preparation of the examination.

The seven required examinations (five specified and two elective) may be taken by any student whenever he thinks advisable, regardless of how many courses he has pursued in residence or the length of time he has been in residence.

Each of the seven examinations is six hours in length— three hours in the morning and three in the afternoon of a given day. Thus, each student must pass forty-two hours of examinations, either all at one examination period of two weeks or spread over several examination periods.

A student who has completed a course is not required to

take the comprehensive examination immediately upon the completion of that course; however, all seven of the comprehensive examinations must be passed within a period of two calendar years after the first comprehensive examination is passed.

Students are identified at examinations by signature and by photograph, and the examinations are thoroughly proctored.

The Board examinations are either published and may be purchased at the University of Chicago Bookstore, or, in the case of small groups, when the number of copies prepared is limited, they are on file in the departmental libraries. Consequently, the student has access to any examination that has been given by the Board.

No fee is charged the first time a student takes any Board examination. If the examination is repeated, a fee of five dollars is charged for the first repetition and ten dollars for each subsequent one. There is no limit to the number of times a student may repeat any one of the examinations to attain a passing grade.

A student, if he wishes, may repeat an examination in order to raise his grade. The higher of the two grades is entered on the student's record: that is, if the second examination gives a higher grade than the first, the second grade stands; if the second grade is lower than the first, the first grade stands. A few students, as a matter of personal pride or to improve their chances for honors or for a scholarship, pay the fee and repeat an examination in an attempt to raise a grade of B to A.

If a student questions the correctness of his grade, he may have his examination reviewed by presenting a petition to the Dean of College Students and making a deposit of five dollars. The deposit is refunded in case the letter grade is raised. The Board examinations are devices for measuring achievement, are not intended to be instruments of instruction, and hence are not returned to the students. Examinations for instructional purposes are frequently given in courses; these papers are carefully corrected and returned to the students, frequently in individual conferences, though the marks are not officially recorded. The only examination results that are made a matter of official record are those of the Board examinations.

The upper-divisional requirements for the Bachelor's degree are stated primarily in terms of two comprehensive examinations—one in the divisional field and one in the chosen departmental field.

STUDENT GUIDANCE AND PERSONNEL WORK

A faculty Adviser, who is selected for each student in the light of his educational needs and aims, takes his responsibilities seriously and is ready at all times to play the rôle of guide, counselor, and friend, but not that of nursemaid or policeman. Each student has at least three conferences with his Adviser during the first year, and at least one conference during the second year. There is provision for as many more conferences as either the student or the Adviser thinks advisable or necessary for the welfare of the student.

The Adviser chosen for the student is specifically trained in a field closely allied to the student's chosen field of specialization or interest, as stated in the student's application for admission; or, if the student is undecided as to his vocational or major scholastic interest, he is assigned to a special Adviser for "undecided" students. It is the specific function of the Adviser to counsel a student concerning the courses he should pursue with a view to fulfilling the requirements of the particular division or professional school of his vocational choice; also to counsel a student concerning any conditions or problems which may directly or indirectly affect his progress in the University. A program is outlined by each student, in consultation with his Adviser, in advance for at least an academic year.

Student personnel reports are sent regularly by faculty members for each student each quarter to the office of the Dean of Students in the College and are available at all times to the Advisers.

Any student in the College is eligible for participation in any and all student extra-curriculum activities, with the exception that in intercollegiate athletics he must meet the requirements of the Intercollegiate Conference, of which the University is a member. Each Adviser is responsible for advising his students regarding participation in extra-curriculum activities.

An excellent Health Service is maintained by the University to serve all students. The staff includes several well-trained and experienced physicians and nurses and two psychiatrists. There is close co-operation between the College Advisers and the staff of the Health Service with a view to serving the best interests of each student.

Offerings in physical education of attractive variety are available for both men and women students on the voluntary basis.

DISMISSAL POLICY

Students are required to give evidence of satisfactory progress for continuation in the College. At the end of each year a student is expected to pass at least one-half of the comprehensive examinations for which he is presumed to be prepared by the courses which he has pursued.

A student who fails to meet these minimum requirements will be denied the privilege of further registration until these requirements are met. Special circumstances affecting any particular case are considered by the Dean of Students in the College. A student who has been denied the privilege of further registration may re-register when he has passed the number of comprehensive examinations that were required for continuance in the College. A student who has been denied the privilege of further registration for residence work is eligible to take any of the comprehensive examinations whenever offered. A student may also be granted the privilege of re-registering if he submits an acceptable record of work done in another institution of creditable standing.

STUDENT-INSTRUCTOR RELATIONSHIPS

The relationship between student and professor has been completely changed by the abandonment of course credits and by divorce of the examination function from the instructional function.

Class attendance is not required but is voluntary on the part of the student. With the syllabus of a course in hand, a College student may find that he has mastered certain parts of a course and may advisedly omit the sessions of the class in which these parts are discussed.

In a course in which effective instruction can be given only with the intelligent and faithful participation of the students, the instructor may notify a student that he will be regarded as a visitor in the course whenever, through lack of interest, adequate preparation, or ability, he has shown himself to be a hindrance to the progress of the majority.

HONORS

Honorable mention for excellence in the work of the College is awarded to not more than the highest 15 per cent of the students completing the work of the College, selected on the basis of their performance in the comprehensive examinations in fulfilment of the requirements for the College Certificate.

TRANSFER STUDENTS

A student who enters the College with credit for a full year or more of college work by advanced standing may, at the discretion of his Adviser, arrange for a modified program under the New Plan. In such case, some of the courses credited by advanced standing may be substituted for comprehensive examinations. A modified New Plan program does not entitle the student to the College Certificate or the Associate in Arts title, but by passing certain prescribed examinations a student may fulfil the requirements for admission to a division.

A student who wishes to transfer from our College to another institution is given a transcript of record that shows his marks on whatever comprehensive examinations he may have taken, and the quarterly evaluations of the student's work in courses by his instructors, which are used by us only for guidance purposes but which may be (and are quite generally) accepted by other institutions as certification of course credits.

APPENDIX A

THE CURRICULUM AND ITS ADMINIS-
TRATION—DOCUMENTS

I

REPORT OF THE COLLEGE CURRICULUM COMMITTEE, SENT TO MEMBERS OF THE FACULTY FEBRUARY 7, 1931, AND ADOPTED, MARCH 5, 1931

(A) REQUIREMENTS OF THE COLLEGE DIVISION

I. Completion of the requirements of the College division shall be measured by comprehensive examinations. In the administration of this system the College Board of Examiners may take into consideration not only the performance of the student in the examinations but also whatever other information may be secured regarding the student's abilities and attainments. (See Glossary (1), appended to this report.)

II. A certificate signifying the satisfactory completion of the requirements of the College division shall be awarded to any student who may desire it, when he shall have pursued a full program of work in the University for at least one academic year and shall have passed the examinations. (See Glossary (2).)

III. In order that completion of the requirements of the College division may signify a wholesome balance between breadth and depth of educational experience, examinations shall be set to demand:

    (1) the attainment of the minimum essentials of factual information and an introduction to the methods of thought and work in each of the four divisional fields—the humanities, the social sciences, the physical sciences, and the biological sciences——such as may be expected of a student who has pursued a general course through an academic year in each of the four divisional fields; (See Glossary (3).)

    (2) the attainment of such mastery of the subject matter, techniques, skills, habits of thought, and methods of work in two

of the four divisional fields as may be expected of a student who has through three quarters pursued in two of the four divisional fields an advanced divisional general course or divisional conference course, or a divisional or subject sequence of courses recommended by a division and approved by the College Curriculum Committee; (See Glossary (4), (5), (6), (7), (8).)

(3) a demonstration in the examinations required under (1) and (2) of the student's ability to express himself with clarity and accuracy in written English;

(4) the mastery of a foreign language at the level of attainment expected of a student who offers two acceptable entrance units in a foreign language, unless the student shall have offered two acceptable entrance units in a foreign language; and a mastery of mathematics at the level of the attainment expected of a student who offers two acceptable entrance units in mathematics, unless the student shall have offered two acceptable entrance units in mathematics.

IV. The examinations for fulfilment of the requirements of the College division may be taken during one examination period or may be spread over several examination periods, subject to the limitation that all required examinations shall be passed within a period of two calendar years. (See Glossary (9).)

(B) The College Curriculum

I. As an aid to the attainment of III (1), above, under (A) "Requirements of the College Division," there shall be offered, in each of the four divisional fields, a general course in the divisional field. (See Glossary (3).)

(1) It is contemplated that each of these general courses will be offered to large groups by the lecture method to the extent that this method may be wisely used.

(2) For each of these general courses a syllabus, with appropriate bibliographical material, and sample examinations shall be prepared and published. (See Glossary (10).)

(3) Each of these general courses shall be under the direction of a faculty member of the division concerned, who shall be responsible for the organization and administration of the course; it is expected that the faculty member in charge of the course

will need to ask, and will receive, the hearty co-operation of other faculty members who are qualified and willing to give assistance in preparing the syllabus and in giving the course. Such assistance shall not be asked as an extra service; necessary and appropriate adjustments of his program of work shall be made in the case of each faculty member who participates in the organization and offering of the course. The person in each instance responsible for the administration of one of these general courses shall have the assistance of instructors sufficient in number to read and correct whatever written work may be required, and to conduct whatever discussion groups, laboratory work, or individual consultations may be necessary for the attainment of satisfactory educational results.

(4) Each of these general courses shall be organized and offered in such fashion as to require of the average student approximately ten hours per week in all the activities and work of the course. The specific proportions of lectures, discussion section meetings, individual consultations, laboratory work, study, and any other types of formal or informal activities, shall be determined in the light of experimentation. The average full-time student would be expected to carry four courses each quarter, devoting ten hours a week to each course, and thus devoting forty hours a week to class periods, discussion groups, laboratory work, consultation, and study.[1]

(5) The person in each instance responsible for the administration of one of these general courses shall report to the Registrar at the close of each quarter for each of the students enrolled in his course that the student has or has not made satisfactory progress, and shall submit whatever other comments he may be able and may care to make about the work of the student. (See Glossary (1).)

(6) Though the work of the general course in any divisional field need be offered in only one manner, small-group instruction covering the syllabus of the general course and conducted by

[1] The provision "to require of the average student approximately ten hours per week in all the activities and work of the course" in this and other sections of this document means in practice merely that the "average" student, who devotes an average of ten hours a week throughout a year to a course should be able to meet the passing standard, D, on the corresponding Board examination.

the conference method for superior students selected by the Advisers and by placement tests shall be encouraged. (See Glossary (5), (12).)

(7) There may be offered in any divisional field one or more sequences of three one-quarter subject courses, so organized that one of these sequences together with three other one-quarter courses would give the equivalent of the general course and a sequence as provided under II, below, for election by students with a special interest in that divisional field.

II. As an aid to the attainment of III (2), above, under (A) "Requirements of the College Division," there shall be offered in each of the four divisional fields: (a) an advanced divisional general course through three quarters (See Glossary (4).) or (b) an advanced divisional conference course through three quarters for students who qualify (See Glossary (5), (6).) or (c) one or more divisional or subject sequences through three quarters approved by the College Curriculum Committee or the College Faculty (See Glossary (7), (8).) or (d) any two or all three of these types of offerings approved by the College Curriculum Committee or the College Faculty.

(1) Experimentation with methods of instruction shall be encouraged.

(2) For each of the courses or sequences of courses offered under II (a), (b), and (c) above, a syllabus, with appropriate bibliographical material, and sample examinations shall be prepared and published. (See Glossary (10).)

(3) These courses may vary in enrolment to whatever extent may be deemed appropriate in view of the methods employed.

(4) The faculty member in each instance responsible for the administration of a course shall have such instructional assistance as may prove necessary for the attainment of satisfactory educational results.

(5) Each of these courses shall be organized and offered in such fashion as to require of the average student approximately ten hours per week for all the activities and work of the course.

(6) The faculty member in each instance responsible for the administration of one of these courses shall report to the Registrar at the close of each quarter for each of the students enrolled in his course that the student has or has not made satisfactory progress, and shall submit whatever other comments he

may be able, and may care to make, about the work of the student. (See Glossary (1).)

(7) A first-year student may be registered for any one of the courses described in this section II of the College Curriculum, with the recommendation of his Adviser, subject to the approval of the faculty member in charge of the course, who may require the student to take a placement test during the first week of the quarter. (See Glossary (11), (12).)

III. As an aid to the attainment of III (3), above, under (A) "Requirements of the College Division," adequate instruction in English composition, suitable to the maturity of students at the College level, shall be provided for those who, as shown by the results of placement tests, need such instruction. (See Glossary (13).) Such instruction as proves necessary shall be intrusted to instructors especially appointed to give it, under the direction of an expert. (See Glossary (14).) This staff shall conduct experiments with different methods of instruction, including that of giving instruction in English composition to a significant number of students, individually and in groups, in connection with, and on the basis of, written work in the College courses, and shall report the results of their experiments to the College Curriculum Committee.

(1) Though some students may demonstrate that they need no instruction in English composition, and some others may need instruction over a considerable period of time, the standard of achievement demanded shall be such that the average student will need instruction for no more than two quarters, with an allowance of ten hours a week for class meetings, individual conferences, and preparation, or the equivalent thereof for a longer period than two quarters.

(2) Placement tests, administered by the Board of Examiners, shall be given at least three times a year, open to any student who desires to ascertain whether he has acquired the habit of writing good English. (See Glossary (13).)

IV. As an aid to the attainment both of III (4), above, under (A) "Requirements of the College Division," and also of II, below, under (C) "Requirements for Admission to a Division," such courses in foreign language, in mathematics, in statistics, and in any other specific training as may prove necessary, shall be offered in such manner as to fit into the four-course program of a full-time student. (See Glossary (15).)

(C) Requirements for Admission to a Division

I. It is contemplated that the requirements for entrance to a division will include, as a minimum, the requirements for the College Certificate or their equivalent.

II. It is recommended that each division, in setting any additional requirements, make its total requirements for admission such that they may be met in two years of College work by the average student who has offered at entrance acceptable units distributed in accordance with the following standard for a four-year high-school program:

> 3 units in English
> 2 or more units in a foreign language
> 2 or more units in mathematics
> 2 or more units in history and the social studies
> 2 or more units in science (physics, chemistry, botany, zoölogy), one of which should be physics or chemistry.

[Several samples of possible student programs were given in (D).]

Glossary and Supplementary Explanations

(1) (A) I, ". . . . whatever other information may be secured regarding the student's abilities and attainments" means that the "comments" mentioned in (B) I (5) and (B) II (6), similar to the comments now secured from instructors on our "personnel cards," may be given consideration, along with the results of the examinations, in passing judgment on a student who, as a candidate for the College Certificate, is a marginal case in the light of his performance in the examinations only.[2]

(2) (A) II ". . . . a full program of work in the University for at least one academic year" has reference solely to the award of the College Certificate, and not to admission to a division. The Committee believes that a certificate or a diploma should be given to no person who has been in residence in the University as a full-time student for less than an academic year. It is contemplated that a student who has been in residence for only one quarter might pass the examinations and be admitted to a division.

(3) "General course," as used in (A) III (1) and in (B) I, means a course dealing with the subject matter and methods of thought

---

[2] To date the College Certificate has been granted to no student who has not passed all required examinations.

and work of a divisional field, and not merely of a single departmental field or a group of departmental fields within a divisional field.[3]

(4) "Advanced divisional general course," as used in (A) III (2) and in (B) II, means a course dealing with the subject matter and methods of thought and work of a divisional field, and not merely of a single departmental field or a group of departmental fields within a divisional field, at a higher level than the "general course" described in (3) above.[4]

(5) "Conference course," as used in (A) III (2), in (B) I (6), and in (B) II, means a small-group divisional course, limited in enrolment to approximately twenty students, providing opportunity and encouragement for each student to progress as rapidly and penetrate as deeply as his interest and capacity may lead and permit; the instructor shall be encouraged to experiment with instructional methods with the group as a whole and with individuals.[5]

(6) "Advanced divisional conference course," as used in (A) III (2) and in (B) II, means a small-group course, as defined in (5) above, but at a higher level.[5]

(7) "Divisional sequence," as used in (A) III (2) and in (B) II, means a sequence of three one-quarter courses, in two or three departmental or subject fields in a divisional field.[4]

(8) "Subject sequence," as used in (A) III (2) and in (B) II, means a sequence of three one-quarter courses in a subject in a divisional field, which subject may lie within a single departmental field or may cut across two or more departmental fields.

(9) (A) IV ". . . . all required examinations shall be passed within a a period of two calendar years," means that if a student should pass part of the required examinations in June, 1932, he must have passed all of the remainder of the examinations by June, 1934, in order to count those passed in June, 1932, as satisfying part of

[3] Technically this provision is violated, but by mutual agreement, in the design and administration of the Introductory General Course in the Social Sciences, since it deals almost solely with economics, political science, and sociology.

[4] Glossary (4) does not apply to Social Sciences II and Biological Sciences II, since the former deals solely with economics, political science, and sociology, while the latter deals solely with botany, zoölogy, and physiology. Both of these sequences, however, fall in the category of Glossary (7).

[5] No such course has to date been offered in this manner.

the requirements. "A period of two calendar years" has no reference to dates of residence work. It is contemplated that all examinations set for the fulfilment of the requirements of the College division will be given during a period of several days two, three, or four times a year, as may later be determined.

(10) (B) I (2) and (B) II (2). It is contemplated that the syllabi and the sample examinations will appear first in mimeographed form with a statement on the title-page that they are tentative and experimental.

(11) (B) II (7). Some limitation of this privilege may be necessary in the first year of operation of this plan.

(12) (B) I (6) and (B) II (7). "Placement test" as used in these sections means a test to determine a student's competence for enrolment in a course.

(13) (B) III. "Placement tests" as used in this section means tests to determine whether a student needs instruction and, if so, what grade of instruction, to reach a certain level of attainment. Placement tests in English composition will be given in Freshman Week in order that students who seem to need no instruction in English composition may be so informed, and in order that those who need instruction may be classified for different types and amounts of instruction.[6]

(14) (B) III. "Instructors especially appointed to give it" is intended to include, not only members of the faculty in the Department of English, but also those members of the faculty in other departments who are (a) willing to assume responsibility for instruction in English composition in connection with their instruction in other departmental or divisional fields, (b) acceptable, as instructors in English composition, to the expert directing the work in English composition, and (c) especially appointed to give instruction in English composition in connection with their instruction in other departmental or divisional fields.[7]

---

[6] The present practice is to give the English composition placement test only in Freshman Week, and the English composition qualifying examination in November and in May.

[7] To date, no faculty member has been especially appointed to give instruction in English composition in connection with his instruction in another department. All faculty members who give instruction in English composition are members of the English Department solely.

(15) (B) IV. It is contemplated that elementary instruction in foreign languages will continue in much the same manner as now given, with such readjustment as is involved in changing from a three-course to a four-course student program. It is also contemplated that the class sections in elementary language instruction will be limited to approximately twenty-five students, or a smaller number if practicable, and thus will be smaller than at present. It is not contemplated that instruction in elementary algebra and plane geometry will be offered in residence, but will continue to be offered in the Home-Study Department as at present.

II

ELIGIBILITY, PROBATION, DISMISSAL, FRESHMAN ASSEMBLIES, AND HONORS

May 7, 1931, the College Faculty, upon recommendations from the College Curriculum Committee, adopted the following:

Eligibility.—Each student in the College shall be eligible for participation in student activities with the exception that in intercollegiate athletics we shall follow the conference regulations. The Advisers are expected to advise their students regarding participation in student activities.

Probation.—The present regulations concerning probation, stated in terms of grade points, are inapplicable under the New Plan. Probationary status has had significance as a warning to the student and has rendered the student ineligible for student activities. It is recommended that probation as an official status be abolished; that eligibility be handled as indicated above; and that each Adviser be responsible for warning students and their parents in writing that a student's work is unsatisfactory whenever such is the case to the extent that a warning is deemed advisable for the student or for the University by the Adviser.

Dismissal.—The present regulations concerning dismissal, stated in terms of grade points and probationary status, are inapplicable under the New Plan. It is recommended that dismissal for poor work be intrusted to the College Board, with instructions to give the matter careful study under the New Plan; to dismiss students for poor work at any time after the end of the student's first year whenever such action is deemed advisable for the student or for the University; to work out policies regarding dismissals for poor work which shall be reported to the College Faculty, with recommendations concerning appropriate legislation on the subject.

Freshman assemblies.—The practice of requiring the attendance of Freshmen at weekly assemblies, at 11 o'clock on Mondays, during the Autumn Quarter, was adopted some four years ago when compulsory attendance at Chapel was abolished. These assemblies have not proved of enough value to warrant their continuance at the expense of reserving one of the best class hours of the day for this purpose. It is recommended that compulsory attendance at Freshman assemblies be abolished.

Honors.—Honorable mention for excellence in the work of the junior colleges has been awarded under the grade-point system to each student who has an average of $3\frac{1}{2}$ grade points (B—) per major taken at the time of admission to senior college. It is recommended that honorable mention for excellence in the work of the College be awarded under the New Plan to not more than the highest 15 per cent selected on the basis of their performance in the examinations for fulfilment of the College requirements.

III

THE COLLEGE EXECUTIVE COMMITTEE

December 7, 1931, the College Faculty, upon recommendation of the Dean, adopted the following:

The Executive Board of the Colleges no longer has a proper place in the list of University Boards under the present organization of the University. It is proposed that there be created an Executive Committee of the College Faculty as follows:

The Executive Committee of the College Faculty shall consist of the Dean of the College, who shall serve as chairman, the Dean of Students in the College, the Advisers of College students, the Registrar, and a representative of each department offering courses in the College that is not represented in the ex-officio members listed above, each such departmental representative to be appointed by the Chairman of the Department and the Dean of the College. The Executive Committee shall assist the Dean of the College and the Dean of Students in the College in determining policies in harmony with the legislation enacted by the College Faculty. This Committee shall also act for the College Faculty in the recommendation of candidates for the College Certificate.

IV

MARGINAL CANDIDATES, ENGLISH COMPOSITION, ENTRANCE UNITS AND SEQUENCE EXAMINATIONS, AND PHYSICAL CULTURE

May 18, 1932, the College Faculty approved the following recommendations from the Executive Committee:

I. That the words "the College Board of Examiners" in (A) I in the action on the College Curriculum be deleted and the words "the College Executive Committee" be substituted therefor.

II. That the College Faculty instruct the College Executive Committee to give careful consideration to the case of each student who, as a candidate for the College Certificate after reports are available on all required examinations, is a marginal case in the light of his performance in the examinations only; to work out policies for the award of the College Certificate on the basis of personnel reports from instructors in the case of a student who in one or two of his examinations has failed by a small margin to attain a passing mark, while in one or more other examinations he has attained a mark or marks above the passing mark by a fairly wide margin; to report these policies, as soon as they may be developed, to the College Faculty, together with recommendations concerning appropriate legislation on the subject.

III. The Curriculum Committee's recommendation that a student's achievement in English be measured by his writing on the comprehensive examinations seems to the Board of Examiners, to the instructors in the general courses, and to the Department of English, to present insuperable difficulties. The present statement in the College requirements that the student shall demonstrate his "ability to express himself with clarity and accuracy in written English" has proved to be inadequate. The College Executive Committee recommends the adoption of the plan proposed by the Department of English for the development in the student of acceptable and reliable habits of writing and for the testing of the attainment of these habits. [This plan involved a complete reorganization of the course in English composition, with an integration of the writing in the English course with the subject matter of, and the writing suggested in, the four introductory general courses, and the development of a special comprehensive examination to give the student an adequate opportunity to demonstrate achievement in English composition.] The Executive Committee also recommends that the College Faculty authorize such further experimentation, with the approval of the Executive Committee, as may prove necessary for the development in the student of acceptable and reliable habits of writing and for the testing of the attainment of these habits.

IV. In fulfilment of the College requirement of a sequence examination in each of two of the four divisional groups in addition to the four general-course field examinations, a student may offer any College sequence examination regardless of whether the sequence examination includes units of work for which the student has offered entrance credit, except that in the humanities group a student may not offer as a College sequence examination one in a foreign language that includes units of work offered to meet the College foreign-language requirement.

V. That the physical-culture requirement be abolished. [This subject had been debated long and earnestly in several previous Faculty meetings.] For the entering class next autumn we should adopt a program which provides; (1) a fair trial of the experiment of conducting physical culture on a voluntary basis; (2) adequate facilities for, and instruction in, intramural sports; (3) physical examinations and health conferences for all College students at intervals more frequent than at present.

V

AN EXPLANATORY LETTER FROM THE DEAN TO MEMBERS OF THE COLLEGE FACULTY, EARLY IN THE SECOND YEAR OF THE NEW PLAN

THE UNIVERSITY OF CHICAGO

The College of Arts, Literature, and Science
Office of the Dean

October 26, 1932

MEMBERS OF THE COLLEGE FACULTY:

This letter is prompted by a number of inquiries from members of the College Faculty regarding some phases of our New College Plan.

Quarterly examinations.—Under our New College Plan a final examination at the end of the quarter is not required. The official schedule of course examinations during the last three days of the quarter does not apply to College courses—those in the 100-group. College courses are presumed to continue on the regular class schedule to the end of the quarter, including the three days devoted to examinations in the upper divisions. An instructor of a College course may give any type of test or examination he may desire to give at any regular class period for instructional purposes or for information on which to base his quarterly reports regarding the progress of his students. Though a large majority of the students now in College courses are New Plan students, we have some old-plan students in College courses; these old-plan students may have some conflicts between upper divisional examinations and the College regular class schedule at the end of the quarter, and it would not be fair to them to give a crucial test for marking purposes during the last three days of the quarter. Ultimately, of course, when the upper divisions are operating solely on the New Plan and have awarded the last degrees under the old plan, we shall be relieved of this present embarrassment from conflict of schedules during the last few days of the quarter.

Quarterly reports.—The following marks are used in reporting the progress of *all students* (old plan and New Plan students, divisional students and College students, alike) in *all College courses* at the end of each quarter:

S, indicating that the quantity and quality of the student's work in a course are satisfactory.

U, indicating that the quantity and quality of the student's work in a course are unsatisfactory.

R, indicating that though the student was registered in the course he did not give the instructor sufficient evidence of the quantity and quality of his work for a report of either S or U.

In some courses effective instruction can be given only with the co-operative participation of students desiring the instruction; in such a course, whenever a student shows a disinclination to co-operate effectively, he may be notified by the instructor that henceforth he will be regarded as a visitor and will be reported R; or, when a student, through lack of adequate preparation or ability, shows himself to be an unreasonable drag upon the progress of the majority who can and do work effectively in a co-operative enterprise, he may be notified by the instructor that henceforth, if he continues to attend, he will be regarded as a visitor and will be reported R. This means that if a student desires to continue to have the privileges of a participant, and not be regarded as a visitor, he is obligated to give evidence to the instructor, whenever and in whatever form requested, that he is not an unreasonable deterrent in the maintenance of a rate of progress which the large majority of participants can and do attain. An instructor is not obligated to devote any more of his time and efforts than he may choose to give to "visitors."

While course credits have been abolished in our New College Plan and the College Certificate is awarded on the basis of examinations administered by our Board of Examinations, it should be remembered that a report of S carries with it a course credit for the old-plan students still with us and for students who may wish later to transfer to another institution. Degrees under the old plan are not to be awarded after the Convocation at the end of the Summer Quarter, 1935.

Weekly class schedules.—The New Plan legislation does not specify for any College course the number of class meetings per week or the specific proportions of lectures, discussion group meetings, individual consultations, laboratory work, study, or any other type of formal or informal activities. Experimentation in an effort to determine the most effective methods and proportions of various methods is encouraged. The New Plan legislation does state, however, that a College course shall be offered in such fashion as to require of the average student approximately ten hours per week for all the activities and work of the course (except the new course in English composition, in which the work of two quarters' standard is spread over three quarters).

Under the present plan a class may meet two, three, four, or five times a week, with the other types of activities requiring, respectively, approximately eight, seven, six, or five hours per week of the average student. The number of class meetings may be varied from week to week in the light of what seems wise as the character of the educational objectives and the appropriate types of activities may vary in different parts of the course. Since we have a number of courses in which small discussion sections are conducted once a week, it seems that we may have to ask for a designation in the quarterly *Time Schedule* of the maximum number of days each week for which a classroom should be reserved for each class, together with a designation of the days, in order that we may register students and provide rooms, without conflicts, for the discussion sections that meet regularly only once a week. Thus a room used fairly regularly by one class four days a week may be assigned for the fifth day to one of the staggered discussion sections of a large lecture course; and a student who registers for a course meeting at a given hour four days a week may register for a discussion section of another course at the same hour on the fifth day.

Yearly student programs.—Virtually all our College courses are now year-courses extending through the three regular quarters of the academic year, while very few College courses are offered in the Summer Quarter. In order to maintain as nearly constant as possible the student and faculty personnel through the three quarters of a year-course, the program of each College student entering in the Autumn Quarter is now planned for the entire year, so that he may continue in the same section of each year-course throughout the year. This will enable instructors to get better acquainted with their students and to render to them more effective instructional assistance than was true last year, when the class-section personnel changed quite generally each quarter. This will also make it possible for instructors to fill out the student personnel reports with greater insight and accuracy as the year progresses, and these reports will thus be of greater value to the student Advisers in the Office of the Dean of College Students.

Though a student who has paid tuition for a full program is privileged to visit any course with the consent of the instructor, a student is entitled to the privileges of a participant only in the courses and the particular sections for which he is registered. In order that class sections may be kept fairly equal in size, instructors should not permit students to attend as participants sections other than those for which they are registered.

Student Advisers.—Nine members of the College Faculty are devoting no small amount of their time and efforts to the educational guidance of College students individually in the Office of the Dean of College Students. At first this guidance has to be based upon the information found in the student's application-for-admission blank, which gives a rather complete account of the student's high-school career. As time goes on, during the student's college career, the Advisers rely more and more upon the quarterly reports by instructors to the Registrar's Office, upon reports from the Board of Examinations, and particularly upon the quarterly personnel reports from instructors to the Office of the Dean of College Students.

In view of the new registration policy, the Advisers will not find it necessary to devote so much time as in the past to the mechanics of registration, and will have more time for educational and personal counseling in their student interviews. Whenever you may discover that a student has an educational or personal problem on which you do not wish, or do not feel qualified, to advise him, you may do him a genuine service by urging him to consult his Adviser, or, if you prefer, by informing the Office of the Dean of College Students in person, in writing, or by telephone that the student seems to need assistance.

A word of appreciation.—All evidence available to date seems to show that the New Plan progressed more smoothly and produced even better results than most of us dared to hope would be possible in the initial year. The opening weeks of the current year have been remarkably free from the confusion among students and faculty alike that characterized the same period a year ago. These gratifying results have been due entirely to the faithfulness and intelligent co-operation of the great majority of the College Faculty. No one appreciates more fully than does the Dean of the College, because probably no one knows as well, the immense amount of time, effort, and genius that many of you put into the original preparation and the recent revision of the numerous excellent syllabi now available for College courses, and that most of you have put into the effective offering of these courses in complete harmony with the spirit of the New Plan. No faculty ever gave better co-operation in better faith or in better spirit than has our College Faculty during the last two strenuous but glorious years.

I shall welcome an opportunity to talk with you individually about any phase or problem of our co-operative enterprise any time at your convenience, either in your office or in mine. If I can be of any assistance to you at any time, please do not hesitate to call upon me.

Again assuring you of my appreciation of the excellent co-operation and effective service that the great majority of you have given, I remain,

Sincerely yours,

C. S. BOUCHER

VI

THE ASSOCIATE IN ARTS TITLE, AND ELECTIVE COURSES AND EXAMINATIONS

April 9, 1934, the College Faculty adopted the following:

I. A proposal, approved by the College Executive Committee and by the College Curriculum Committee, to award the title Associate in Arts with the College Certificate, as was done previously (prior to 1918) by the University of Chicago, and as is done at the present time by approximately half of the more than five hundred junior colleges of the country.

II. A proposal, approved by the College Curriculum Committee, to change the requirement, "The attainment of such mastery of the subject matter, techniques, skills, habits of thought, and methods of work in any two of the four fields as may be expected of a student who has pursued through an academic year in each of two of the four fields a second-year general course or a sequence of three quarter-courses in a subject or an approved combination of subjects within the general field," to read: "The attainment of such mastery of the subject matter, techniques, skills, habits of thought, and methods of work in any two divisional or departmental fields as may be expected of a student who has pursued through an academic year in each of two divisional or departmental fields a second-year general course or a sequence of three quarter-courses in a departmental subject or an approved combination of subjects in a divisional field."

This proposal, if adopted, will enable a student, who so desires, to offer his two elective sequences in the same divisional field. In the case of Romance languages it will be interpreted to mean that a student may offer a sequence in each of two languages, but not two sequences in the same language.

The change regarding the two unspecified examination fields was adopted in order to give the student somewhat greater freedom (in two-sevenths of his College program instead of in one-seventh), to pursue special interests, or special needs for his chosen upper divisional work. It was felt that, in the prescription of examinations in English composition and in each of the four divisional fields, enough was prescribed to insure breadth of educational experience—a respectable minimum of contact with the major fields of thought—without requiring him to elect his two additional examination fields from two different divisional fields.

APPENDIX B

YEAR-COURSES AND YEAR-SEQUENCES OFFERED IN THE COLLEGE

Each year-course or year-sequence runs through the Autumn, Winter, and Spring quarters. Art 101, 102, 103, for example, is a sequence of three quarter courses offered in the Autumn, Winter, and Spring quarters, respectively. Nearly all College courses are numbered in the 100 group. In a few instances the numbers for quarter courses used under the old plan have been continued in use under the New Plan. In the cases of the second-year courses in the biological sciences and in the social sciences, they are designated as "Biological Sciences II" and "Social Sciences II," respectively.

INTRODUCTORY GENERAL COURSES AND ENGLISH COMPOSITION

Introductory General Course in the Biological Sciences.
Introductory General Course in the Humanities.
Introductory General Course in the Physical Sciences.
Introductory General Course in the Social Sciences.
English 102A, B, C.—English composition.

ELECTIVE YEAR-COURSES AND YEAR-SEQUENCES

Art 101, 102, 103.—Introduction to Art: historical, practical, and theoretical.
Biological Sciences II.—A three-quarter sequence in botany, zoölogy, and physiology, with emphasis on laboratory training.
Chemistry 104, 105, and 120 or 130.—General Chemistry and Elementary Organic Chemistry I or Qualitative Analysis I; emphasis on laboratory training.
Classics of the Western World 101, 102, 103.

English 130, 141, and 131 or 132.—Introduction to the Study of Poetry Shakespeare, and Drama or Fiction.

French 101, 102, 103.—First-year college French; equivalent of the first two years of high-school French.

French 104, 105, 106.—Intermediate French; second-year college French; equivalent of the third and fourth years of high-school French.

French 107, 108, 109.—Introduction to French Literature.

Geography 101, 102, 103.—A descriptive and explanatory survey of man's occupation and utilization of the earth.

Geology 101, 102, 103.—Geologic Processes, Historical Geology, and Common Minerals and Rocks.

Geology 101, 102, Astronomy 101.—Geologic Processes, Historical Geology, and Descriptive Astronomy.

German 101, 102, 103.—First-year college German; equivalent of the first two years of high-school German.

German 104, 105, 106.—Second-year college German; equivalent of the third and fourth years of high-school German.

German 107, 108, 109.—Introduction to German Literature.

Greek 101, 102, 103.—First-year college Greek.

Italian 101, 102, 103.—First-year college Italian.

Latin 101, 102, 103.—First-year college Latin; equivalent of the first two years of high-school Latin.

Latin 104, 105, 106.—Second-year college Latin; equivalent of the third and fourth years of high-school Latin.

Latin 107, 108, 109.—Third-year college Latin.

Mathematics 101, 102, 103.—Plane Trigonometry, College Algebra, and Plane Analytic Geometry; or Mathematics 104, 105, 106.— Elementary Mathematical Analysis.

Military Science and Tactics 101, 102, 103.—Basic course for a commission in the Officers' Reserve Corps.

Music 101, 102, 103.—History, Theory, and Appreciation of Music.

Philosophy 101, 102, 103.—Movements of Thought.

Physics 105, 106, 107.—Mechanics, Heat, Sound, Electricity, Light; emphasis on laboratory training.

Social Sciences II.—Second-year course; an intensive study of a number of problems raised in the first-year's work.

Spanish 101, 102, 103.—Elementary Spanish; first-year college Spanish; equivalent of the first two years of high-school Spanish.

Spanish 104, 105, 106.—Intermediate Spanish; second-year college
  Spanish; equivalent of the third and fourth years of high-school
  Spanish.
Spanish 107, 108, 109.—Introduction to Spanish Literature; third-year
  college Spanish.

All courses in advance of those listed above, or in departments not listed above, are offered in the upper
divisions.

APPENDIX C

REPRESENTATIVE STUDENT PROGRAMS OF COURSES AND EXAMINATIONS

I

An average student interested in the biological sciences.

FIRST-YEAR COURSES

Introductory General Course in the Biological Sciences
Introductory General Course in the Humanities
English 102 (composition)
Chemistry 104, 105, and 120 or 130

SECOND-YEAR COURSES

Introductory General Course in the Physical Sciences
Introductory General Course in the Social Sciences
Biological Sciences II
German 101, 102, 103 (first-year college German)

EXAMINATION SCHEDULE

English qualifying examination, May, first year
Biological sciences examination, June, first year
Humanities examination, June, first year
Chemistry 104, 105, and 120 or 130 examination, June, first year
Physical sciences examination, June, second year
Social sciences examination, June, second year
Biological Sciences II examination, June, second year
German 101, 102, 103 examination, June, second year

The German 101, 102, 103 is used to meet the foreign-language requirement of the Division of the Biological Sciences.

II

A superior pre-medical student, who entered with two units of German and with trigonometry, physics, and chemistry, and passed the English qualifying examination and the physical sciences general examination without taking the corresponding courses.

First-Year Courses

Introductory General Course in the Biological Sciences
Biological Sciences II
Chemistry 104, 105, and 120
Introductory General Course in the Humanities

Second-Year Courses

Introductory General Course in the Social Sciences
Physics 105, Zoölogy 205, Physics 106
Chemistry 130, Chemistry 241, Zoölogy 220

Examination Schedule

English qualifying examination, November, first year
Biological sciences general examination, June, first year
Biological sciences II examination, June, first year
Chemistry 104, 105, 120 examination, June, first year
Humanities examination, June, first year
Physical sciences examination, September, after first year
Social sciences examination, June, second year

A superior pre-medical student may register for both Biological Sciences I and II in his first year. A superior student is thus able to fulfil the requirements for entrance to our Medical School at the end of two years, though most students require three years to do so—a year in addition to the two years usually needed for completion of requirements for the College Certificate.

III

An average student, interested in the humanities.

FIRST-YEAR COURSES

Introductory General Course in the Humanities
Introductory General Course in the Biological Sciences
English 102 (composition)
French 104, 105, 106 (second-year college French)

SECOND-YEAR COURSES

Introductory General Course in the Physical Sciences
Introductory General Course in the Social Sciences
Art 101, 102, 103
French 107, 108, 109

EXAMINATION SCHEDULE

English qualifying examination, May, first year
Humanities examination, June, first year
French 104, 105, 106 examination, June, first year
Biological sciences examination, September, after first year
Social sciences examination, June, second year
Art 101, 102, 103 examination, June, second year
Physical sciences examination, September, after second year

French 107, 108, 109 is in addition to College requirements and is in anticipation of divisional requirements. The student offered two entrance units in Latin as well as two units in French and hence has the second foreign-language for requirements of the Humanities Division.

IV

A superior student, interested in the humanities, who entered with four units in Latin, and passed the English qualifying examination without taking the English composition course.

First-Year Courses

Introductory General Course in the Humanities
Introductory General Course in the Biological Sciences
Greek 101, 102, 103 (first-year college Greek)
Latin 107, 108, 109 (third-year college Latin)

Second-Year Courses

Introductory General Course in the Physical Sciences
Introductory General Course in the Social Sciences
Greek 204, 205, 206 (in the Humanities Division)
Philosophy 101, 102, 103

Examination Schedule

English qualifying examination, November, first year
Humanities examination, June, first year
Biological sciences examination, June, first year
Latin 104, 105, 106 examination, June, first year
Physical sciences examination, June, second year
Social sciences examination, June, second year
Philosophy 101, 102, 103 examination, June, second year
Greek 101, 102, 103 examination, June, second year

The Latin 107, 108, 109 and Greek 204, 205, 206 are in anticipation of, and count on, the requirements of the Division of the Humanities for the Bachelor's degree. Greek 101, 102, 103 meets the Humanities Division requirement of a second foreign language.

The Latin 104, 105, 106 and the Philosophy 101, 102, 103 examinations meet the College requirement of two elective sequence examinations.

V

A below-average student interested in the humanities.

First-Year Courses

Introductory General Course in the Humanities
Introductory General Course in the Biological Sciences
English 102 (composition) (failed)
Spanish 101, 102, 103 (first-year college Spanish) (dropped in mid-year)

Second-Year Courses

Introductory General Course in the Social Sciences (failed)
English Literature 130, 141, and 131
Spanish 101, 102, 103 (repeated)

Third-Year Courses

Introductory General Course in the Physical Sciences
Introductory General Course in the Social Sciences (repeated)
English 102 (composition) (repeated)

Examination Schedule

English qualifying examination, May, first year—failed
Humanities examination, June, first year
Biological sciences examination, June, first year
English qualifying examination, November, second year—failed
Social sciences examination, June, second year—failed
English Literature examination, June, second year
Spanish 101, 102, 103 examination, June, second year
Physical sciences examination, June, third year
Social sciences examination, June, third year
English qualifying examination, May, third year

With three repeated examinations, and with barely passing marks in the others, this student required three years to attain the College Certificate, and is not recommended for admission to an upper division.

VI

An average student interested in the physical sciences.

First-Year Courses

Introductory General Course in the Biological Sciences
Introductory General Course in the Social Sciences
English 102 (composition)
Chemistry 104, 105, and 120 or 130 (or physics or mathematics)

Second-Year Courses

Introductory General Course in the Humanities
German 101, 102, 103
Physics 105, 106, 107
Mathematics 101, 102, 103 or 104, 105, 106

English qualifying examination, May, first year
Biological sciences examination, June, first year
Social sciences examination, June, first year
Chemistry 104, 105 and 120 or 130 examination, June, first year
Humanities examination, June, second year
Physical sciences examination, June, second year
German 101, 102, 103 examination, June, second year
Mathematics 101, 102, 103, or 104, 105, 106 examination, June, second
   year

This student offered two units of Latin at entrance.
The Physics 105, 106, 107 and German 101, 102, 103 are
for, and in anticipation of, requirements in the Division
of the Physical Sciences and are in addition to completion
of requirements for the College Certificate. This student,
by taking three sequences in physical sciences and by
working independently on the parts of the Introductory
General Course in the Physical Sciences not covered in the
courses he took, was able to pass the examination on the
general field without taking the course.

VII

A superior student, interested in the physical sciences,
who passed the English qualifying examination without
taking the English composition course, and passed the
physical sciences general examination without taking the
course.

First-Year Courses

Introductory General Course in the Humanities
Introductory General Course in the Biological Sciences
Mathematics 104, 105, 106
Chemistry 104, 105, and 120 or 130

Second-Year Courses

Introductory General Course in the Social Sciences
Physics 105, 106, 107
Chemistry (divisional sequence)
Mathematics (divisional sequence) or German 101, 102, 103

English qualifying examination, November, first year
Humanities examination, June, first year
Biological sciences examination, June, first year
Mathematics 104, 105, 106 examination, June, first year
Chemistry 104, 105, and 120 or 130 examination, June, first year
Social sciences examination, June, second year
Physical sciences examination, June, second year

He has anticipated divisional requirements to the extent of a year's sequence each in physics, chemistry, and mathematics or German.

VIII

A below-average student interested in the social sciences.

FIRST-YEAR COURSES

Introductory General Course in the Social Sciences
Introductory General Course in the Biological Sciences
English 102 (composition)
Mathematics 104, 105, 106

SECOND-YEAR COURSES

Introductory General Course in the Humanities
Introductory General Course in the Physical Sciences
Mathematics 104, 105, 106 (repeated, because failed)
Social Sciences II

EXAMINATION SCHEDULE

English qualifying examination, May, first year
Social sciences examination, June, first year
Biological sciences examination, June, first year
Mathematics 104, 105, 106 examination, June, first year (failed)
Mathematics 104, 105, 106 examination, June, second year
Humanities examination, June, second year
Physical sciences examination, June, second year
Social Sciences II examination, June, second year (failed)
Social Sciences II examination, September, second year (failed)

This student must pass the Social Sciences II examination, or some other elective sequence examination, for completion of the College requirements; admission to the Division of the Social Sciences is doubtful.

IX

A superior student interested in the social sciences, who passed the English qualifying examination, the social sciences general examination, and the French 104, 105, 106 examination without taking the corresponding courses.

FIRST-YEAR COURSES

Social Sciences II (and visits the social sciences introductory course periodically)
Introductory General Course in the Humanities
Introductory General Course in the Biological Sciences
Philosophy 101, 102, 103

SECOND-YEAR COURSES

Introductory General Course in the Physical Sciences
Divisional sequence
Divisional sequence
Divisional sequence

EXAMINATION SCHEDULE

English qualifying examination, November, first year
Social sciences general examination, June, first year
Social Sciences II examination, June, first year
Humanities examination, June, first year
Biological sciences examination, June, first year
French 104, 105, 106 examination, June, first year
Physical sciences examination, June, second year

This student has anticipated a year's work in the division and will probably graduate in three years or less. He entered with four units in French and was able to pass the French 104, 105, 106 examination without taking the course in college.

APPENDIX D

SCHEDULE OF LECTURE AND DISCUSSION SECTIONS FOR THE FOUR INTRODUCTORY GENERAL COURSES, THROUGH THE AUTUMN, WINTER, AND SPRING QUARTERS, 1934-35

Course	8:00	9:00	10:00	11:00	1:30	2:30
THE BIOLOGICAL SCIENCES		Disc. secs.: F., a; M., b, c	Disc. secs.: F., d; W., e	Lect. A: W., Th., F. Disc. secs.: M., f, g, h, j; Tu., k, m, n, o	Lect. B: W., Th., F. Disc. secs.: M., p, q, r, s; Tu., t, u, v, w	Disc. secs.: M., x
THE HUMANITIES	Disc. secs.: W., a	Lect. A: Tu., W., Th. Disc. secs.: M., b, c, d, e, f; F., g, h, j, k	Disc. secs.: M., m; F., n	Disc. secs.: F., o; M., p	Lect. B: Tu., W., Th. Disc. secs.: M., g, r, s, t, z; F., u, v, w, x	Disc. secs.: W., y
THE PHYSICAL SCIENCES	Disc. secs.: F., a, b	Lect. A: Tu., W., Th., F. Disc. secs.: M., c, d, e, f, g	Disc. secs.: F., h, j	Lect. B: Tu., W., Th., F. Disc. secs.: M., k, m, n, o, p	Disc. secs.: M., q, r	Lect. C: Tu., W., Th., F. Disc. secs.: M., s, t, u, v, w
THE SOCIAL SCIENCES I	Lect. A: M., Tu., Th. Disc. secs.: W., a, b, c, d; F., e, f, g, h	Disc. secs.: Th., j; F., k	Lect. B: M., Tu., Th. Disc. secs.: W., m, n, o, p; F., q, r, s, t	Disc. secs.: F., u; M., v	Disc. secs.: Th., w; M., x	Disc. secs.: Th., y; M., z

Honor sections, review sections, special-training sections, and office conferences do not appear on this schedule.

APPENDIX E

EXCERPTS FROM REPORTS BY FACULTY MEMBERS

Some excerpts from informal (though written) reports made periodically by many members of the College Faculty to the Dean of the College.

I

The members of our staff make a particular effort to develop acquaintanceship with the individual student's abilities and needs. Personal interviews with students are of unquestionable value. Some resistance, or perhaps mere hesitation, has to be broken down at the beginning of the year or when students first enter a discussion group. General invitations to visit instructors during office hours are likely to be met by a skepticism resulting from the usual high-school student's fear of being suspected by his fellow-students of attempting to curry favor if he takes advantage of the invitation. Hence, two things should be kept in mind if personal interviews are to have constructive, helpful results. The first is that the student must be furnished with an obvious reason for first seeking an interview with the instructor, and the second is that he must at this interview and subsequent ones learn to regard the instructor as a helper and not as a dispenser of grades.

A. *Interviews regarding whole-volume readings.*—To bring about the first, papers on whole-volume readings serve as admirable means. Much of the value to be gained from writing a paper is lost if it is handed back to the student with only a criticism in writing. As supplementary to the written criticism, the instructor should make the most of any opportunity to discuss with the student the main issues of the book in question and the student's ideas concerning them. Papers in this way often serve as a valuable means of breaking down the student-teacher attitude and supplanting it by a friendly, informal one. Often problems besetting the Freshman during the period when new ideas are coming to him so thick and fast as to unsettle him to the point of discomfort can be thrashed out in a personal interview with the reciprocal advantage of furnishing sympathy and understanding to both student and instructor. A perfunctory handling of papers, on the other hand, results in perpetuating cold and impersonal relations on both sides.

As an example, the case of a Freshman who had been shocked into vigorous thinking by reading in quick succession Hoover's *American Individualism* and Norman Thomas' *America's Way Out: A Program for Democracy* might be cited. With the zeal of the newly illumined he attempted to "show up" what he regarded as the abysmal ignorance and gross prejudice of his parents. In an interview concerning his papers on these books he confided his troubles to his instructor, saying that his attempts to convert his parents to his viewpoint (which was the innocuous one of substituting a social viewpoint for an individualistic one) had had disastrous results. They were so incensed, he said, that they wanted to "throw him out," accusing him of being a "communist." As he had been studying the various forms of socialism and knew the difference between socialism and communism, his opinion of the intelligence of his parents had fallen to the zero point. The instructor, from a fuller experience and longer perspective, was able to point out to the student that his experience was generic and not specific, that younger generations inevitably had certain difficulties with older ones but that it was the better part of wisdom and courtesy for him not to be too condescending in his attitude toward his parents, as they had undoubtedly had the same sort of difficulty with their parents and he would, no doubt, have some agonizing experiences with his children. A boy who came to the interview bitter and rebellious toward his parents finally saw, after a friendly and informal discussion of his problems, that older persons have a great deal to give to younger ones, and vice versa, and that no one has the right to cram his views down another person's throat. Moreover, the student began to see the value of recognizing the place of courtesy in family discussions, instead of getting "mad," which he said was the usual result of his approach to any controversial question at home. This interview resulted in a friendly relationship of lasting quality between instructor and student.

Another case was that of a student who in written and class work demonstrated complete indifference and laziness. In personal interviews concerning his papers, however, he showed a good deal of intelligence. Finally one day, after some informal conversations, it became evident that the boy had no goal whatever and seemed to think education for the sake of education was useless. Much as may be said for the latter, it was evident that here was a boy who had to have something to shoot at or he wouldn't shoot at all. It was not very hard to interest him in consular service, to send for information, to indicate the necessity of a broad, cultural training and a sound factual foundation in the social sciences (in which he claimed to be interested "more than in other subjects") for such work. In a short time his work showed infinite improvement. To be sure, he has transferred his interest from consular service to municipal government and city managership; but, at any rate, he now sees himself as a possible contributor to a world in need of intelligent handling and no longer does he drift along, doing only enough work to "get by." On the contrary, he not only does the "indispensable" readings but explores allied territory. He has also been very active in organizing a special discussion group.

A good deal is said about the "total situation" by psychologists dealing with industrial questions. Surely the importance of knowing some of the personal problems affecting the quality of a student's work is very great. Admittedly, it is always a question how far a discussion leader should go into such matters. It seems to me this problem naturally solves itself in time by the degree of friendliness and helpfulness each student may or may not feel in his or her instructor. Under the New Plan there is surely every incentive to help the earnest and serious student to advance as fast as his abilities permit and, by marking the trees on the trail, to help him to tread bypaths of interest. The possibilities of greater initiative and individuality which the New Plan develops make individual attention to the "total situation" desirable whenever a student indicates a desire for help in solving problems affecting his work.

B. *Interviews regarding quarterly tests.*—Quarterly tests furnish another valuable means of checking the progress of a student, not merely as far as the tangible written result is concerned, but the interview concerning the results of the test gives the discussion leader an opportunity to discover how the student who is timid in class discussion has reacted to the lectures and readings, to indicate where his work may need strengthening, and so forth. The student who relies on doing as little reading as possible can be made aware of the folly of his ways by a discussion of his answers to specific examination questions which indicate superficiality in his work, lack of understanding, too many outside duties or diversions, or some other more or less remediable situation.

C. *Accessibility of classroom to office.*—Too much cannot be said in favor of having a discussion leader's office near the classroom. It has frequently been my experience that a student follows me into my office for a continuance of discussion begun in the classroom; whereas if the office were in another building this would not happen so often. . . . .

II

When the New Plan was first under way, many pre-medical and pre-legal students complained of having to "waste" time taking the social science general course. It was foolish, even doctors and lawyers told them so, not to mention upperclassmen! We took every possible opportunity to connect social-science discussions with various fields of work, and gradually these students saw that housing and crime and banking and legal aid and social, economic, and political problems of all kinds had an enormously large connection with law and medicine and business and industry—and, indeed, every field of work. The interdependence of our increasingly complicated economic and social structure became a living picture which demonstrated the fact that no profession today can live in an air-tight compartment. This year we no longer hear, "But I am a pre-medic. Why should I have to take social sciences?" Indeed, many of the pre-medics and pre-legal students are exceptionally interested in social sciences now. It surely will be a different world when engineers and lawyers and doctors and physicists and other "specialists" go out into their professions equipped with some knowledge of their connection with, and duty to, an interdependent civilization. . . . .

III

A few students expressed a desire to know more about unemployment insurance, considering the fact that unemployment insurance bills have been laid before twenty-seven state legislatures. Accordingly we organized a small group (the average attendance has been eight) to discuss various forms of social insurance. The first quarter, however, the group decided to devote to a discussion of the *President's Report on Social Trends*, as the material in this report was of even more immediate and widespread interest. We are now studying and discussing the reasons why Great Britain adopted unemployment insurance, going into the background of her "poor laws" and the various unsatisfactory methods of dispensing relief before insurance was introduced. The group, while small, continues its interest; and the contacts made with students are worth while. . . . .

IV

Last winter a group of about fifty students went to Druce Lake for a week-end conference on our present-day social and economic problems. Several faculty members went along; and they helped to guide discussion, which, because of the subject and the point of view of the first speaker on the program, Mr. Reinhold Niebuhr, became quite controversial. Mr. Niebuhr maintained that our economic organization has in it the germs of destruction and nothing can save it—in other words, complete collapse is inevitable and any "patchwork" measures are completely futile. Mr. Gideonse took issue with this point of view and held that many things could be done to reform our present organization. The students "warmed up" particularly the next day (Sunday), when Mr. Mullenbach was discussion leader and they were better acquainted. . . . .

The last week-end in April between fifty and sixty undergraduates, four faculty members, and several graduate students and speakers went to Lakeside for a week-end conference on international relations. The first session was Saturday afternoon, when Rev. James Yard, who has lived in China fifteen years, spoke on the Manchurian situation. The discussion was only fair, as Mr. ———, a Chinese student, became rather heated on the failure of the United States to intervene on behalf of China, and discretion probably dictated more or less silence. Moreover, it was a warm spring afternoon, we were sitting out under the trees, and Mr. Yard had much to say; so it was easy to be lazy. On Saturday evening Mr. Clark Eichelberger, of the League of Nations Association of the Midwest, spoke on the functions, achievements, and frustrations of the League. The discussion was lively, and the students showed surprising background and understanding. When an English graduate student showed skepticism, he was driven to cover until, finally, in self-defense, he said he had belonged to the British League of Nations Association for some years and was in reality deeply in sympathy with the League's aims. The consensus of student opinion was in favor of our joining the League.

Sunday morning we broke up into three discussion groups after Mr. Gideonse and Mr. Clifford Utley (of the Chicago Council on Foreign Relations) had addressed the entire group on current European problems. Mr. Gideonse, Mr. Utley, and I led the three groups. In the group I had we discussed the Chinese-Japanese situation and Mr. ———, a Japanese student, was given an opportunity to explain Japan's militaristic attitude. The students were very courteous but very searching in the questions they asked.

Students who have discussed the conference with me think the best sessions were the League of Nations evening and the Sunday morning three-group sessions. They were very enthusiastic about their discussions with Mr. Utley and Mr. Gideonse.

At this conference, as well as at the Druce Lake conference, the New Plan students stood head and shoulders above the others. This was so noticeable in relation to both their grasp of the subjects discussed and their phrasing of questions that one of the old-plan students said to me, "We old-plan students are at a disadvantage at these conferences, for you can see what a difference the New Plan training has made when you hear the Freshmen and Sophomores in discussion."

V

Surely no one can accuse the New Plan of regimenting or routinizing the instructor. On the contrary, it furnishes rich opportunities for initiative and experimentation, and no instructor can justly attribute to it any contribution toward a tendency on his part to go stale. In other words, dry rot may attack any instructor under any scheme; but the New Plan has in it potent antitoxins for the counteracting of such germs.

In the first place, there is a healthy feeling on the part of the students, that this is *their* education and they have a right to express disapproval of any phase of it which does not measure up to their standards. The instructor therefore becomes a living Suggestion Box, which function is not conducive to worshiping the *status quo*. Let a lecturer duplicate material, become verbose, or pad, and the discussion group leaders are bombarded with complaints. Let the instructor be maladroit in allowing one or two embryonic orators to monopolize the discussion hour, and he hears about it! Let some of the examination questions show carelessness in phrasing or fuzzy thinking in arrangement, and the student does not suffer in silence. A healthy, critical attitude is maintained, and the wise instructor encourages it. After all, are we not working out an educational experiment by co-operative effort?

In the second place, the plan furnishes ample opportunity for experimentation in conducting discussion groups. Sometimes several students enter the classroom with questions left over from a dormitory discussion or with skepticism concerning something heard in a lecture or read in a book. Occasionally a group volunteers to act the parts of persons of divergent viewpoints who discuss a matter of common interest to all of them. For example, one day Hobbes and Locke and Spencer and Bentham and Mills and Rousseau and Paine and Kropotkin (impersonated by as many students) sat on the banks of the River Styx considering their theories of government. Another day a group imagined themselves at dinner, discussing the controversial question of "Government in Business." One of the high spots of the latter was the students' own recognition of too much heat and not sufficient objectivity and detachment for a sophisticated, cultivated group of dinner-table companions!

Discussions and the interest they arouse in the more eager students lend zest to the instructor's academic life. No, there is no reason for any discussion leader to become "routinized" in a system that encourages initiative on the part of all.

VI

First of all, the success of the Plan, when compared with other schemes under which I have taught, is still marked if success is to be measured in terms of active interest and spontaneous participation by the students. This is always, of course, true of the top of the class; but it is so much more true than under any other scheme that I am familiar with that it deserves special mention. Students continue to come for personal discussions of problems that have arisen in their readings and discussions, they show far more interest in current social phenomena around them, and they continue to ask for, and participate in, special discussion groups on current problems related to our subject matter. . . . .

VII

Perhaps the most striking changes brought about by our reorganization has been the new emphasis upon general education. In our set-up this objective of providing a general education is the primary concern of the College. We confidently believe that a general education, such as we are attempting to provide for our students, is not only the best preparation for life, in case the students leave at the end of two years at college and do not go on with advanced work, but is also the best preparation for more specialized work if students wish to go on toward a Bachelor's or higher degree.

We believe a general education should deal educationally with the whole person, or, as the recent report of a committee put it, with men and women as knowers, actors, and appreciators. We are aiming, in so far as an educational institution can, to produce well-rounded men and women, equipped with accurate knowledge, acquainted with the best that has been produced in all of the fields of human activity, and able to think independently and clearly. To this end we have given our students in the College, as elsewhere, freedom to develop their talents to the utmost.

For one thing we have freed the students from compulsory class attendance and formal day-to-day class requirements, in the hope of making them into self-governing, responsible persons equipped with initiative and with sound habits of controlling their own lives. We do not treat them as infants but as adults, hoping thereby to develop their resourcefulness and their sense of responsibility to themselves and to the community. From our experience so far we find that we are justified in thus breaking with the academic past in America. . . . .

But we need not await the final outcome to note some of the results. If interest is a measure of the success of our plan, then the plan is an unquestioned success. The campus is alive with intellectual activity. Students are not merely attending lectures and reading books; they are thinking, writing, and participating in the movements in the city and the nation which aim to make this is a more satisfactory world to live in. Some of them may find it harder to make a living in the years to come than those before them who were born in an age of plenty and of high-powered salesmanship and executives. But even though the University may have failed to provide them with a magic and infallible formula for making a fortune, it will have taught most of them a good deal more about how we live in the twentieth century than college students ever knew before.

VIII

In my opinion the personal conferences between instructor and student constitute one of the most valuable features of the present administration of the Introductory General Course in the Social Sciences. Without them the majority of those taking the course would find it exceedingly difficult to maintain the required pace. In these conferences elementary difficulties are discussed and clarified, while the student whose problems are on a somewhat higher level finds in them an opportunity to advance and defend particular interpretations and criticisms. . . . . While it is true that during pre-examination weeks the number of those seeking personal conferences increased somewhat, there was a steady and considerable flow of students into the staff office all the year round. Many came with specific questions; others, and the number of these was surprisingly great, invited discussion of certain of the larger aspects of the course. Frequently, too, students sought the instructor's advice on personal or extra-curricular matters which affected only indirectly the progress of their studies.

One of the notable features of the course this year was the organization of "special-interest" sections by the various instructors. I formed one early in the autumn, and it has continued to meet right through the current quarter. The general topic of discussion was Fascism; and every member of the group, which numbered about ten, presented a paper on some special aspect of the subject and then conducted the discussion under my supervision. The interest in the project has throughout been keen, and every member has participated actively in the discussions. The meetings took place every other week and generally lasted two hours. I am planning to carry on this work indefinitely, inasmuch as the members of the group have indicated their willingness to continue. Participation in the group's activity entailed the setting-aside of some time regularly for reading and reflection on the topics announced beforehand at the meetings. The discussions, led in rotation by the various members of the group, were, on the whole, stimulating and I enjoyed them thoroughly. The group was alert and critical and allowed no dubious assertions to go unchallenged. . . . .

While many of the students under the New Plan at first placed a very mistaken interpretation on the academic freedom which is now theirs a very considerable number of them have responded to the challenge by developing very excellent study habits. It is my impression that the New Plan students not only do more work than their old plan predecessors, but approach their academic problems with greater alertness and understanding. The necessity of integrating and synthesizing data garnered from various fields of learning has provided the more intelligent and industrious students with that intellectual experience which, under existing educational conditions, to a large extent is reserved for post-graduate study.

IX

The New Plan has been a fine thing for me personally—it has given me a chance to broaden and co-ordinate my own knowledge, and has stimulated my interest in teaching and the problems of education. . . . . One thing definitely that may be claimed for the humanities course is that it is a general course and that it contemplates primarily, not subjects, but civilizations or stages in the development of man. Another thing that may be definitely claimed for the humanities course is that this feature of it has been very successful. I could offer the objective results of the comprehensive examinations to substantiate its success, for they have, on the whole, revealed a familiarity with and appreciation of the field of humanities that the graduate students in humanities on the whole could not equal. The measure of success which I have the deepest faith in, however, is more subjective—it is what I think I get out of a class, and I think I get more out of a class under the New Plan than I did either at the University of Chicago before the New Plan or at ————. Nowhere do I appreciate this fact so much as when I teach Shakespeare, whom, obviously, I have taught under all three conditions, which at least is the right word to use in referring to ————. Under the New Plan, there is in the humanities course only one discussion session devoted to a play of Shakespeare's. Yet in ten minutes' time I can get across the general dramatic development that is necessary to understand Shakespeare's plays. The students already know the classical drama of the Greeks. They know, in addition, of the humanistic revival of classical art and literature in the fifteenth century. And there is still time left to draw out from the students in what ways Shakespeare followed the classical traditions and in what ways he followed the native English tradition. What is most important, these students are able quickly to realize the spirit in which Shakespeare wrote. They have behind them a background of Renaissance culture, with its love of bold assertions, pageantry, and color. They have seen these things in the history of the Renaissance, in its paintings, in its architecture; I think they see these things quickly in its language. This, I realize, is the testimonial type of evidence, but then I am always more certain of my testimonials than I am of my figures. . . . .

I am thoroughly convinced of the academic soundness of the general course; I am thoroughly convinced the humanities course as it has been planned is a successful general course. But I also feel that some changes, many of them simple, would considerably increase its impact upon the student. And, besides, certain changes should be contemplated always to keep the teachers awake.[1]

Perhaps the feature of the New Plan, both in its theory and actuality, that has proved itself without any reservation has been the removal of compulsory class attendance and prescribed class work.

Let me start off realistically by admitting that there is a group of students who should go to class regularly and who should work regularly but who do neither. For the most part it is made up of a class of fairly well-to-do, idle drifters who will drift through a life of social aimlessness, no matter what administrative measures are adopted. . . . . Nevertheless, a percentage of this group who takes unwise advantage of the academic freedom of the New Plan has possibilities of redemption. This percentage is made up of the homesick, the lovelorn, the disappointed; it is made up as well of students who only temporarily have turned "collegiate." All of these students, as I have said, have possibilities of redemption; and at this point we come for a moment to the subject of instructors, who shouldn't be above saving a soul now and then. There is really nothing menial or manual about the job; and, sometimes, amazingly enough, a soul can be saved, although only by an instructor— never by a full professor. Especially under the New Plan should the rôle of the instructor be a very personal one; for the New Plan, in its main outlines, is an impersonal system, with the burden of proof on the large lecture classes and the student's own initiative and independence.

If I have given a good deal of attention to this group who does not use its academic freedom wisely, I have done so, not because this group is as large numerically as it believes itself to be, but because I believe a little attention will reduce this group even further. Certainly the vast majority of the students has learned or already knew that freedom is something to be used. The lecture attendance, for instance, seems to me remarkable, although I can give more accurate testimony as to the attendance at discussion groups, where I know the exact number on the roll. If five are absent from a class of thirty I know the word has got around that I haven't much to offer that week. In other words, I feel badly if I have more than three or four absent from a class. Some instructors note a seasonal variation in their attendance, the low level occurring at the middle of the quarters. Undoubtedly, there are varia-

---

[1] Several of the changes suggested by this and other staff members have been adopted and are now in practice.—AUTHOR.

tions in attendance, and undoubtedly some of them are due to external causes; but I prefer to hold myself accountable for them. My assumption has the value of making me teach better than I otherwise would.

The academic freedom of the New Plan is good, not only for the students, but for the teachers. It smokes them out when they tend to get in a hole. It is good for the teachers in still another way. It takes the policeman's badge off them. It frees them of the onerous task of turning in an alarm every time a student cuts a class—and this, and other things like it, make a difference. My relationship with students has never been so pleasant and efficient as it has been under the New Plan.

The discussion group, at least in the humanities course, has the possibility of performing the most valuable function of education—that of developing a critical approach to the material which the student will read or hear of in the lectures. In other words, it should be concerned primarily with methods—historical, literary, philosophical, and artistic. As an example, the student will read a good deal about the history of Renaissance art, and he will be lectured to for a week upon the subject; but the function of the discussion group leader is to appear with some reproductions of Renaissance art and to try to draw out of the students a set of critical values that can be applied to art and then to get the students to apply these standards to the specific reproductions at hand. And so on. In the last analysis, the purpose of the discussion group is critical and inspirational, or at least so I have always felt. It should attempt to get the students to realize values, it should get them to participate in and familiarize themselves with these values by applying them to specific cases; it should get them excited over values and specific cases. Otherwise, the history of human culture will be unfolded to them and they will have none of it themselves. May I say again I believe that, as a staff, we were much more effective in our discussion groups this year than we were the year before.

Of course, all of us who are concerned primarily with running discussion groups feel that our bounds of effectiveness are definitely limited by at least two factors that are beyond our control. We believe, for one thing, that we could get far better results if we could expect more papers from the students. Obviously, one of the best ways to learn criticism is to be criticized, but under the present arrangement we are not able to criticize adequately more than a few papers from each student during the year. Pathetically enough, some students ask me if I will criticize extra papers if they will write them; and of course I always am glad to, since the number of these extra papers does not become alarmingly great. One other boundary we all feel limited by is the fact that we meet the students only once a week. Personally, I know I should like to have two meetings a week, but perhaps my feeling of deprivation is at root only wounded vanity—I'm not sure whether I feel badly because I believe the students are slighted or because I believe I am slighted.

X

My own experience as a student and as a teacher has led me to believe in the great value of a more than perfunctory willingness on the part of the instructor to put himself at the disposal of students outside of class hours. We have always maintained ample office hours in our group, but in addition to formally specified periods most of us have spent considerable time in individual appointments or in chance meetings. Personally, I do not consider this time wasted, even (or especially) when conversation has not stayed within the limits of our course work. I believe that students appreciate this ease of access; certainly they avail themselves of it freely. In the beginning there are few customers; and I try to make it a point of returning papers in my office instead of in class, until I meet as many as possible of my students.

XI

My "special-interest" section in philosophy contained about twenty students, most of them of superior ability. The way in which these young students took hold of a rather difficult subject, and one in which they had had no previous training, was a revelation to me. This was one of the most enjoyable classes that I have ever had, and I hope that these sections will be continued next year. The "special-interest" sections require considerable work on the part of the instructor. But the students are very appreciative and responsive, and the instructor is well repaid for his efforts.

APPENDIX F

EXHIBITS IN THE PHYSICS MUSEUM

In the *Syllabus* for the Introductory General Course in the Physical Sciences is printed the following list of exhibits in the Physics Museum, with space for the student's notes on each exhibit:

1. Jumping Rings—"Forceless (?) Motion"
2. Inertia Balance—"Mass without Weighing"
3. Force Table—Motionless Force
4. Transfer of Momentum—"The Wisdom of the Spheres"
5. Acceleration—The Falling Fork
6. Reaction Wheel—"Recoiling Rails"
7. Angular Momentum—Winding Up a Spin
8. Planetarium—Seasons in Sequence
9. Perpetual Motion—(You can't get something for nothing)
10. Kinetic-Potential Energy. The Energy Twins
11. Chemical Heat, Mechanical Energy
12. Prony Brake—(How fast can you work?)
13. Mechanical Advantage. Levers—(Save your back)
14. Mechanical Advantage. Wedge in Block. Tons from a Blow
15. Mechanical Advantage. Inclined Plane—(The longest way up is the easiest)
16. Mechanical Advantage. Wheel and Axle—(Look at for a couple of moments)
17. Mechanical Advantage. Block and Tackle—(That long easy pull)
18. Mechanical Advantage. Worm Gears—(All automobiles have them)
19. Cartesian Diver—The Diving Bottle
20. Hydraulic Press—Force or Pressure, Which?
21. Pascal's Tubes—An Ancient Paradox
22. Bernoulli Principle (Another old chestnut)
23. Ball on Jet—(It hangs from the air)
24. Cavendish Experiment—Weighing the Earth

25. Standard Meter Bar—(It couldn't have only one end)
26. Analytical Balance. Weighing Balances
27. Model Watch Escapement—Tick-Tock
28. Steam Engine
29. Steam Turbine
30. Liberty Motor
31. Transmission of Power
32. Mechanical Work into Heat—(Working makes it warm)
33. Brownian Movements—(See the invisible)
34. Molecular Motions in Solids—(Vibrations of matter)
35. Molecular Motions in Gases—(The little ones are lively)
36. Balloons *in Vacuo*—(Inflation by depression)
37. Barometer *in Vacuo*—Superhurricane
38. Baroscope—Lying Balance?
39. Tompion Barometer
40. Weather Charts
41. Modern Barometer
42. Aneroid Barometer—(Up 10 miles by pulling the handle)
43. Magdeburg Hemispheres—(All the King's horses couldn't pull 'em apart)
44. Von Guericke Vacuum Pump—(We do it better now)
45. Modern Vacuum Pumps
    a) Sectioned Oil Pump
    b) Mercury Diffusion
    c) Ionization Gauge
46. Geyser—"Young Faithful"
47. *a*) Mercury and Alcohol Thermometers
    b) Sense of Touch and Temperature
48. Thermal Expansion Ball and Ring
49. Vapor Pressure Thermometer—(Are your hands warm?)
50. Thermal Expansion of Wire—(Heat does a stretch)
51. *a*) Temperature Control—Thermostat Relay—(In every modern schoolroom)
    b) Temperature Control—Sign Flasher—(Signs of the times require these)
52. Temperature Control—(Thermal ups and downs)
53. Temperature Control—Bimetallic Thermometer
54. Pulse Glass—(The pulse has nothing to do with it)

55. Pith-Ball Electroscope—(The Greeks gave it its name)
56. Electrophorus
57. Static Machine—Artificial Lightning—(Spare the rod and burn up the house)
58. Floating Magnet
59. Mysterious Magnetizing Coil—(Can you guess this one?)
60. Oersted Experiment—Magnetic Merry-go-round
61. Magnetic Coil Compass—(Magnet or motor)
62. Forces on Parallel Wires—(Repulsion or attraction by the yard)
63. Sturgeon's First Magnet
64. Henry "Quantity" Magnet
65. Henry Large Magnet—(This will jolt you)
66. Jacobi Motor—(It's somewhat out of date, but still it runs)
67. Henry and Modern Telegraph—(Telegraphs, old and new)
68. The Henry Motor—(The beginnings of the telephone bell)
69. Faraday Coil—(Kick and back-kick)
70. Henry's Commutator
71. Henry's Intensity Magnet
72. Henry's Quantity Galvanometer
73. Tangent Galvanometer—(Why "tangent"?)
74. Electrodynamometer
75. Kelvin Electric Balance—(Current by the pound)
76. D'Arsonval Galvanometer and Body Resistance—(How's your resistance?)
77. Electric-Power Comparison—(Save money—read your meters)
78. Simple Transformer—(No battery for this lamp)
79. Stepdown Transformer—Power Distribution—(There's one for nearly every house)
80. Horngap—(Yes, it *is* hot)
81. Direct-Current Dynamo
82. A. C. Dynamo
83. Magneto and Lamp—(From elbow grease to electricity)
84. Barlow's Wheel—(Most motors are not as simple as this)
85. Foucault Currents—(Watch your speedometer)
86. Spinning Dollar—(It's not really a dollar)
87. Induction Motor—(You have to work to drive a current)
88. Cenco-Kelvin Wave Model—(Waves from dumb-bells)
89. Bell *in Vacuo*—(Watch for silence)

90. Longitudinal Wave Model
91. Limits of Audition—(Test your ears)
92. Tuning Fork and Resonator
93. First Edison Phonograph
94. Sound Filters
94a. Resonant Forks—(Responsive singing)
95. Practical Acoustics
96. Sound Beats—(Gongs that beat)
97. Ordinary Mirror, Double Reversing Mirror—(See yourself as others see you)
98. Michelson's Velocity of Light—(The swiftest thing in the world)
99. Michelson's Early Apparatus
100. Hartyl Disc—(Tie light into knots)
101. Critical Angle of Refraction, Water to Air; Total Reflection
102. Optics of Eye—(Here's the inside of your eye)
103. Development of Microscope—(A wonderful instrument from a small beginning)
104. Diffraction Grating—(Taking light apart)
105. Interferometer—(Of all devices the most delicate)
106. Vertical Interferometer—(To measure the earth)
107. Polarized Light—(Colors from colorless things)
108. Spectra of Constituents of the Air—(See that you breathe)
109. Projection of Continuous Spectrum—(Guess what the source is)
110. Radiometer and Chart of E. M. Range—(The keyboard of invisible colors)
111. Resonance
    a) The Fickle Spring
    b) Station PMUC. Tune in!
    c) Sympathetic Pendulums
112. Electrical Discharge in Vacuo—(Visible vacuum)
113. X-Rays—(Can look through you)
114. Radioactivity—(Atomic splashes)
115. Edison Effect—(Light and electricity in bottle)
116. Thermionic Tubes —(Etheric telephone)
117. Cathode Rays—Richlmear Propagation—(They go straight)
118. Cathode Rays—Cathode Ray Heat—(They're hot)

119. Cathode Rays—(Cathode rays fluoresce; they cause light)
120. Cathode Rays—Cathode Ray Magnetic Deflection—(They're magnetic)
121. Cathode Rays—Negatively Charged
122. Construction of Photo Cell
123. Photoelectric Effect—(Listen to light)
124. Crystal Structure
125. Atom Model

APPENDIX G

SAMPLE OUTLINES OF BIOLOGICAL LABORATORY DEMONSTRATION EXHIBITS

I

The gross outline of the main content of a series of seven exhibits in physiology:

Complete anatomical charts with "keys"
Blood coagulation
Blood slides (white and red cells)
Circulation in frog's foot
Blood counting
Tissue slides (blood vessels)
Blood plasma
Centrifuged whole blood and oxilated blood
Sheep's heart dissected to show valves and cavities and musculature
Beef heart to show valves working
Anatomy of dissected dead dog
Cast of human thorax and abdomen
Metal lung models
Blood pressure on man and on dog
Artificial respiration on dog
Heart sounds in man
Heart beat in open thorax of dog
Effect of vagus on heart and blood pressure
Effect of sciatic on heart and blood pressure
Effect of phrenics on diaphragm
Action current of heart (muscle-nerve preparation)
Movies of movements of gastro-intestinal tract
Salivary secretion in dog on stimulation of chorda tympani
Peristalsis in rabbit
Gastric juice—its reactions and proteolytic powers
Whole pouch stomach dog

Urine secretion and removal of sugar and albumen
Mechanical structure and anatomical relationships of kidneys
Postural and body-righting reflexes (rabbit and rooster)
Decerebrate pigeon
Dissected central nervous system (brain, cord, nerve roots, ganglia and meninges) of dog—also hypophysis and eye
Models of brain and various sections through it
Dissected ox eyes
Human brains
Sheep brains sectioned

II

A detailed outline of a single exhibit in embryology:

1. *Gametes*
   Guinea pig sperm—living material—microscopes
   Guinea pig egg cell—prepared slide of ovary
2. *Dogfish embryology*
   1. 7-mm. embryo—slide showing gill slits and arches. Note on gill slits and arches
   2. 30-mm. embryo showing large yolk sac. Note on dogfish egg and yolk sac
   3. 12-cm. embryo showing reduced yolk sac
3. *Amphibian embryology*
   1. Live *Necturus* or *Cryptobranchus* in aquarium as example of a tailed amphibian
   2. Cleavage and embryogenesis series of *Cryptobranchus*, with legends and diagrams
   3. *Frog metamorphosis*
      a) Frog eggs as they are gathered shortly after laying
      b) 8-mm. tadpoles
      c) 8-cm. tadpoles—short hind legs
      d) Same—hind legs well developed
      e) Same—forelegs present
      f) Dissected tadpole to show gut of early metamorphosis
      g) Same—gut of later metamorphosis
      h) Same—gut of young frog
      i) Four stages in development of frog skeleton

4. *Reptilian embryology*
  1. Four stages in the development of the alligator
  2. Several stages in the embryology of the snake
5. *Chick embryology*
  1. 33-hr. chick—slide
    Diagram of chicken egg. Note on the bird's egg
  2. 48-hr. chick—slide
  3. 72-hr. chick—slide
  4. Chick—4½ days—bottle
  5. Chick—5½ days—bottle
  6. Chick—7 days—bottle
  7. Chick—10 days—bottle
  8. Chick—14 days—bottle
  9. Chick—16 days—bottle
  10. 55-hr. living chick embryo on yolk under long-armed binocular
  11. 50-hr. chick model
  12. 55- to 74-hr. chick removed from the yolk, placed in warm saline on a warming stage and under a binocular scope to observe the circulation of the blood in the vitelline veins and arteries. A liberal supply of properly incubated eggs is necessary, since the specimen has to be changed frequently to make the exhibit a striking one
6. *Dissection of pregnant guinea pig*—uterus opened to show the placenta
7. *Mammalian embryology*
  A. *Pig*
    1. 5-mm. pig—slide—shows arches and clefts
    2. 8-mm. pig—bottle
    3. 10-mm. pig—bottle
    4. ⎫
    5. ⎬ Successive stages of pig—jars
    6. ⎪
    7. ⎭
    8. 60-mm. pig showing amnion. Note on amnion
    9. and 10. Cleared pigs to show ossification centers. Note on bone development
  B. *Mammalian embryos for comparative study*
    1. Calf
    2. Dog
    3. Rat
    4. Opossum

C. *Human embryology*
1. Human female reproductive tract—normal
2. Human pregnant uterus—diagram showing relation to placenta
3. Human embroy—16-mm. embryo and membranes, to show chorionic villi
4. Human embryo—to show yolk sac and form of early embryo
5. Human embryo—50-mm. amnion and yolk sac intact
6 and 7. 90- and 100-mm. embryos and placentas.
8. Human embryo—about 4–4½ months
9. Pair of human twin chorionic vesicles—one with embryo removed, the other with the embryo intact
10. Models of human embryo and of the pregnant uterus
All other specimens numbered and in museum

D. *Twinning in mammals*
1. See No. 10 under C
2. Freemartin calves
3. Armadillo quadruplets
Charts on the laboratory walls:
72-hr. chick. Embryology of the pig. Diagram of the pregnant uterus and placenta formation in human. Armadillo quadruplets. Freemartin calves

III

A detailed outline of a single exhibit in bacteriology:

Media
Plain-agar and blood-agar slants and plates
Nutrient broth in tubes and flasks
Beef heart and brain broth for anaërobic cultures
Sugar broths with indicators
Milk medium with indicator
Semisolid medium containing various bacteriostatic dyes for differential culture
Agar agar in granular and shredded form

Equipment and methods
Autoclave, oven, Bunsen burner, inoculating needle, pipettes and pipette cans; Berkefeld and Seitz bacterial filters; broth cultures before and after filtration, Spray anaërobic plate cultures, anaërobic jar cultures

Display cards outlining methods and principles in transference of cultures, in sterilization, filtration and aërobic and anaërobic cultivation of bacteria

Plates and broth tubes demonstrating methods of obtaining pure cultures from mixtures of bacteria, by streaking on the surface of semisolid media and by serial dilution in broth

Morphology

Outline of principal morphological types; rod and coccus types demonstrated microscopically; capsulation, flagella, and spore forms shown microscopically; living motile bacteria shown in a hanging drop. Dark-field technique, motile organism (*Bacillus proteus*)

Metabolism

Fermentation of sugars, acid formation with gas, acid formation without gas, growth without change in the sugar; protein decomposition by bacterial action, acid and alkaline changes in milk, clotting of milk, digestion of milk clot, hydrogen sulphide formation by protein decomposition

Hemolysis by bacterial enzymes in tubes and on blood-agar plates

Phosphorescence (demonstrated in the dark room) on semisolid medium and in broth cultures

Chromogenesis, bacteria and molds; *Bacterium prodigiosum, Bacillus pyocyaneus, Staphylococcus aureus, Torula rosea, Sarcina lutea, Rhizopus orizae*

Organisms

Bacteria in milk (raw and pasteurized), serial dilution plates to show actual numbers of viable organisms. Outline of method of pasteurization and advantages

Bacteria in fecal matter; plates to show *Bacterium coli* colonies and *Bact. typhosum* in contrast (Endo's plates)

Bacteria in the normal throat, blood-agar plate culture. Outline of significance of throat organisms and possibilities of dissemination

Anthrax organism in blood smear, anthrax septicemia

Bacillus tuberculosis, agar slant cultures

Molds and yeasts, *Saccharomyces cerevisae, Penicillium roqueforti, Rhizopus orizae*

Protozoa and helminths; malaria organisms within red blood cells; living motile trypanosomes (*Trypanosoma lewisi*) in rat blood, stained trypanosomes (*Tryp. equiperdum* from the mouse), hookworm, male and female (*Ancylostoma duodenale*)

Biological processes and products

Phagocytosis, stained smear of pus from cases of gonorrhoea, showing diplococci engulfed by white blood cells

Agglutination of typhoid bacilli by immune serum

Antiserum (Botulinus Antitoxin A and B)

Animals

Various normal and experimental animals with display cards indicating their use in the study of particular diseases. Canaries (being used in malaria study—mosquito larvae and pupae are shown in conjunction therewith), mice, rats, guinea pigs, rabbits, pigeons, monkey

APPENDIX H

EXAMINATION RESULTS—REPORTS AND TABLES

The tables presented in the following pages have been taken from, or have been constructed from, reports prepared by the Chief Examiner, Dr. Louis L. Thurstone, and members of his staff, and by the Registrar, Mr. Ernest C. Miller, and members of his staff. The data given in the following pages are but representative samples from a vast quantity in my files.

In contemplating the tables and statistical analyses, one should keep in mind not only that each Board examination is six hours in length—three hours in the morning and three hours in the afternoon of an announced day—but also that each examination is deliberately framed so that it will be impossible for any student to write a completely perfect paper. In several instances, however, we have been astounded at the near approach to perfection of the papers written by some students.

The first official Board examinations under the New Plan were given in June, 1932.

I

GRADES MADE BY 2,109 STUDENTS TAKING ONE OR MORE COLLEGE COMPREHENSIVE EXAMINATIONS FROM JUNE, 1932, TO SEPTEMBER, 1934, INCLUSIVE

Examination	Number of Students Taking Each Examination	Number of Students with Each Letter Grade Now on Record					Average Passing Grade	Average Grade Now on Record, Including Failures	Total Failures by All Students	Average Failures per Student
		A	B	C	D	F				
Biological Sciences I	1,586	184	291	708	261	142	2.27	2.07	241	.152
Humanities	1,352	134	254	629	220	115	2.24	2.05	187	.138
Physical Sciences	1,113	135	217	457	226	78	2.25	2.09	131	.118
Social Sciences I	1,482	173	251	677	236	145	2.27	2.05	239	.161
English Qualifying	1,767	166	420	641	299	241	2.30	1.98	691	.391
Biological Sciences II	231	29	46	80	57	19	2.22	2.04	31	.134
Social Sciences II	368	41	64	165	62	36	2.25	2.03	49	.133
Art 101-2-3	23	....	10	8	4	1	2.27	2.17	1	.043
Chemistry 101-2-3	23	....	4	6	5	8	1.93	1.26	8	.348
Chemistry 101-4-5	35	4	7	11	6	7	2.32	1.86	7	.200
Chemistry 104-5-20	252	36	52	83	65	16	2.25	2.11	31	.123
Chemistry 104-5-30	42	2	6	16	12	6	1.94	1.67	6	.143
English 130-31-41	171	21	36	65	27	22	2.34	2.04	28	.164
English 130-32-41	88	9	20	37	11	11	2.35	2.06	13	.148
English 131-32-41	1	1	....	....	....	....	4.00	4.00	....	....
French 101-2-3	172	16	37	67	30	22	2.26	1.97	27	.157
French 104-5-6	126	9	23	51	29	14	2.11	1.87	16	.127
French 107-8-9	45	5	6	19	11	4	2.12	1.93	6	.133
French 107-9-18	1	....	1	....	....	....	3.00	3.00	....	....
French 107-9-60	3	2	....	1	....	....	3.33	3.33	....	....
French 109-18-60	1	....	1	....	....	....	3.00	3.00	....	....
Geography 101-2-3	200	10	41	73	39	37	2.13	1.74	47	.235
Geography 101-11-4	17	....	5	6	4	2	2.07	1.82	2	.118
Geological 101-2—Astronomy 101	27	2	6	6	5	8	2.26	1.59	8	.296
Geology 101-2-3	23	3	7	6	5	2	2.24	2.04	3	.130
German 101-2-3	201	31	39	78	27	26	2.42	2.11	29	.144
German 104-5-6	39	7	12	5	8	7	2.56	2.10	8	.205
General Honors 110	2	....	....	2	....	....	2.00	2.00	....	....
Greek 101-2-3	11	4	3	3	1	....	2.91	2.91	....	....
History 171-2-3	136	13	33	44	32	14	2.22	1.99	24	.176
Italian 101-2-3	7	2	1	4	....	....	2.71	2.71	....	....
Latin 101-2-3	5	2	2	1	....	....	3.20	3.20	....	....
Latin 104-5-6	5	1	2	1	....	1	3.00	2.40	1	.200
Latin 107-8-9	11	4	3	3	1	....	2.91	2.91	....	....
Mathematics 101-2-3	94	16	20	29	17	12	2.43	2.12	14	.149
Mathematics 104-5-6	61	4	12	24	13	8	2.13	1.85	10	.164
Military Science 101-2-3	44	9	13	15	3	4	2.70	2.45	4	.091
Music 101-2-3	12	2	1	5	2	2	2.30	1.92	2	.167
Philosophy 101-2-3	61	8	14	15	20	4	2.18	2.03	5	.082
Philosophy 103-4-206	1	....	1	....	....	....	3.00	3.00	....	....
Physics 105-6-7	10	1	....	6	1	2	2.13	1.70	2	.200
Physics 111-12-13	4	1	1	1	....	1	3.00	2.25	1	.250
Spanish 101-2-3	45	6	15	14	6	4	2.51	2.29	5	.111
Spanish 104-5-6	22	4	6	5	5	2	2.45	2.23	2	.091
Spanish 107-8-9	11	2	4	4	1	....	2.64	2.64	1	.091
Totals	9,931	1,099	1,987	4,071	1,751	1,023	2.27	2.04	1,880	.189
Percentage	100	11.07	20.01	40.99	17.63	10.30	.....	.....	.....	.....

II

SUMMARY OF DISTRIBUTION OF GRADES ON THE COLLEGE COMPREHENSIVE EXAMINATIONS, SPRING QUARTER, 1934

Examination	No. Registered	No. Absent	No. Taking Examination	No. Passed	No. of A's	No. of B's	No. of C's	No. of D's	No. Failed	Percentage Passed	Percentage Failed
General Courses:											
Biological Sciences...	727	34	693	622	86	121	302	113	71	90	10
Humanities.........	546	12	534	480	52	95	241	92	54	90	10
Physical Sciences....	539	34	505	454	49	90	208	107	51	90	10
Social Sciences.......	727	32	695	604	83	102	321	98	91	87	13
Total..........	2,539	112	2,427	2,160	270	408	1,072	410	267	89	11
Sequences:											
Biological Sciences, II	151	5	146	136	13	29	54	40	10	93	7
Social Sciences II....	231	11	220	195	24	33	108	30	25	89	11
Art 101-2-3.........	10	1	9	8	0	2	3	3	1	89	11
Chemistry 104-5-20..	88	6	82	69	9	9	22	29	13	84	16
Chemistry 104-5-30..	42	0	42	37	3	6	16	12	5	88	12
English 130-31-41....	80	9	71	57	5	14	30	8	14	80	20
English 130-32-41....	56	4	52	47	8	13	22	4	5	90	10
French 101-2-3......	103	6	97	78	9	19	31	19	19	80	20
French 104-5-6......	50	3	47	40	7	11	25	7	7	85	15
French 107-8-9......	27	3	24	22	2	4	10	6	2	92	8
Geography 101-2-3...	134	5	129	103	9	19	52	23	26	80	20
Geology 101-2-3.....	16	0	16	14	1	3	8	2	2	87.5	12.5
Geology 101-2—Astronomy 101......	21	2	19	12	0	2	5	5	7	63	37
German 101-2-3.....	113	8	105	89	16	17	44	12	16	85	15
German 104-5-6.....	15	0	15	11	4	6	0	1	4	73	27
German 107-8-9.....	1	0	1	1	0	0	0	1	0	100	......
Greek 101-2-3.......	8	0	8	8	1	3	3	1	0	100	......
History 171-2-3......	15	3	12	11	0	3	4	4	1	92	8
Italian 101-2-3......	5	0	5	5	2	0	3	0	0	100	......
Latin 101-2-3........	5	1	4	4	1	2	1	0	0	100	......
Latin 104-5-6........	2	0	2	2	0	2	0	0	0	100	......
Latin 107-8-9........	2	0	2	2	1	1	0	0	0	100	......
Mathematics 101-2-3.	29	1	28	25	1	5	13	6	3	89	11
Mathematics 104-5-6.	42	2	40	34	0	8	17	9	6	85	15
Military Science 101-2-3...............	20	1	19	16	2	4	9	1	3	84	16
Music 101-2-3......	15	2	13	12	2	4	5	1	1	92	8
Philosophy 101-2-3...	39	9	30	27	4	6	10	7	3	90	10
Physics 105-6-7......	11	1	10	7	0	2	4	1	3	70	30
Physics 111-12-13....	1	0	1	1	0	0	1	0	0	100	......
Spanish 101-2-3......	19	0	19	17	2	3	8	4	2	89	11
Spanish 104-5-6.....	7	0	7	7	1	2	2	2	0	100	......
Spanish 107-8-9.....	9	1	8	8	1	2	4	1	0	100	......
Total sequences..	1,367	84	1,283	1,105	128	234	514	239	178	86	14
Total general courses and sequences.......	3,906	196	3,710	3,265	398	642	1,586	649	445	88	12
English Qualifying Examination..........	584	17	567	485	48	95	256	86	82	89	11
Grand total...	4,490	213	4,277	3,750	446	737	1,842	735	527	87.7	12.3

III

COLLEGE COMPREHENSIVE EXAMINATIONS, SPRING QUARTER, 1934

	NUMBER OF STUDENTS WHO TOOK (EXCLUSIVE OF THE ENGLISH QUALIFYING EXAMINATION)						
	1 Exami- nation	2 Exami- nations	3 Exami- nations	4 Exami- nations	5 Exami- nations	6 Exami- nations	Total
Number of stu- dents..........	260	339	745	116	11	3	1,474
Total number of examinations taken in each group..........	260	678	2,235	464	55	18	3,710

IV

PERCENTAGE OF STUDENTS RECEIVING EACH LETTER GRADE IN THE FOUR GENERAL INTRODUCTORY COURSES

GRADE	BIOLOGICAL SCIENCES					HUMANITIES					PHYSICAL SCIENCES					SOCIAL SCIENCES					GRAND TOTAL
	6–32*	9–32	12–32	6–33	To-tal	6–32	9–32	12–32	6–33	To-tal	6–32	9–32	12–32	6–33	To-tal	6–32	9–32	12–32	6–33	To-tal	
A......	10	9	12	10	10	11	5	0	9	9	12	26	6	9	10	11	8	8	10	10	10
B......	19	0	12	18	18	18	10	16	17	17	19	17	24	18	19	20	14	20	16	18	18
C......	45	34	8	44	43	46	38	23	47	45	44	14	34	45	43	43	42	20	44	43	44
D......	13	18	31	16	15	13	22	19	16	15	14	13	6	17	15	14	19	12	17	16	15
F......	13	39	39	11	14	12	24	42	11	13	11	30	30	11	12	12	17	40	13	13	13
Total	100	100	100	100	100	100	100	100	100	100	100	100	100	100	100	100	100	100	100	100	100
No.†	385	44	26	610	1,065	418	58	31	470	977	198	23	33	374	628	404	36	25	507	972	3,642

* Examination dates: June, September, December, 1932, and June, 1933.
† No. of examinations written.

The percentage of students receiving each letter grade is nearly the same in each of the four general courses in the June examinations and for the total of the examinations given on the four dates.

V

INTERCORRELATIONS OF GRADES

EXAMINATION	BIOLOGICAL SCIENCES		HUMANITIES		PHYSICAL SCIENCES		SOCIAL SCIENCES		PSYCHOLOGICAL EXAMINATION	
	June, 1932	June, 1933	June, 1932	June, 1933	June, 1932	June, 1933	June, 1932	June, 1933	June, 1932	June, 1933
Biological Sciences........	.....	.....	225	222	60	75	210	263	364	530
Humanities....	.73	.74	.....	.....	110	104	246	95	384	300
Physical Sciences........	.86	.89	.72	.69	.....	.....	121	121	190	336
Social Sciences.	.77	.79	.84	.76	.71	.67	.....	.....	379	449
Psychological Examination*	.49	.43	.64	.48	.58	.39	.52	.35	.....	.....

* The American Council on Education Psychological Examination, given in Freshman Week at the opening of the Autumn Quarter.

Numbers to the left of the blank diagonal are coefficients of correlation, and numbers to the right are the numbers of students on which the coefficients are based.

The correlations among the general courses are fairly high, especially those between physical sciences and biological sciences.

The correlation between:

Social Sciences I, June, 1932, and Social Sciences II
in June, 1933, was .79 (163 students).

Biological Sciences I, June, 1932, and Biological Sciences II
in June, 1933, was .69 (90 students).

English Qualifying, at an earlier date, and Humanities
in June, 1933, was .48 (251 students).

English Qualifying and Psychological Examination
in 1932–33, was .57 (sample—130).

Psychological Examination, at an earlier date, and Social Sciences II
in June, 1933, was .41 (162 students).

VI

THE NUMBER OF QUARTERS IN WHICH STUDENTS HAD BEEN
REGISTERED IN THE CORRESPONDING COURSES FOR THE
EXAMINATIONS ON THE FOUR FIELDS OF THE INTRODUC-
TORY GENERAL COURSES, OFFERED IN JUNE, SEPTEMBER,
AND DECEMBER, 1932

NUMBER OF QUARTERS IN COURSE	NUMBER OF STUDENTS RECEIVING EACH LETTER GRADE						PERCENTAGE OF STUDENTS RECEIVING EACH LETTER GRADE					
	A	B	C	D	F	Total	A	B	C	D	F	Total
3............	153	252	636	211	241	1,493	10	17	43	14	16	100
2............	6	17	32	11	12	78	8	22	41	14	15	100
1............	7	18	19	11	3	58	12	31	33	19	5	100
0............	10	18	20	4	0	52	19	35	38	8	0	100
Total.....	176	305	707	237	256	1,681	10	18	42	14	15	100

Note that there were no failures among those who took
examinations *without* course registration. The 16 per cent
of failures of the students who took examinations after
three quarters (registration for the entire course) included
several students who failed the examination in a given
field more than once.

Note also that the proportion of high grades, A and B,
was much higher for those students who took examinations
without registering for the course or after only one quarter's attendance than for those who attended the full three
quarters.

These facts show that the superior students are taking
advantage of the opportunities offered under the New
Plan.

VII

COMPARATIVE ACHIEVEMENT OF MEN AND WOMEN STUDENTS

EXAMINATION	PERCENTAGE OF TOTAL GROUP				MEAN SCORES						PERCENTILE RANK OF MEAN SCORES					
	June, 1932		June, 1933		1932			1933			1932			1933		
	Men	Women	Men	Women	Men	Women	Total	Men	Women	Total	Men	Women	Total	Men	Women	Total
Biological Sciences I..	65	35	58	42	349	318	339	377	338	360	54	35	48	53	38	48
Humanities..........	52	48	53	47	196	189	192	652	630	642	52	46	49	54	48	49
Physical Sciences....	69	31	60	40	102	95	100	197	176	188	56	42	51	60	42	52
Social Sciences I...	60	40	68	32	197	191	195	231	227	229	48	40	46	54	46	50
Biological Sciences II	....	....	76	24	....	....	....	1,381	1,258	1,351	....	....	....	52	32	45
Social Sciences II...	....	....	64	36	....	....	....	37.3	37.6	37.4	....	....	....	52	54	53
Psychological Examination*	60	40	60	40	208	191	201	225	207	218	54	42	49	54	42	50

* The American Council on Education Psychological Examination, given in Freshman Week at the opening of the Autumn Quarter.

This table indicates that the performance of the men is superior to that of the women in each of the examinations except Social Sciences II.

VIII

DISTRIBUTION OF SCORES AND LETTER GRADES, SOCIAL SCIENCES I EXAMINATION, JUNE, 1934

Grade	Score	Frequency	Total Number	Percentage
A	690–99	2		
	680–89	0		
	670–79	0		
	660–69	2		
	650–59	5		
	640–49	3		
	630–39	4	83	12
	620–29	8		
	610–19	5		
	600–609	8		
	590–99	10		
	580–89	9		
	570–79	10		
	560–69	17		
B	550–59	24		
	540–49	17		
	530–39	15	103	15
	520–29	24		
	510–19	23		
C	500–509	26		
	490–99	28		
	480–89	35		
	470–79	25		
	460–69	24		
	450–59	40	320	46
	440–49	33		
	430–39	40		
	420–29	35		
	410–19	34		
D	400–409	24		
	390–99	32	98	14
	380–89	25		
	370–79	17		
F	360–69	25		
	350–59	12		
	340–49	13		
	330–39	15		
	320–29	8		
	310–19	4		
	300–309	3		
	290–99	2	91	13
	280–89	2		
	270–79	4		
	260–69	1		
	90–94	1		
	40–49	1		

IX

SOCIAL SCIENCES I EXAMINATION, SEPTEMBER, 1934

Grade	Frequency	Percentage
A...................	4	5
B...................	7	9
C...................	24	31
D...................	15	19
F...................	28	36
Total...........	78	100

DISTRIBUTION OF GRADES OF STUDENTS ACCORDING TO NUMBER OF QUARTERS REGISTERED IN THE COURSE

Quarters Registered	A	B	C	D	F	Total
0................	3	3	5	0	4	15
1................	1	0	0	0	1	2
2................	0	1	3	2	5	11
3................	0	3	15	11	15	44
4................	0	0	0	2	1	3
Uncertain........	0	0	1	0	2	3
Total.........	4	7	24	15	28	78

DISTRIBUTION OF GRADES OF STUDENTS REPEATING THE EXAMINATION

Previous Grade	Present Grade					
	A	B	C	D	F	Total
C................	0	2	0	0	0	2
F................	0	0	4	9	13	26
Total.........	0	2	4	9	13	28

An index of the reliability of the examination was obtained by correlating the raw score of the morning section with the raw score of the afternoon section. This correlation was .81, which indicates a reliability coefficient of .90 for the entire examination.

X

RELATIONSHIP BETWEEN LETTER GRADES ON EXAMINATIONS
IN THE FIELD OF THE INTRODUCTORY GENERAL COURSE IN
THE PHYSICAL SCIENCES, THE NUMBER OF QUARTERS REG-
ISTERED IN THE COURSE, AND THE ELECTION OF PHYSICAL
SCIENCE DEPARTMENTAL SEQUENCES, JUNE, 1934, AND SEP-
TEMBER, 1934

NUMBER OF QUARTERS IN COURSE	NUMBER RECEIVING EACH LETTER GRADE					TOTAL NUMBER OF STUDENTS	PERCENT- AGE OF STUDENTS	NUMBER ELECTING PHYSICAL SCIENCE SE- QUENCES	PERCENT- AGE ELECTING PHYSICAL SCIENCE SE- QUENCES
	F	D	C	B	A				
June, 1934									
4 or more....	1	3	2	....	....	6	1.2	0	0.0
3............	43	94	173	76	38	424	83.9	94	22.2
2............	5	6	21	6	7	45	8.9	27	60.0
1............	....	1	3	5	3	12	2.4	7	58.3
0............	....	4	7	4	2	17	3.4	12	70.6
Home-Study Department	....	....	1	....	....	1	0.2	......	....
Total ...	....	....	....	....	....	505	100.0	......	....
September, 1934									
4............	1	2	....	....	1	4	5.3	0	....
3............	6	21	10	1	1	39	52.0	5	....
2............	2	3	1	....	....	6	8.0	0	....
1............	2	2	1	1	2	8	10.7	3	....
0............	1	1	3	5	5	15	20.0	7	....
Data lacking..	....	....	....	....	....	3	4.0	......	....
Total ...	....	....	....	....	....	75	100.0	......	....

XI

From the report to the faculty on the June, 1934, "Comprehensive Examination on the field of the Introductory General Course in the Humanities," prepared by the humanities examiner, Mr. John M. Stalnaker, the following data and comments are quoted:

PERCENTAGE OF STUDENTS RECEIVING EACH LETTER GRADE
IN THE COMPREHENSIVE EXAMINATIONS ON THE FIELDS OF
THE FOUR INTRODUCTORY GENERAL COURSES IN JUNE, 1932,
1933, AND 1934

EXAMINATION	GRADE						NUMBER OF STUDENTS
	A	B	C	D	F	Total	
Biological Sciences:							
1932	10	19	45	13	13	100	385
1933	10	18	44	16	11	100	610
1934	13	18	44	16	10	100	693
Total	11	18	44	15	11	100	1,688
Humanities:							
1932	11	18	46	13	12	100	418
1933	9	17	47	16	11	100	470
1934	10	18	44	17	10	100	534
Total	10	18	46	16	11	100	1,422
Physical Sciences:							
1932	12	19	44	14	11	100	198
1933	9	18	45	17	11	100	374
1934	10	18	41	21	10	100	505
Total	10	18	43	18	11	100	1,077
Social Sciences:							
1932	11	20	43	14	12	100	404
1933	10	16	44	17	13	100	507
1934	12	15	46	14	13	100	695
Total	11	16	45	15	13	100	1,606
Total:							
1932	11	19	45	13	12	100	1,405
1933	10	17	45	16	12	100	1,961
1934	11	17	44	17	11	100	2,427
Grand total	11	17	45	16	12	100	5,793

INTERCORRELATION OF GRADES, JUNE, 1934

Examination	Biological Sciences	Humanities	Physical Sciences	Social Sciences	Psycho-logical Examina-tion*
Biological Sciences.....	....	237	82	368	440
Humanities............	.74	....	162	74	389
Physical Sciences......	.87	.62	....	121	428
Social Sciences........	.74	.81	.71	....	537
Psychological Examina-tion...............	.49	.46	.49	.41	....

* The American Council on Education Psychological Examination.

Numbers to the left of the blank diagonal are coefficients of correlation, and numbers to the right are the numbers of students on which the coefficients are based.

The complete examination was divided into twenty-five parts: the essay and eight other parts in the morning section, and sixteen parts in the afternoon section. A following table gives the perfect score on each of these sections, together with the obtained average score, the variability of the scores, and the correlation between the section and the score on the total examination.

Perhaps a note concerning the measure of variability, sigma, is appropriate. Sigma gives the number of score units one must go on either side of the average to include approximately two-thirds of the students. Of the 100 points possible on the essay, the average score was 47.5; the sigma is 18.8, which indicates that two-thirds of the students received scores between 29 (47.5–18.8) and 66 (47.5 plus 18.8). The variability of this weighted essay score was the largest variability among the parts. In general, the sections will contribute to the total score roughly in proportion to their variabilities and not in proportion to the total possible score per part, nor even to the obtained average score. For this reason, the variability is an important consideration.

DISTRIBUTION OF SCORES, HUMANITIES EXAMINATION,
JUNE, 1934

Grade	Score	Number	Total Number	Percentage
A	780–99	1	53	9.9
	760–79	5		
	740–59	6		
	720–39	8		
	700–719	12		
	680–99	21		
B	660–79	24	97	18.2
	640–59	29		
	620–39	21		
	600–619	23		
C	580–99	24	236	44.2
	560–79	43		
	540–59	31		
	520–39	34		
	500–519	34		
	480–499	34		
	460–479	36		
D	440–59	44	93	17.4
	420–39	32		
	404–19	17		
F	380–403	12	55	10.3
	360–79	11		
	340–59	13		
	320–39	5		
	300–319	5		
	280–99	2		
	240–59	3		
	200–219	1		
	140–59	1		
	100–119	2		
Total		534		

The correlation between the part and the total indicates the extent to which the part predicts the total. If we as-

LIST OF HIGHEST STUDENTS

	Raw Score	Percentile	Percentage of Total Possible
Total possible....	906	....	100
Student As———......	785	100	87
Student Sh———......	774	100	85
Student Fi———......	772	99	85
Student Pe———......	768	99	85
Student Ir———......	765	99	84
Student Kl———......	762	99	84
Student In———......	747	98	82
Student Sa———.....	744	98	82
Student Sm———.....	744	98	82
Student Ka———......	743	98	82
Student La———......	743	98	82
Upper quartile.......	614	75	68
Median.............	529	50	58
Lower quartile.......	453	25	50
Lowest score........	103	0	11

COMPARISON OF A AND F STUDENTS

	A Students		F Students	
Number of students..............	53		55	
Average Psychological Examination* percentile................	79		34	
	No.	%	No.	%
Number who have passed other examinations:				
Biological Sciences.............	46	87	27	49
Physical Sciences..............	30	57	17	31
Social Sciences................	29	55	16	29
English Qualifying.............	46	87	31	56
Sequences: One only...........	15	28	14	25
Two only...........	25	47	4	7
Three only..........	1	2	.....	......
Four only..........	1	2	.....	......

* The American Council on Education Psychological Examination.

Because the use of books was allowed in the morning section of the 1934 examination, some interest attaches to a comparison between the June, 1933, and the June, 1934, examination. The following comparisons show that the effect of "open book" on the results is not great. The value of the use of books is perhaps twofold—better examination questions are written, and the students do a more valuable type of studying, even to the keeping of more elaborate and analytical notes. Such values are not shown in the following figures:

CORRELATIONS

Examination	June, 1934	June, 1933
Psychological Examination* and total examination..	.46	.48
Morning and afternoon objective..............	.85	.83
Psychological Examination* and morning total.....	.54	.50
Psychological Examination* and morning objective..	.57	.50
Psychological Examination* and afternoon total....	.46	.55
Total objective and morning essay..............	.55	.79
Morning total and afternoon total..............	.84	.88

* The American Council on Education Psychological Examination.

AVERAGE SCORE EXPRESSED AS A
PERCENTAGE OF THE TOTAL
POSSIBLE SCORE

Examination	June, 1934	June, 1933
Morning essay........	48	48
Morning objective....	60	66
Morning total........	57	60
Afternoon total.......	60	58
Grand total..........	59	59

DISTRIBUTION OF LETTER GRADES OF STUDENTS WHO
WERE REGISTERED IN THE COURSE 0, 1, 2, 3,
AND 4 QUARTERS

Grade	0	1	2	3	4	Total
A.	1	2	2	48	....	53
B.	2	2	1	92	....	97
C.	3	4	18	210	1	236
D.	1	2	8	81	1	93
F.	1	3	1	50	....	55
Total.	8	13	30	481	2	534

XII

The English Qualifying Examination given in May,
1934, consisted of four parts in the morning (three hours)
and six parts in the afternoon (three hours); the essay parts
totaled 180 minutes—the semi-objective parts 40 minutes
and the objective parts 140 minutes. The examination was
taken by 571 students, with grade distributions as follows:
A, 8 per cent; B, 17 per cent; C, 48 per cent; D, 15 per
cent; and F, 14 per cent. The Examiner included in his
report the results of item analyses.

The following is quoted from the report of the humanities examiner, Mr. John M. Stalnaker, on the English
Qualifying Examination given November 10, 1934, merely
because it is the latest report available. The group taking
this examination in May is more "regular" in personnel,
i.e., primarily composed of Freshmen, most of whom have
pursued the course in English composition.

REPORT ON ENGLISH QUALIFYING EXAMINATION, NOVEMBER 10, 1934

Section and Time	Description	Possible Score	Average Score	Sigma*
Morning section: I. Essay (120 minutes)	The directions read: "Compare the positions of the authors of the two extracts given below. Make the comparison point by point; that is, present in turn the major issues of the controversy concerning reforestation, indicating the ideas of both authors with respect to each issue."	77	35.7*	14.0
II. Grammar (15 minutes)	Each of a series of 26 sentences is to be marked satisfactory or corrected by a change of a single word.	26	18.4	3.5
III. Sentence Structure (15 minutes)	Each of a series of 25 sentences is to be classified according to the type of sentence fault it represents. A list of possible faults is given.	25	17.1	4.3
IV. Wordiness (25 minutes)	Each of a series of 16 sentences is to be rewritten; all unnecessary words are to be omitted, but all the ideas of the original retained.	32	18.0	5.9
Afternoon section: I–II. Organization (60 minutes)	From a series of statements, an outline is to be constructed which adequately develops the purpose given.	18	10.0	3.8
III. Construction Shifts (40 minutes)	The student makes a specified change in each of a series of 28 sentences, together with any other changes necessitated.	58	40.2	7.9

* The sections are weighted in proportion to the sigma. Thus, the essay (with a sigma of 14) has roughly one-half the weight of the total objective (sigma, 26); the essay had half the time (two hours) of the total objective (four hours). In the objective total, only four students scored below 90. In the essay, five students scored zero.

REPORT ON ENGLISH QUALIFYING EXAMINATION,
NOVEMBER 10, 1934—*Continued*

Section and Time	Description	Possible Score	Average Score	Sigma*
IV. Word Change (40 minutes)	In each of 17 paragraphs, the student is to find the one word which has been changed to destroy the meaning of the paragraph.	17	12.8	3.2
V. Unity-Coherence (15 minutes)	The order of the sentences in each of two paragraphs is to be changed so as to make each paragraph a logical, coherent unit.	17	11.4	3.1
VI. Diction (15 minutes)	The errors in idiom and diction contained in a short passage are to be underlined.	34	16.9	5.3
Total objective...	....	227	144.6*	26.0

The two-hour essay was read twice independently, and the sum of the two grades was used for the essay score. In case of a disagreement in the two judgments of over 2 points on the 11-point scale used, the paper was read by a third reader, and twice the median score used as the final grade. The reliability of the reading, determined by correlating the two independent readings before any third reading was done, is .73. Of course, the actual reliability is higher than this because not one reader's judgment was used, but two. The estimated reliability of the combined grade is .84. Twenty-seven papers were read three times because of the discrepancy between the original two scores. The difference of the first two grades was in these cases usually 3 points; but in three cases, it was 4 points and in one case 5 points.

The readers felt that the system they decided on for

reading the papers was not so satisfactory as had been hoped; but in spite of this feeling of dissatisfaction, the reliability was higher than usual for a paper of such length. The readers also commented on the superior quality of the essays; in particular, the mechanics of writing were generally good. In grading the papers, the readers allowed 2 points for completeness, 3 for the interpretation of the material, 3 for mechanics of writing, and 3 for coherence.

This November examination was of particular interest because it was expected that most of the students who were recommended, on the basis of the Freshman Week placement test, to take the qualifying test at once would do so. After the grades had been assigned, it was found that 71 of the 96 recommended students had taken and passed the examination. In addition, 67 other Freshmen took the examination (none were from the group of F students on the placement test); the results are given in the accompanying table.

ENGLISH QUALIFYING EXAMINATION, NOVEMBER, 1934

GRADE	FRESHMEN		NOT FRESHMEN*	TOTAL
	Recommended	Others		
A..............	16 (22%)	5 (7%)	9 (9%)	30 (13%)
B..............	26 (37%)	7 (10%)	12 (12%)	45 (19%)
C..............	27 (38%)	44 (66%)	34 (34%)	105 (44%)
D..............	2 (3%)	7 (10%)	21 (21%)	30 (13%)
F..............	....	4 (6%)	23 (23%)	27 (11%)
Total.......	71 (100%)	67 (100%)	99 (100%)	237 (100%)

* Two of these students were "recommended" students of a year ago. One received A, the other B, on the qualifying examination. Besides Sophomores this group included many advanced-standing and old-plan divisional students.

The essay part of the test correlated with the total objective .48. Records were available for 134 students who had taken both the 1934 placement test and the November qualifying examination. (Four of the Freshmen who took this examination had not taken the placement test; their grades were A, B, C, and F.) The correlation, based on these 134 cases, between the qualifying and the placement-test scores was .58, a fairly high validity coefficient for the initial form of the placement test. The next placement test will be revised and improved on the basis of the results of this qualifying examination and that to be given in May, and only those items retained which have high predictive value.

As soon as certain types of parts (not the same items) of the objective test have been used several times, analyses are made. The sentence-structure, grammar, and construction-shifts parts of the November examination were built of carefully analyzed material. Only the successful types of items are duplicated. The November examination will in time be completely analyzed, item by item; and the May examination should have, as a result, a successful objective section.

As usual, many errors made by the students were the result of a careless reading of the directions.

XIII

Abstracts of data taken from the records of some of the students who have completed the requirements for the College Certificate, or the requirements for the Bachelor's degree, or both, in less than normal time. In each instance the student entered as a Freshman.

J. C. was in residence for a full program during the three quarters of 1932–33, and for a half-time program in the Autumn Quarter, 1933, a total of three and one-half quarters. He passed five College examinations in the spring, 1933, and the other two in June and September, 1934. His average on all examinations was C.

E. P. was in residence four quarters, from the Autumn, 1931, to the Autumn, 1932, inclusive. He passed two examinations for the College Certificate in June, one in September, and one in December, 1932, and three in June, 1933, with an average slightly below B.

A. M. was in residence the three quarters of 1932–33 for a regular program. He passed one College examination in December, 1932, one in May, four in June, and one in September, 1933, with an average slightly above C.

C. C. was in residence during the Autumn and Spring quarters of 1931–32, and the Winter and Spring quarters of 1933–34, a total of four quarters. He passed three College examinations in June, 1932, and the remaining four in May and June, 1934. His average on all examinations was B—.

J. V. was in residence during the Winter and Spring quarters of 1933 and of 1934, but was registered for a full program during only one quarter. His total residence program equaled a full program for three and one-fourth quarters. He passed four College examinations in the spring, 1933, and the other three a year later, with a C+ average.

I. R. was in residence for full work during the three quarters of 1932–33. He passed one College examination in September, and one in December, 1932, four in June, and one in September, 1933, with a B+ average.

M. S. was in residence during the Autumn Quarter, 1931, for full work, during the Winter and Spring quarters of 1933 for half work, and during the Autumn Quarter, 1933, for full work, making the equivalent of three quarters of full work. He passed one College examination in December, 1931, one in September, and two in December, 1932, two in June, and one in December, 1933, with an average slightly below B.

R. B. was in residence for full work during the three quarters of 1933–34. He passed one College examination in December, 1933, four in May and June, and two in September, 1934, with an average slightly below B.

R. R. was in residence during the three regular quarters of 1933–34, registered for more than a full program each quarter. He passed one College examination in December, 1933, one in February, four in June, and one in September, 1934, with an average of C+.

T. S. was in residence during three quarters, 1933–34, registered for more than a normal program each quarter. He passed one College examination the month he graduated from our University High School,

June, 1933, five in May and June, and one in September, 1934, with an average of B+.

W. G. was in residence for five quarters from the winter, 1933, to the spring, 1934, inclusive. He passed one College examination in February, three in June, and one in September, 1933, and two in June, 1934, with six grades of A and one B.

D. M. was in residence for a normal program of courses in the three quarters of 1933–34. He passed all seven College examinations within a period of three weeks in May and June, 1934, with an average of B—.

F. B. was in residence for four quarters from the Autumn, 1931, to Autumn, 1932, inclusive. She passed two College examinations in June, and one in September, 1932, one in May, two in June, and one in December, 1933, with an average slightly above D.

J. E. took the Bachelor's degree after having been in residence eight quarters, two and two-thirds academic years, during the period from the autumn, 1931, to the spring, 1934, inclusive. She qualified for the College Certificate in September, 1933, with an average slightly above C, and passed her Bachelor's degree comprehensive examinations in May, 1934, with a B average.

L. K. took his Bachelor's degree after two years (six quarters) of residence work, from the autumn, 1932, to the spring, 1934, inclusive. He qualified for the College Certificate in June, 1933, with six A grades and one B. He took the Bachelor's degree in June, 1934, with a grade of B on his comprehensive examinations, and registered at once for graduate work.

G. M. entered in the autumn, 1931; qualified for the College Certificate in December, 1932, with an average slightly above B on the seven examinations; attempted the Bachelor's comprehensive examination in August, 1933, but failed; came up again in March, 1934, and passed with a grade of B. He had been in residence nine quarters (three academic years), including the Summer Quarter, 1933.

E. R. took the Bachelor's degree after nine quarters (three years) of residence, 1931–34, with a B— average on the seven examinations for the College Certificate, and B on the Bachelor's degree comprehensive examination.

W. S. entered in the autumn, 1931, qualified for the College Certificate in June, 1933, with an average slightly better than C, and qualified for the Bachelor's degree in June, 1934, with an average of C on the comprehensive examinations.

R. W. entered in the autumn, 1931, qualified for the College Certificate in June, 1933, with a B average, passed the departmental comprehensive examination for the Bachelor's degree in May, 1934, with a B grade, and the divisional comprehensive examination in August, 1934, with a C grade.

F. W. entered in the autumn, 1931; qualified for the College Certificate in June, 1933, with a B average; qualified for the Bachelor's degree in June, 1934, with a grade of B on the departmental comprehensive examination and C on the divisional comprehensive examination.

L. D. entered as a Freshman in the Autumn Quarter, 1933; passed all seven examinations for the College Certificate with a B average, and the Social Sciences divisional comprehensive examination with a grade of C, in June, 1934; passed the political science departmental comprehensive examination with a grade of C in December, 1934; during the present quarter (Winter, 1935) he is taking the additional elective courses necessary to meet the remaining divisional requirements, and will take his A.B. degree in March, 1935, if the social sciences division will waive the requirement of a year of residence in the division; he will then have been in residence in the University five quarters (three in the College and two in the social sciences division), a total of one and two-thirds academic years.

XIV

COMPARISON OF THE AVERAGE GRADES RECEIVED BY STU-
DENTS ON THE COLLEGE EXAMINATIONS AND THE AVERAGE
NUMBER OF QUARTERS SPENT IN THE CORRESPONDING
COURSES FOR THE FOLLOWING GROUPS OF STUDENTS: THOSE
WHO COMPLETED THE COLLEGE REQUIREMENTS (A), WITH
HONORS; (B), IN FEWER THAN SIX QUARTERS; (C), WITH D
GRADES IN FOUR OR MORE OF THE SEVEN COLLEGE EXAMI-
NATIONS; AND (D), ALL STUDENTS WHO HAVE TAKEN ONE OR
MORE COLLEGE EXAMINATIONS

	Number of Students	Average of Passing Grades Only	Average of All Grades, Including Failures	Number of Failures per Student	Average Quarters Registration in Corresponding Courses before Passing
Group A.........	94	3.56	3.46	0.191*	2.55
Group B.........	34	2.52	2.32	0.618	1.99
Group C.........	46	1.39	1.10	1.870	2.98
Group D.........	2,109	2.27	1.18	0.891	2.68

* All in the English Qualifying Examination.

SAME AS PRECEDING TABLE BUT EXCLUDING THE
GRADES ON THE ENGLISH QUALIFYING
EXAMINATION

	Number of Students	Average of Passing Grades Only	Average of All Grades, Including Failures	Number of Failures per Student	Average Quarters Registration in Corresponding Courses before Passing
Group A.........	94	3.64	3.64	0.000	2.72
Group B.........	34	2.54	2.50	0.088	2.09
Group C.........	46	1.36	1.16	1.065	2.99
Group D.........	2,109	2.30	1.98	0.564	2.78

INDEX

[PRINTED IN U·S·A·]